Finding Your Serenity

Angela Timms

DEDICATION

For Oscar.

ACKNOWLEDGMENTS

With thanks to Niall Smith and all the animals including some totally amazing goats who have helped to make life how it was over all those years.

i

NOTES

INTRODUCTION

In the Beginning there was the Word. Since then there have been a whole lot more words but where have they got everyone? What do we want out of life? Happy is the person who is content with what they have, where they are and who they are with.

Here I hope to take you through a time of questioning but also a time of finding your inner peace even if life won't give you the space you really need. Yes it is lovely to take a walk in nature and to have time to meditate for hours but in a world where the bills have to be paid and there are responsibilities these things are not always possible. Well not in the classic sense but there are always ways to get around that and find your peace in the middle of the maelstrom which is everyday living. I know as I've been there and done that. I worked in London for many years and endured the Underground and enjoyed the restaurants and bars as well as having a full time job first as a Legal Secretary and then as a Secretary in a Patent and Trade Mark Attorneys. That meant years of running the gauntlet of the Underground, terrorist scares and trying to enjoy a social life. I've survived three divorces and many house moves and the stresses in life caused by others. I've walked miles in other people's shoes as I've been in similar situations so what I have included here is tempered with a reality of what is possible when you have time constraints as well as a wish to look after yourself.

At the end of the day only you can look after yourself as you are the one who knows what you are really thinking and how any situation truly affects you.

In the latter part of this book I have compiled a list of facts and fables about plants and other "tools" which are available to make your life easier, to help with your well-ness and generally to give you a feel of the way that nature is there to support and protect (as well as being a tooth and claw creation). In a world of plant abundance which historically our ancestors would have enjoyed there was very little problem finding the plants that they needed day to day. They had no medicine or any other option than to use the resources they were given. In a limited world where our land is cultivated and our "wild land" managed and limited such plants are not as abundant as they would have been.

Without care, if we encourage a "plant revolution" of many more people using these plants without any form of control or sensibility then they will soon be wiped out and we could be adding them to the endangered species list. At best that could lead to a few years' glory before the wide menu is cut back again. That is why wisdom to know what not to take and teachings like leaving the "Grandmother Plant" are important. This teaching dictates that you never take the first plant that you find that you are looking for. You always take the second, then you guarantee that there is always one plant to continue.

I've watched goats grazing. When they find something they like they stop and have some but they move on. In an area where they are not confined by space they will happily do this which ensures that the plant survives. Sometimes they take a few leaves, sometimes a lot more and then they move on to the next tasty plant. When they run out of abundant food because they are limited by the area they have available to graze they will of course wipe everything out. Before the Enclosure Acts this was not an issue, some would wander for miles and eat what they wanted. When they have enough land this is what they do, they choose a route, follow it sometimes day after day and then they change that route to try new places and new food before returning to the old route at a later point. We too are now limited and space where these plants can grow is limited so we have to be wise enough to know when to leave enough plants to carry on even though our "grazing" is now limited.

Fortunately laws are in place to protect many of these plants and it is illegal to pick flowers and plants from many public wild places. That is how it has to be. There is nothing stopping you cultivating these plants yourself though and many companies sell seeds from wild plants which you can grow at home.

I had time to do research into plants and it opened up a whole new world of magic and mystery to me. It also lead to an understanding of some "older ways" that had been a thing of story and fable.

Everyone knows something and nobody knows everything. For the bit in the middle there are books and in this age the Internet if you have access to it. With these resources everyone can know the bit of everything that they need at one particular moment in time. Unless you are a quiz genius or a "Chaser" from the TV Show you have no need to fill your head with everything. You just need to know where and how to find what you want to know when you want to know it. You aren't necessarily smart or intelligent just because you have learnt a lot of facts from books. You may be Learned but it doesn't make you Intelligent or Wise. Wisdom comes from knowing what you can do with the facts and tools you have available. Intelligence shows you what to do but it is Wisdom which dictates whether you should actually do it or not. If you give yourself the space to listen then you will be able to know. Unfortunately in the madness of deadlines, timelines and appearances to others sometimes this question doesn't get asked and thereby comes the problem. Deep down you know what you should do. Acting contrary to this nature causes a dis-ease which can lead to deeper routed problems. Here we set out to try and find out what has been causing you to worry and freeing you to be able to Speak Your Truth, even if it is only to yourself.

–

2 FREATIVITY – FREEING YOUR CREATIVITY TO BE WHO YOU ARE

ARE YOU OK?

Is this the moment when even an honest person is put in a position to lie? That is if it is an honest question. Sometimes it is almost an "hello". Sometimes it is something to say when there is nothing else to say.

All too often it is easy to say. "Fine thank you." This is the time when inside you are screaming. "No!"

Everyone feels down sometimes. We all get a dose of the blues or brought down by the weather. Sometimes it can be a lot more and then you need someone to offer a hand to pull you out of the far too deep to climb out of hole.

If it is the "Beastly Blues" then you may feel bad but life doesn't change. Your sleep patterns, appetite and launch into the day are not affected.

Putting a brave face is often necessary. It gets us through the Blues even if it doesn't get us over or out of it. Very handy when you have work or a necessary engagement to survive.

Even then you do have to be honest with yourself. You are feeling down. Yes it happens but it still feels awful and is debilitating.

There are times and places where you can't share your feelings. There are people we cannot share out feelings with for professional or personal reasons. But, everyone needs someone or somewhere to honestly express how they feel in an intimate and non-judgmental way. There is no point burying it and denying it and if you have nobody to tell then write it down in a Thought Journal.

If you don't want a permanent record then take a piece of paper and a pen or pencil and write exactly how you feel! If appropriate also why you think you feel that way and what or who may have caused it. You can add to it at any time, it is your writing. You can cross bits out. You can write what you like as when you feel better and happier you can burn it and it is gone, taking the negativity with it.

If it is the Beastly Blues then you can fight it. What better excuse to treat yourself, spoil yourself and be kind to yourself.

If it is clinical depression you can fight that too if you make yourself carry on. Turn the frown upside down is a highly irritating and annoying statement when you genuinely feel down through clinical depression and you have no idea why you feel that way. That is the difference between clinical depression and being upset because awful things have happened and the mood is totally justified. There is no cause you can deal with. It just is, it is there and you have to find ways to deal with it after you have recognized the monster for what it is.

Smiling does help though.

If the Beastly Blues or Clinical Catastrophe happens regularly then writing a list in your Thought Journal of what you have to do each day and making yourself do the actions, even if unwillingly, means you have least won a bit of the war. You may not have the motivation but you know that soon enough that motivation will come back.

If you have good friends and family you can tell about your feelings then that is perfect. If not then your Therapist if you have one can help or a Reiki Therapy with a Qualified Reiki Master may help to raise your spirits. Reiki may also help with any sleep problems or help with the space to speak you truth about how you feel in a confidential and non-judgmental situation.

Prevention is better than cure. In a Beastly Blues situation you may not be able to work out any external influences. When you feel better you may be able to ferret out what may be instigating the mood.

Of course you could be in a situation which causes a perfectly explainable attack of the Beastly Blues. In this situation there can only be the question as to whether the situation can be cured or must be endured. Either way addressing and accepting the cause is the first step to recovering your personal power.

You are worth being happy. You deserve to be happy and if it is the case there is no pleasure or security in feeling the negativity. If there isn't someone who can throw you an emotional rope you may have to make one bit by bit.

Baby steps, forgive yourself and be kind to yourself and proud of anything you can get yourself to do to get yourself back to happiness.

THOUGHT JOURNAL

Thoughts are fleeting and sometimes the best thoughts fly away in a moment.

Having a Thought Journal to hand is a safe place to download ideas and to write what you feel needs to be permanently recorded so you can go back to it later.

Journals are becoming ever more popular and their power and use cannot be denied. In this world of internet spying your written word on a sheet of paper at least can't be hacked!

It can inspire you to do things so you have something to write about. It can be your confidant when nobody else is around.

A Journal is your private place where you can focus on your ideas and ideals without censorship or comment. You can set your goals and track your progress. On paper you will be able to walk through problems. Or it can be a record of how you feel. You can also have more than one Journal if you would like to split up your topics.

You have an appointment with your Thought Journal daily and that is your time to write things down and to track your progress.

The journal can contain what you want it to contain. Perhaps a "To Do List" to get yourself organized and cross off what is done. Perhaps you can list the good things that have happened or things you are looking forward to.

A Thought Journal can help you to clarify and identify what you are thinking and feeling. It is a way to reflect.

If the thoughts are on paper it gets them out of your head. Writing will also help to focus your attention and one thought can lead to another.

The only "rule" is that it must be private. Nobody other than you reads the words. The words are your downloaded mind and yours alone. Free of the confines of worry about appearances and correct grammar you can let loose the worries that grab your mind in their grotesque grip. When you write in your journal you are free.

This is your place far from the madding crowd where you are with your best friend, yourself.

What you write and your thoughts are private. They are not for show or "Likes". This is your appointment with yourself where appearances, grammar and spelling do not matter.

As with Reiki Therapy you do have to want any changes you are asking yourself to bring about. Writing them down makes you see them, understand them and makes them part of you, if only as words to start with.

TELL YOURSELF YOUR TRUTH

If you speak your heart will listen so choose those words well. You can convince yourself that anything is possible, because when it doesn't relate to anything actually impossible and relates to something you could do then you possibly could.

Positive affirmations are your arsenal to fight against self doubt. So when you see one, hear one, read one, or think one, write it down. That energy is then yours.

I would recommend carrying a "Think Book" with you on your new adventure in life. This is a small notebook, not your Thought Journal, which you can keep in your pocket, handbag or in the glove compartment of the car. This is a book where you can capture those words and ideas before they slip off into the ether never to be remembered again.

Like a spare memory chip the "Think Book" can store these for you until you want to see what you wrote. Then you have them to act upon later and to perhaps be a catalyst that will bring what you could, will or should do. You can also download them when you have the chance into your Thought Journal for further comment.

WHO AM I?

How do you define yourself?

Try describing yourself as if you were describing someone you know to a friend. Did you describe yourself as the best or worse of how you see yourself?

This is your writing for yourself so be honest.

You are also possibly "many people" by necessity. I don't mean that you have any mental disorder. You are the person at work, the friend, the parent and the brother or sister. In each situation you are the aspect of you which you need to deal with that situation. If you welcome this and accept it then it is a powerful tool.

Each of those personas comes with expectations which makes it hard to be "you". The real "you" uninfluenced by any situation may have to hide behind many masks to get you through the day, earn your salary or help to be accepted into a pre-conceived idea of who you should be or who you think that you are.

When you were a child you thought as a child because you could. Your "inner censor" didn't know the rules and as you learnt them you began to temper your actions to be in harmony with those around you. At the same time the "inner you" was exposed to the attitudes of others which began to drive your wants and needs.

A basic human need is to be accepted and that leads in the formative years to a desire for things that will help you to fit in and a perception of success.

Successful is the person who is totally happy with who they are, where they are and who they are with. The basic emotional needs are sated and life is fine.

At the end of the day when you close your eyes you are alone with yourself. At the end of the day finding your Serenity where the "yourself" is happy means you have to find a calm which survives whatever is going on around you.

Are you "you" or are you a reflection of others and how you think they see you?

If you had time on your own would you be different? How much of "you" is the creation of circumstances, either following or rebelling?

Only in the peaceful silence with no extraneous influences can you meet the real you. This however takes shrugging off pre-conceived ideas and projected expectations.

Evaluating yourself is not necessary as in many ways you are not going to know who you "are" or how you would deal with something until you are faced by a situation you have to deal with. Even then it can depend on whether or not you have an "audience".

In a time of Social Media we are invited to put ourselves on screen for everyone to look at. But, how honest are you? Do you select and write about what you really like or do you choose things that you think will make people like, admire or respect you?

If you have started a Thought Journal then you might like to answer some of these questions to help you think about who you are. Answer them honestly, it is only for you and nobody is going to read it.

> How do you spend your time?
> How would you spend that time if you could do anything?
> What dominates your thoughts?
> What inspires you?
> What are your goals?
> What would you study if you had the chance?
> What would you read if you had the time?
> Is your relationship a good one?
> Is your home a calm sanctuary?
> Do you have time for yourself?
> Where would you go on holiday if you could?
> What are your achievements?
> What are your professional achievements?
> What are you good at?
> What are your strengths?
> What are your positive traits?

Firstly answer the above questions for yourself and then if you have someone who knows you well perhaps you could ask them to answer the questions about you.

CONSTANTLY CHANGING

Every day you are exposed to new situations, ideas and ideals. This is a constant evolution from cradle to grave.

Serious "life changing" events do just that. Little events do as well. You cannot unsee or unknow anything and unless you are very careful you cannot shield yourself from these "events".

If you look around you now, a fraction of a second later that scene is different in many different ways. There are specs of dust which land on things, a sound is added or goes or something else seemingly trivial which makes that moment changes.

It is like that for what you think, say or do. One thought, word or action can change your day and if said or done to another can change their day too. You have the "power" to change how they feel as much as others have the power to change how you feel. What you say will always be a part of them as it is a fraction, if even a moment, of their life. So, everything you say is important as is everything someone else says to you is important.

SELF LOVE

If you don't look after number one you can't look after number two. I'm hearing that a lot these days, particularly relating to those who care for others.

How can you expect someone else to love you if you don't love yourself.

Loving yourself means being kind to yourself. That in turn gives you a more balanced way of living. If you don't look after yourself you can't look after anyone else.

Most people expect self love to be taking time to meditate or do all the "restful" things you may love to do. But taking time out for many who are busy can add to the daily stress of increased workload packed into less time when you get back from a lovely long break or neglect everyday tasks where your time is limited anyway.

Self love sometimes can be seeing these problems and working them out so that you can have "guilt free" time with no repercussions. If it is at work perhaps to talk to a manager or "boss" and explain the situation and see if there is a way of dividing up that work or finding someone to cover it while you have a break which in turn would also mean that others can have a break and do the same.

If you were someone else how would you advise yourself?

Writing lists of reasons why you love yourself could well end up like a Curriculum Vitae writing session. I'm sure you have summed yourself up enough times in a positive way for many of your daily situations, reviews and job interviews.

In a busy life situation finding that space is essential. I used to find it by reading a good book on the Underground but that depends on either getting a seat or developing the skills of a circus performer to hold onto the rail, hold onto a book and turn the pages. Also a good book can make you miss you stop which doesn't aid stress relief at all. Of course there is always reading digitally off of your phone or tablet. That is a bit easier.

I sometimes used to get off of the Underground train a stop before the one closest to work so that I could walk a bit before work. I was pleased that there were a chain of little parks alongside the walk through Barbican to Grays Inn. Also walking through Covent Garden Market early had an amazing feeling to it, watching things opening up. This works if you are on the Underground as one stop is not that far.

WHO DO I REALLY LIKE TO BE WITH?

The first person you have to like to be with is yourself. That is the person you spend the most time with. Do you like that person? Would you like that person if you had a choice?

There are many types of friends and some are more genuine than others. But I am sure you already know this and are aware of how you think of your friends.

Are they real friends? Are they "vampiric" friends who only want your friendship for your support and to add to their numbers and you leave your time with them feeling drained? Do you look forward to hearing from them? Are they there for you when you need support even if it is just a supportive message?

How do you define a friend?

How much "quality" time do you spend with them?

DIGITAL DETOX

Don't panic!

It is said that 72 hours without the digital world is optimum. It makes it sound like a virus that infests your system and takes over your life which "dies" in 72 hours!

Taking time away from the demands means stepping away from the addictions it causes. Is it your master and is it dictating that you keep grabbing for your phone or laptop and "having a look". That cheeky check to see if anyone has liked your post or whether you have messages fuels the addiction and causes an opportunity for disappointment.

The "Likes" will still be there later and the digital world will be yours to tap into whenever you choose to return. The furious need it can create when removed can leave a place of peace in its wake. A serenity that you have time to yourself without having to be emotionally on call for whatever someone may write or post.

A real conversation, hearing real words which vibrate and resonate with the psyche is much more beneficial. But, the internet has its place and many lonely people feel so much better when they can get a message across the miles which doesn't get lost in the post. Seeing real body language which indicates what people are feeling is far better and there is no need to choose an emoji to show you.

I took many years away from the "madding crowd" in a place with poor internet. This gave me a choice. Yes you can get angry that your basic human rights are not being delivered correctly or you can wake up and smell the roses, or grass or whatever else you enjoy smelling when you aren't sitting tied to a keyboard or with your concentration tied to a little box. Real animals play and they are not doing it to be photographed to get likes. You see an image of something funny it is for you, not to capture to share. They are doing it because they can.

Dance like nobody's watching
Sing like nobody's listening
Work like you don't need the money

I have no idea who first said that but it is a good way to be.

Not such a great way to get likes on TikTok but far better for your own personal peace and satisfaction.

How often do you do something or say/write something just to put it on Social Media? Then you submit your work for marking and the approval of your peers.

That is why the Thought Journal where you write for yourself is so important. That is where you can write uncensored and without seeking approval as the main reason for it is that it is the un-hackable place only you can see.

THE ROCK ON WHICH YOU BUILD

What "nurtures" and supports you? Is it "you" or do you need to rely on family and friends to give you "strength".

Looking after your foundations is always a good idea. This can be defining your beliefs or a myriad of other things.

Knowing what you rely on is a first step to securing "it" and making sure you have that support into the future. It is also the first step to ensuring it doesn't have too much control over you, you aren't too reliant on it and you can increase that support by increasing your reliance on yourself.

If you identify the friends and family who support you, keep them close. Others can come and go but those who genuinely help you, whether by word or deed are your true friends. It may be that they quietly help you. So listen, watch and learn to know who are the real friends and who are the "users" who just want to add you as a number.

MEDITATE ON THAT

Meditation has long been proven to aid Wellbeing. Blessed be those who have the time but for many Meditation is a luxury there just isn't time for.

If you are short of time then having a quick way of calming, perhaps a candle holder you use and familiar things you associate with what meditation you can manage. It will help you get into the mindset faster if your time for Mediation is limited.

CHANGE YOUR LIFE?

Do you really need to?

There can be a lot of pressure to change your life. Changing your life is easy. You can sell your house. You can sell your car. You can resign from your job. All these things will change you life but is that wise?

It is easy to redesign your life but there is a reassurance in keeping your life the same and altering yourself. You don't have to "throw the baby out with the bathwater" by which I mean that sometimes you don't have to make drastic changes across the board to find the happiness which is eluding you.

Perhaps you just need to accept and acknowledge the things in your life you want to keep.

The question is whether the aspects of life should and must change or be made to change.

Before you launch into any major life shift it is wise to try and assess your motives. It may be to alleviate your boredom, give you something to plan and discuss but when you have changed will that too become mundane and boring and will you regret the sacrifice of the old life?

If you need a change, you need a change. It can be as dramatic or small as you need it to be.

You deserve anything that is going to make you happy and if that is to change everything or anything then that is what you need to do. Not doing it will be much more damaging as regret is a niggling monster who can haunt the quiet moments you may have.

As long as you address your motives and make sure your reasoning is sound then it is time to take your future into your own hands.

ADDING TO YOUR ARSENAL

Every day you gain more experience even if it doesn't feel like it. As the senses are battered with news, views and comments your mind is processing all that information.

For more specific development you may have to choose to do a course or find someone to show or tell you.

Depending on what you would like to learn it could be very liberating to tell others of your plans. Just voicing the need can open up possibilities and start to manifest the answers. It is also a way to get support from those you care about. That is reassuring in itself. Speaking it is the first stage to getting things started and that is the first weapon you may need to combat the inner critic or any doomsayers and psychic vampires you may have in your life.

DON'T WORRY, BE HAPPY

Do you want to be happy?

What is your definition of happy?

Are you content but not happy?

What is missing in your life which means you are not happy?

Everyone is different and therefore what makes you happy is going to be different to what makes someone else happy. To know if you are happy you have to know what makes you happy.

Life will always get in the way and a total idyllic happiness may just be the stuff of novels.

Real life is gritty and we have to claim happiness where we can. A degree of contentment helps. This is being happy with who you are, where you are and who you are with.

Something that makes you laugh can make you happy. Perhaps your favourite comedian or film will put that smile on your face.

Laughing with friends about something daft to anyone else can be the best medicine of all. That time is precious and the happiness it brings is not time squandered. Afterwards you will be happier, more able to cope with the world and any darkness the world throws at you.

If exercise makes you happy and music makes you happy then dance to music. At home, on your own, for sheer pleasure. Where the music is bright the feet will follow and the heart won't be far behind. The beauty of dancing alone is that you don't have to be any good at it. You are not dancing to please others, you are doing something for you. A nice little biproduct is keeping fit but don't dwell on that or you will ruin your fun.

How do you face situations? Are they a challenge or source of woe? If you flip how you see a situation into seeing it as a challenge or a test it makes it far less personal and less of an attack on your happiness. The blessing is that when you succeed you will feel better about yourself and those around you.

THE WHOLE PICTURE

If you sit for a moment then that moment is filled with sight, sound, scent, sense and emotion.

What you see has an effect on how you feel. That relates to everywhere you are. Around you can be serene or discord. This relates to all situations so choose places which make you feel good.

The rooms in your house are your Sanctuary. This is one place you do have control over. It may take time and effort but every room should make you happy. That doesn't have to be an expensive change if your rooms don't make you happy. Perhaps you just need to tidy up, release the things that don't make you happy and rearrange the rest so that the image you see is no longer discordant.

Sounds fill your senses and can create emotion. Grating sounds and irritating sounds diminish your personal power by distracting thoughts and causing irritation. If you can remove the source of the irritation then great. If not then you may have to add music to drown them out.

Music can fill your life when you want it to. A whole library now fits on a phone. If you enjoy it then you should enjoy it whenever you can. Music which raises the spirits is a valuable tool.

The Sound of Silence – The most blessed sound of all and the hardest to attain. The time when you can think undistracted.

Scent which is unpleasant is never going to allow you to feel happy. An arsenal if incense, scented candles and sprayable aromas can soon deal with that but best of all is to find the source and deal with it.

Sense is an odd one as it comes from you. It is what you "feel" about a place. If there is disharmony then there is something there which needs dealing with.

Emotion is a complicated collection and reaction to all that is going on in your life. Recognising it and enhancing the positive emotions through all the other aspects of that moment gives you control.

Be kind to yourself. If you were someone else in the same situation what would you say to that person?

Are you thankful for all the good things that you have and the gifts you have been given? Perhaps spend a moment to list them in your Thought Journal.

Are you hanging onto things, ideals and people which do not make you happy? Can you let go or would letting them go bring even more unhappiness?

HAPPY EATER

Food Intolerance

If your gut is upset that will ruin your day and upset any good mood. That is blindlingly obvious but it can also cause mood swings, irritability, nausea, lack of focus, hyperactivity, nervousness and aggression. You can help yourself to avoid this by trying to avoid colouring, sugar, nitrates, preservatives and additives.

Many nutrients can lift your mood and without causing too much trouble as you can pick food which contains them. Calcium, Chromium,

Folate, Iron, Magnesium, Omega 3, Fatty Acids, Vitamin B6, Vitamin B12, Vitamin D and Zinc.

Green Tea contains L-theanine which relaxes the mind which can reduce anxiety which in turn obviously improves your focus and concentration.

Spinach is a source of magnesium and calcium which calms the nervous system. It is a bit disappointing for Popeye the Sailor that it is not quite as good as it was billed in the War Years as the decimal point was put in the wrong place but it still has beneficial properties.

Pumpkin seeds are another source of calming magnesium and zinc. They can keep the blood sugar stable which helps to reduce the release of stress hormones.

Happy Food: Chicken, Turkey, Bananas, Oats, Strawberries, Lentils, Avocadoes, Spinach, Grapes, Sesame Seeds, Raw Nuts, Salmon.

IN THE DARK ABOUT THAT ONE

We need to be in the dark sometimes. The body produces the hormone Melatonin when we are in darkness.

Just a quick search of the Internet will reveal companies selling Melatonin as a sleep aid. It is a hormone which occurs naturally in our bodies and is prescribed for insomnia for patients with learning difficulties.

It helps us to fall asleep quickly and to be less likely to wake up during the night. This can be an issue of course if you do not like sleeping in a dark room. You can get it on prescription or if you fear sleeping in the dark you could set aside some time to Meditate in the dark.

Of course you could address the reasons why you can't sleep in the dark. This is particularly prevalent in children who fear the monsters in the cupboard and under the bed.

Many years ago I introduced the idea of Frixians to some friends of mine. I created the idea of Frixians being alien spirits which inhabit soft toys to look after children and protect them from such fears. The idea is that a bear or soft toy given with love from someone who cares about them carries that spirit and can protect them from all the unseen nasties which could creep up on them in the dark.

This expanded to Widget the Frixian writing stories and books. She visited the Vale of Rheidol Railway on their Ghost Train, The Dr Who Exhibition in Cardiff and came on a tour through France to Spain in 2021.

TO DO OR NOT TO DO

Is the "To Do List" a helper or a threat?

The satisfaction of crossing something off when done cannot be denied but the list in the first place can be daunting. As one task is completed another appears. And so it goes on.

The reward for effort is a shorter list but perhaps it would be better to have more than one list and not to add to a list already created. Then the lists can be completed quickly and you will feel less overwhelmed.

Some things are essential and if you don't do them the situation gets worse. Some things "would be nice" so they can be lower priority. Do and it will be done. There is only one answer, get on and do what you need to do and then reward yourself afterwards.

HAPPY MEMORY JOURNAL

Raising your energy to a positive level can attract positive things into your life.

Gathering your Happy Memories into a Journal can give you a focus of happiness and also show you how much happiness you already have in your life.

People, places, celebrations, they all empower you. Pictures of the past which empower your future.

Print them off, cut them to shape and glue them in your journal and write around them and then you have a collage of positive and happy feelings which these people, places or events have inspired.

That Journal can be your happy place and inspiration to get out and make more happy memories to add to it. It is also your happy place when things go wrong and you need a quick place to "escape" to.

BLESS THIS HOUSE

Your home is your Sanctuary, your Nest, your Cave. It can be a blessing or a curse.

The stress of decorating if you have been there a while or just moved in and the whole stress of buying it in the first place adds to your daily "stress quota". Once bought and done however it can be a source of peace and tranquility.

Colour has a great effect on how you feel so if you want to add colour to your home then do a bit of research first. How do you want to "feel" in a particular room and how is that colour going to enhance your wellbeing in that room? Or do you want a feeling which is energetic, "jazzy" and "out there" as you have other places where you relax or you do not need to relax.

There is a lot of focus on relaxing, pastels and other colours but perhaps that is not the feeling you want. The colour ranges now are vast enough and so therefore are the choices. If you are unsure then you can always paint white and use colour wall hangings for that quick change rather than having to decorate to get a new feeling. I have even heard of roller blinds which are used for photography. There is no reason why these couldn't be used to change a decoration on a whole wall if you are unsure of the decoration you want or you like to change your décor on a regular basis.

When does Art become Clutter?

There is a fine line between having all the things you love on view and feeling that a room is cluttered or too busy.

Conversely there has been a movement to throw out the ornaments and live minimally.

There are benefits to both.

Psychometry is the ability to discover facts about an event or person by touching items associated with them. So when you are given a gift or take something into your home which once belonged to someone else you are taking their "energy" into your home. That item is also a visual memory of that person or the time when you were given it. It can be a memory of a place where you purchased it and the people who were with you then. That item could be reassuring every time you see it, reminding you of happy times and people you care about without you even knowing it.

It can also be a lot to dust so if your time is limited I would recommend a cabinet and put things you care about in there.

The unwanted gift can also cause stress. If you don't like it then those glances at it bring and internal "jar" to your day. Putting the "thing" out of sight while the giver is not around is the best answer as it means that if you feel awkward about it you can put it back when they visit. Best to make a note of this somewhere they won't read it so you don't forget though!

The things you have around you are your personal art collection. There is "art" in everything. Someone had to design and make it, however cheaply you may have bought it. The quality of the materials part dictates its "cost" etc but its value to you personally is all that is important when you look at it.

Your home is the one place which you have control over. If you are in a couple then of course the items in it have to be things you both love.

Those items have to "earn their space" and looking at them has to add to the happiness quotient of your day.

There are other ways to "populate" your house. You may prefer to put pieces in your house which mean nothing to you but you feel happy about them because you are keeping up with the latest trend.

The Victorian era saw tables and mantle pieces covered with ornaments and photos in elaborate ornate frames. Many of the Victorian Houses had servants and if you want a dust free home with a lot of ornaments you may feel that you need one once you've finished your dusting!

If you are sensitive to the energy then dusting an item which is associated with a loved one either still with you or passed over can bring that touch with their energy you can no longer feel "in real life". As photos go more digital the energy of physically touching a photo is lost but in new ways that digital image can still be reassuring.

They say that 25 degrees is the ideal temperature to put you in a good mood. With the rising fuel costs keeping a house at this temperature could well put you in a bad one when you get the bill. Perhaps having the heating on for a specific time or heating a place which is your happy place for a Meditation could carry you through the rest of the day in less warm conditions.

CLEAR THE CLUTTER

What is clutter? "To cover or fill with an untidy collection of things."

Every image we see has an effect on how we feel. The things around us should bring us joy and boost our positive thoughts as the eye is drawn to them.

They may carry memories or be decorative such that they bring a smile.

There is a point where this beautiful security and mind boosting resource becomes a different thing altogether.

There is energy in a house and the things you choose to put in it are your way of making it yours and reflecting yourself.

When other items start creeping in then they bring discord. They also cancel out the power of the positive reassuring things as they become lost in the general vision of "stuff".

If you look around you and the room does not bring you a feeling of peace or creativity then it could be time to evict the mischief makers, tidy them away or get rid of them completely so the things that matter can be seen or displayed where they can help your mood, reassure you or just look nice.

Of course a good "smudging" never goes amiss. Even if you are not trained in the Art of Smudging it always helps to light the bundle of sage and focus your intent on the house being rid of negative influences. A little incense or a scented candle can also help to reaffirm the positive ambience of a room or house which will also go a long way to making you feel better.

THE HOME GYM

In a time strapped world the trip to the gym can be a release and pleasure if you have that time. It is semi-social as there are other like minded people around and the exercise releases endorphins and mood regulating serotonin.

If you don't have the time to regularly visit a gym then there are plenty of activities in your day you can adapt and perhaps make a little more challenging to have the same effect. You can also get equipment at home but of course there is none of the interaction there is at the gym.

Just another way to isolate ourselves and become more solitary.

If the exercise bike is your preference then cycling to work or the station if that is possible could be an alternative. Perhaps a bit of alternative thinking? Many years ago I went to the Big Green Gathering. The stages were powered by fixed bikes which generated what was needed and the audience took turns on the bikes to keep the music playing and the lights on. I am stunned that by now the home exercise bike isn't linked to a power generating system which could power the house or charge up the electric car. I proposed to the Government years ago that gyms could be mini power stations.

TAKE A BREAK WITH A WELLNESS HOLIDAY

There are many ways to combat stress and in trying to obtain them there is a certain degree of stress as well.

Needing a break is something we all feel from time to time. A bit of sun to help with SAD. A night under the stars with no street lights and a place to sleep where it is comfortable and dark.

Mini Getaways are becoming increasingly popular and micro retreats are taking the travel industry by storm.

The long, three week, family holiday is becoming a thing of the past for some people. Working at home gives more family time and the need for the long family holiday is not so great. What is popular now is the one week in the sun or more frequent mini breaks of 2 or 3 days on a more regular basis.

They are great for a guilt free few days where the workload doesn't pile up so much in your absence and great for singles too tied up in work for the longer holiday.

Unwind retreats are great for making new friends too and talking to real people face to face who may have a lot in common with you.

They are also great for getting out of your comfort zone and taking a walk on the wilder side.

Sleeping in a Yurt, in a comfortable bed, under the stars with nothing you "have" to do but plenty you could do could be just the break you are looking for to cope with the day to day mundanity, eat-sleep-repeat lifestyle which may have taken over your life.

Cooking with others on a BBQ brings out the Animal Spirit and sitting around a camp fire with like minded people in the evening and doing what YOU want to do all day could be the liberation you need. If that is sleep then nobody is going to wake you up unless you ask them to. You would have space to do what you need to do to relax which may well be essential in this work-orientated world.

Many places also offer the option to lock away your mobile phone for the 72 hours necessary for a "detox".

HARD DAY AT THE OFFICE

Ours is not to do our die, ours is just to pacify.

The days come and go. From the moment you are launched from the comfort of your bed to the moment you walk back through the door at the end of your working day your life is dictated to you.

Just remember that you are in control. You got that job because you were the best person to do it and you still have your own personal power. That is proven at the end of the month when money appears in your bank account which is yours to do what you want with (after the bills are paid of course).

Unless you have actually done it you will never understand the Heaven and Hell which is commuting. You can go to the gym before work, you can write in a journal and all those things do help but what will really help in that situation is how you think about it and what it is "for". For example your time on the Underground or train. If you can this is your time to read, listen to music on your headphones and think and write with nobody bothering you. It is your time away from the family and anyone who would want to ask a question or break into your thoughts. In the madding crowd it is actually a peaceful place where you can do something you want to do without disturbance.

You are going to a place where there are basically like minded people and together you are there to make something work. It doesn't matter what that something is. The world is a machine and every business and place of work are cogs in the machine. Everyone is a part of the whole and without one part the machine doesn't run smoothly. So everyone is important.

The work may be dull but you can get to know colleagues and that makes the day go quicker. It also gives the day a purpose.

When lunchtime comes you have time to yourself. This is the chance to be yourself and enjoy a bit of space. Depending on where you work this can be an interesting or dull time. Either way it is a chance to take a break, get some exercise and get something to eat.

Then when you get home it is time for you. This is where the "rituals" you set up for yourself are important.

There are five aspects of self-care: Physical, Emotional, Psychological, Spiritual and Professional.

Your needs "need" to be prioritized but if time is limited you will have to be organized. Any new habits have to dovetail with the tasks you have to do using what energy you have left from the day.

You could start by making small changes to what you eat. Couple this with increasing what you physically do. Easy if you live alone, not so easy if you live in a family and you aren't the person who cooks. Daily affirmations can help as well if you can find somewhere (even the bathroom) to speak them. Or you can write them in your Thought Journal.

There should be boundaries and home is home. Once you are home you may be able to manage meditation and fit it in with your social life. This is probably harder if you work from home as there is always that temptation to go and do something if you think of it. Perhaps it would be better in that situation to have a notebook, write it down and then you can do it when you are back on work time, not you time.

A bit of self-care has to be essential. You can put it on your To Do List if that helps. It can be as simple as an early night in response to mood swings and tiredness to be able to take your mood with you rather than allowing it to influence others.

If you feel stressed, treat yourself. It has to be something that helps you and everyone is different so only you will know what you would consider a treat.

For your lunchtime you could plan a different thing every day. Plan it, write about it, do it and then write about it in your Thought Journal to start making memories. Your lunch hour is your time, away from family and friends and the best time to do things by yourself and to spend time with yourself. Care Jars can also help with this as you could write ideas for weeks to come, cut them up, put them in the jar and then draw them out when you need inspiration.

KEEPING CONTACT

We have so many ways to communicate now so there is no excuse. Pick up that phone and speak to someone you haven't spoken to for a while if you want to.

Modern life isolates us from family and friends by allowing us to move away from our home town and be wherever we like. That may be stimulating and lead to the life you want but it does leave gaps and it does have a price.

It has been shown that phoning family members at least three times a week helps to lower the level of depressive feelings. Hearing a real voice is important.

USE IT NOW

I was told a story at the College of Psychic Studies about a woman who bought herself a beautiful silk slip. She loved it and kept it in the box it came in as she didn't want to ruin it and she was saving it for a special occasion to actually wear it.

Sadly she passed away before she could wear it and her husband ensured that she was buried in it as that was the last special occasion she would ever have.

Every day should be special and stashing things away for later and a special occasion if you don't actually have a plan for such an occasion usually means that they rarely get used. It is a great way to make a special day out of a mundane one if you wear something you like and that could even cheer you up.

FASTING

There are various fasting options:

1. 5:2 the original and well known approach to intermittent fasting. Eat well for five days, diet for two.
2. 16:8 Fast for 16 hours a day and eat during an eight hour window.
3. Alternate Day: Fast for an entire day every other day. That should be 500 calories or none.
4. OMAD – One Meal A Day

FACE THE MUSIC

Social Media, love it or hate it it is there.

Does it enhance your day or give you unrealistic expectations?

The difference is how you feel about it. It is a tool or a tyrant?

It has its pro's and con's. If you are busy it is a quick way to catch up with friends and let them know you care even if you would never have the time or ability to physically visit them.

There is no demand or urgency that there is with a phone call and if you put the two together in a video message or arranged video call it can actually help avoid the stress of the demanding phone ringing. A message can be answered when you want to answer it. In the meantime posts from friends pop up on your feed and you know they are ok or not, if not then you can contact them and help. A quick like or emoji shows you still care. If you have time to chat then it is easy to send a message and arrange something.

Who you have on your friends list is your decision. If you are someone who needs to see a vast number of "friends" then that is how you are. If you have never spoken to them or met them then in truth they are just a number and the value in that is what you put on it.

If they are all people you know and care about then the situation is quite different. The loving and supporting feeling of seeing posts from your loved ones enhances your day.

The spite and misery caused by some on Social Media is well documented. The satisfaction of blocking them cannot be denied but you have to have the mental strength to claim your personal power by doing so. It is one situation where you can do what you may love to do to some people "in real life".

Wandering onto groups can be a minefield for the emotions. Everyone has views and because of the glorious variety of this world there will be people who will anger and frustrate you. They offer you something which is intended to upset you but you have the ultimate power. They aren't really there, you can walk away, block them, delete the thread. It is a box in your room. You have that power, you can walk away from it, log off or simply message on the thread that you don't want to be involved with the "debate" any further. Life is too short for it to be wasted on "Stressmakers" who obviously have nothing better to do or crave your attention. Forget them and move onto something more interesting like the washing up!

POWER OF POSITIVE THINKING (MANIFESTATION)

Your Thought Journal is a great place to write your Affirmations. These are positive comments which make you feel better and which put the right sort of "ask" about what you want in life.

If you have a goal, write it down. You can then focus your thoughts and energy on it.

EXERCISE

Find a small amount of time when you won't be disturbed. Sit calmly with the words you have written in front of you. Relax. Then take a deep breath and visualize breathing in the words. See the words rise up from the page and float towards you.

Then breathe out all your doubts and fears about your goal. Breathe out all those conversations where doubts have been introduced. Breathe out all the distractions.

When your mind is clear and you are focused on your goal write down what you need to do to achieve it, in the order you need to do them. You can set yourself a time limit for this. Perhaps a minute as you don't need to overclutter the plan.

In turn visualize the steps completed and the feeling that will be your reward. Visualize sharing this with those who have supported you.

Achieving the "goal" is the goal but there is no reason why you can't enjoy the journey and the anticipation of achieving that goal.

MANIFESTING THE DREAM

We are made of energy as is everything else. If we manifest good we need to offer good energy.

Belief: For anything to work you have to believe.

The energy that flows through nature is part of us. We have that link and as, at the base of things there is a variable "soup" which forms into "things" because it uses that pattern, if we can harness our natural "power" we can influence what "is" and manifest what we need.

Making a Request

Be clear about what you want and word it succinctly. Be beyond doubt that it is what you want. Your Thought Journal can be useful for this. Write it, Say it, Visualise it, Affirm it, Think it, Pray for it, Meditate on it. The more you do the better. The more energy you put into it the swifter it will become an option.

But remember, you get what you need, not always what you want.

Speak in the Now

The Universe exists in the now so you need to think in the now. Take the request from your future and work on manifesting it in the now.

Good Vibrations

If you want something good to manifest you have to be working at the highest vibrations. It may help to have a Visualisation you do first which gets you to your happy place.

Words Matter

Think before you attempt to Manifest something and choose your words carefully. Give your energy to positive words and starve the negative ones so they can't grow alongside your positive dream. This also utilizes the Law of Attraction and like attracts like.

Kindness is it's own reward

What you send out into the Universe will affect you first.   If your

Manifestation request is fueled by revenge it will only hurt you. Love based requests will empower your request and yourself.

WINTER WARMERS

Cold weather and dark nights bring glorious woollies and party lights.

Whether they are solar or plugged in the mysterious twinkle of fairy lights can brighten the darkest garden or window. As long as they are not specifically Christmas Lights then their happy glow can brighten the darkness.

If you miss the sunshine you can either book a winter break or possibly buy a natural light bulb. Candles of course are an amazing brightener if used with caution and they also bring a little warmth too.

Seasonal Affective Disorder (SAD) can seriously impact your life if the Winter has an effect on your mood. Christmas and the Winter Festivals were strategically placed to bring a sparkle to the dull days and something to look forward to.

SAD is most common in countries like the UK. Those living furthest from the Equator in Northern Latitudes have the highest susceptibility.

With the advent of Working From Home this doesn't have to be an issue if you are in a position to pick up your laptop, jump on a plane and have the occasional two or three day break in the sun. Just having that "Sun Break" can help whether you are able to continue working or have it as a holiday! Many apartments which are holiday homes in the summer rent out by the month in the winter to people doing just that, escaping the dull weather for the winter season.

Symptoms include a drop in mood, loss of activity and energy, problems sleeping, anxiety, panic attacks, stress, poor appetite, overeating, weight gain, frequent colds, and a loss of sex drive. Couple this with an unwillingness to socialize, comfort food cravings and a lack of concentration and no wonder the winter is such an emotionally dark time for many.

A lack of the hormone Seratonin causes much of this so ifyou can get a good day's sunshine and darkness at night to get the Melatonin which gives you a good night's sleep you are well on the way to a happier life.

Colour Therapy can help as if you surround yourself with bright "sunshine" colours and flower pictures the colour helps to stimulate your mind. There are also "Sunshine Lamps" or Day Light Lightbulbs which are also supposed to help.

MAKE IT YOURS

There is a lot of advice available in magazines. Each of course is totally viable and useful but unless you do nothing else then fitting it all in can be stressful in itself, particularly when those around you start complaining about the time your are hidden away.

Harvesting ideas for yourself can help with this glorious variety of wondrous things. Again your Thought Journal or another notebook could help to create your own selection of what feels right for you personally. You can build your own arsenal of tools.

Your Wellbeing Toolkit should be what you need it to be and full of the parts of the whole menu offered that you feel comfortable with. These should be things which resonate with you and most importantly what you have time for or can make time for.

LAUNCH INTO YOUR DAY?

Or gently wander from the arms of Morpheus into the well trodden path.

Sleep, Eat, Work, Eat, Work, Play, Eat, Repeat

The working week. Interspersed with small talk at the Coffee Machine and if it is your pleasure socializing in the evening or a quiet night in. Quiet being all the things you enjoy at home.

Along with the Care Jars which may enhance your day, if you feel you are on "repeat" you could try a Jar of Wishes.

One day when you have time or when you have time to think about it you could write down things you would like to do in your lunch hour and would have time for. Keep on writing until you have a few. Cut them out, put them in a jar and then once a week draw one out and make yourself go and enjoy whatever it is. Go out and release that Dopamine!

For the evening you could do the same but obviously you have more time (possibly) and you can extend it over a few evenings with some good sleeps in between.

Then of course you will have more to write in your Thought Journal and speak about when it comes to conversations.

SING ALONG

There have been clinical trials but the power of music to change your mood is blindingly obvious.

Whether listening to music or singing along the "right" sort of music can improve your immune system, reduce anxiety, "cheer you up" and distract you from what is worrying you.

The words of a song can often strike a chord and help to make you realise that you are not alone and other people have felt the same way.

This gives you another "tool" you can use to empower your day. If you associate different songs or pieces of music with a feeling or a person then playing that music conjures the emotion or memory of that person. If you want or need that emotion or to remember that person (or pet) then play that music as a "short cut".

PAINKILLER PANIC

Drugs such as Ibruprofen can be dangerous if you take them without food. This has created a night time problem of not eating too many calories while eating enough bulk to work with the tablets.

After my father nearly died from the side effects of Ibruprofen I have become overly cautious as seeing him have to have a "bag" for the rest of his life is incentive enough.

I can't give you an exact recipe as it is usually what I have around and a few choice purchases to top that up. I use a one pot cook and I add no oil, sugar, butter or fat to it.

The base ingredients are usually a chopped cabbage, parsnips (optional as usually only added when I have some), Onions, Birds Eye Chilies (as many as you dare), Bulb of Garlic, Shallots (sliced thinly), carton of Passata or tube of tomato concentrate and anything else which would go with it.

Then comes the fun bit as anything that goes into a casserole, chili or other one pot cook is fair game. I usually add herbs, coriander seed, cayenne pepper, salt (optional), pepper, Worcester Sauce, gravy pot and anything else in the kitchen that would suit.

Top up with mineral water to just beneath the top of what you are cooking and bring to the boil and boil until the ingredients are soft. Add leafy greens such as spinach and then simmer with the lid on for about half an hour. You can visit it in between and stir in the spinach when it is steamed soft.

The resulting pot of vegetables is low calorie and therefore you can have a bowl when you take your tablets. If you make too much you can always freeze it and defrost what you need for a day. It is also handy for a snacking pot if you get hungry and don't want to eat anything too calorific.

The amount of chilies you add is up to you. I also add bell peppers if I have any and beansprouts and celery would also go well in the pot..

ESCAPE THE MUNDANE WORLD

We are creatures of imagination and for many there is nothing better than to escape into a good book. In my time I've read plenty and most of them on the Underground on the way to work.

Being on the train or bus can be seen as a stressful time or you can flip it as it is the one time when family and friends are not entitled to your time. If you sit in your "bubble of unreality" where you are lost in a book and keep that thought strong enough you don't get bothered. The benefit is that most people don't speak to each other on the train or bus so you are guaranteed to be able to sit there with your book and be away with it, "in" the story and seeing it unfold in front of you.

How can the rest of the day trap you when you have that freedom? You can step into worlds where magic is real, dragons are more commonplace and if you like that sort of thing someone else's life is worse than yours. There are books for everyone! Fiction, Reality and you can also learn something and the important thing is that you shut everyone else out.

If you feel that you might not get a seat then there are also talking books. Shut your eyes, forget the world and enjoy it!

GONE BUT NOT FORGOTTEN

Proof of Survival with the help of a Medium

This is firstly information given to you by whoever is doing a reading for you about a loved one who has passed over. This is of course useless for both of you if you lead the situation. The Medium needs to know they have found the right spirit for a start!

You also need to know that the Medium is genuine. Let him or her prove to you that what you are seeing is real and never reveal any information you aren't told by the Medium first.

When someone "passes over" they don't go to the other side straight away. They often wait for the funeral but sometimes if they have unfinished business they can either stay longer or come back.

They can come back for a "visit" depending on who they are and their relationship with their place of the dead.

The Proof of Survival I was taught was more an opportunity for a person who has passed over to give information or a message. Being a Clairvoyant that basically means working with my Guide to meet with the person who has passed over and then working out what is important from images they show me.

As I use a photograph I have been given to get the right spirit of course describing them is useless. There has to be verification and obviously I have no idea what is important as it will be pictures of all manner of things which are important to them and sometimes in a scene so what is important has to be worked out.

An example was a lady in a uniform similar to a nun who stood beside a Vintage Style car. She then took me upstairs in a house. The garden and house were immaculate, as was the bedroom. There was a beautiful old chest of drawers.

She opened the bottom drawer and took out some black lacquer boxes with oriental designs on them and opened each one to show me the jewellery inside. The jewellery seemed important to her.

From the start I was saying what I saw as I had no idea what it meant but the poor girl I was reading for was in tears. Her mother had passed away. She had been a nurse way back when and she had had a black car. The daughter had been wondering whether to sell the jewellery in the lacquer boxes.

That can be the sort of information the dead wish to impart. Or there can be nothing. It is possible or rather very likely that the person has done all they need to do. Their time is done and they are gone to the other side. That is the Blessed Situation as the Spirit is content to move on to whatever comes next and the relative or friend has to accept that. They may be disappointed but if there is no message there is no message.

BE CREATIVE

Everyone is creative in one way or another. If you lay out your desk in a certain way you are creating the "look" you want. If you lay out your food on a plate to look "nice" you are being creative. If you doodle on a post it note that is Art. Choosing an ornament for your home is buying a piece of Art. It doesn't have to be expensive or signed by the artist. Someone created and made it so that you like it and by welcoming it into your home and that special space in your life you are making it important. Art is very personal and one person's masterpiece may not be understood by another. That is the beauty of it. As children we could draw and paint what we liked without fear of criticism. As adults we worry more and sometimes too much. If you like it, that is all that is important really.

Let yourself be creative. Find your personal space. Find out who YOU are. What do YOU like? Free yourself from what people expect you to be and then you will achieve all that you can be. All very easy to say, not so easy to do. When time is limited and you have responsibilities taking time out for yourself is never easy.

People talk about blockages stopping them being creative. With Lockdown people have found time where they didn't have time before and it has liberated creativity. So "spare" time is a big blockage. Or shall I call it un earmarked time. That is the time to yourself where you can do something creative which you may feel day to day is a "waste of time" when there are other choices. Your inner critic is probably very vocal that you are wasting time. But, it is YOUR time to "waste" and creativity is valuable. Tell your critic to leave you alone (and the rest of the family if they are bothering you but in a "nice way" as the last thing you need is ill will!).

To find out what you really want you have to ask yourself. You could be the one standing in your own way. It will bring you the freedom to do what you want to do and sometimes it is worth looking at why you do things and how they come about, those things which "get in your way". Some people need to suffer and feel safe in their suffering. With success comes responsibility and throwing away that security blanket. Some people are not blessed with good health and there are barriers in their way but that is no boundary which can't be worked on, they just have to try harder than most to do the same thing. So the success is all the sweeter.

Sometimes you have to let life make your decisions for you as well. It takes courage to accept the gifts you are given. It takes intelligence to notice them and it takes wisdom to know what to accept and what to leave well alone.

Only you can change your life. Nobody can do it for you. Situations and the actions of others can give you challenges or opportunities but only you can decide how you deal with this. You have to want to change or you will be a "tourist" who is swept along by the life river. If this is what makes you happy then you don't need to change your life at all so accept that and enjoy the ride. If it doesn't make you happy then there is a time to question what you can change and what you cannot.

In a world of chaos and chattering voices, doubts, anxiety, depression and chemically induced worry (caffeine and alcohol) sometimes you need to put your hand up and say "No More!". In a world of Emotional Vampires and those who gain their strength by what they perceive as Personal Power by the submission of others there comes a time when you have to realise what they are doing and say "No more!". In realizing what they are doing you gain your personal power. If it is someone you love and they aren't going to change you have to realise what they are doing and then there is nothing they can do. Then you are "gifting" them the control if it makes them happy when you don't need to challenge them but keeping control of the things which are important when it is important to you. There is great value in making someone think it is their idea.

RECOVERING YOUR LIFE PATH

We all have plans, hopes and dreams when we are young. Even if we do not totally have direction, we have an idea. Sometimes that idea is to be a rebel and to bury and destroy any ideas you have yourself or the hopes and dreams and contentment of others.

Life can shape that idea until one day perhaps we look up and you are somewhere quite different to where you really want to be and perhaps you are not quite the person you know you can be either.

Then it is time to recover that Life Path which can be as drastic as you feel is necessary.

VISUALISATIONS & MEDITATIONS

A Visualisation is a little "film" in your head which brings about feelings. In your mind you are always free to imagine and a visualization is your chance to imagine something. This gives a degree of freedom as you can go there any time you like and anywhere you like. Even if you are squashed on a crowded train clinging to the metal pole and wishing the torment would be over! Instigating a Visualisation takes you to a better place so that the time your body has to endure the "boredom" of being stuck is irrelevant. You are in your happy place and enjoying that time which you have to yourself!

If you would like to try this visualisation then I have put the words on Youtube for you as obviously once you have your eyes closed you can't read it!

I would like you to sit up straight, put your feet firmly on the floor and gently rest your hands on your lap, palm upwards. Please now close your eyes and listen to the words.

"I would like you to imagine light shining down on you from above and washing over you. It starts at the top of your head and gently flows over and through you. Over your head, over your face, down your neck, chest, down your arms to the tips of your fingers, down past your waist, down your thighs, over your knees, calf and finally your ankles and into your feet. This light is flowing away any stress or anxiety you may have had and bathing the negativity away, it is washing away in the current of light and leaving you.

I now want you to see yourself walking down a quiet country leafy lane. The birds are singing and either side of the road is bursting with green growth. The odd wild flower adds colour and you can smell its scent in the gentle breeze, mixing with all the smells of the lane, the grass, the trees.

To your left there is a break in the trees which opens out onto a green pasture. You leave the lane and cross the pasture until you come to a wall with a gate in it. You open the gate and step in. The gate is of your choosing and different for everyone. This is YOUR space. Beyond the gate there is a garden. It is a garden of your choosing, it is how you like it and grows the plants and flowers that you like. If you like ponds, it has a pond. If you like fountains, it has a fountain. Walk into your garden and smell the soil, the plants and the gentle breeze. If it doesn't feel quite right, then imagine the garden as bare soil and build the garden up as you would like it, put in the paths you like and the structures you like. This is your place, what you like is how it is. In the back of the garden there is a waterfall, taller than you are.

You can build a wall around your garden and put in a gate or door. It is your secure place and if you would like a wall, put one there.

43

As you cross the garden to the waterfall you can hear the water falling and feel the gentle chill as you step under it. Feel the water wash down over your head, shoulders, down your arms, over your body, down your legs and over your feet. The water is taking all the stress and worry away, it is filling you with energy, washing it in and washing away tiredness.

You can stay under that waterfall as long as you like, feeling the water tumbling down over your skin. When you are happy to leave, feel the water drain away from you, step away from the waterfall, feel the sun drying you and then leave your garden, close the gate behind you knowing that any time you want to go back there, you can. It is always there, waiting for you and nobody else."

That could be a very useful exercise if you are ever stressed and need to relax very quickly. With practice you will be able to take yourself straight to that waterfall and wash away any tension.

Holding back and denying your true self can cause you to be uncomfortable in your life. Part of you that is your creative side is likely to be crying out to be "noticed". If it isn't "noticed" it can be a disruptive element even if you don't know it is there. We see stress and other issues as being mind effecting but they can have a physical effect as well. Releasing that creative beastie can unblock aspects in your life, allowing your body to function better.

You are designed to do things, it is when you start restraining that ability that there is a dis-ease. Depression, anxiety and sleeplessness are all symptoms that something is not quite right. In a world of restraint this is not surprising.

Many of us want to be more "ourselves". Maybe you sense that you can be more creative or do so much more but somehow you feel unable to use the skills that you have. Your dreams elude you and perhaps your life feels flat. Perhaps you have great ideas, wonderful dreams but you are unable to act on them. Then even the mundane becomes hard work and too much effort.

There will be no quick fix. This can also be a bit of a rollercoaster ride emotionally as well. We will take it gently and remember that you are feeling these emotions because you are waking up and accepting that you want more from life than the routine you have already and this can be a very intense feeling. Or you may take to it as a blessed liberation, feel energized by it all and romp ahead with new plans and ideas which dovetail with the responsibilities and successes you have already.

You have to WANT to be free of situations and you have to WANT to be yourself. Some people are very comfortable to say that they would like to do something but they are blocked from doing it by a whole list of reasons. Sometimes it is they themselves who are writing that blocking list.

Being successful, being creative and being healthy and happy is a big responsibility. It is taking a step out from under the duvet of sympathy and the security that people will feel sorry for you, or where you feel safe in the mundanity of life, and realizing that you are taking the responsibility for being all the things that YOU want to be.

There may well be resentment, there may even be a little anger from those around you. You are shedding a vulnerability and making yourself stronger. By doing that you are showing them that they could do it as well. You may also be showing them that you don't need them. Needing and wanting are two different things. When you lose the reliance on someone you can then truly "want" them to be there for no other reason than you actually enjoy their company and/or love them.

It could be that you give others the permission to make a change in their life too. That is their journey and their path to overcome. You can't focus on others. The whole point here is that you have to focus on yourself in relation to the world, not the world influencing you.

You are quite literally giving up life as you know it as nothing will appear the same again. If it is the chance you want to take then you are taking a step into a life of autonomy, resilience, expectancy and excitement where you can make and execute concrete creative plans.

You take this journey for yourself to live out and achieve YOUR dreams, hopes and ambitions. Or it may be that you find out you are actually happy exactly where you are, doing what you are doing and you just need that extra inner freedom and space to do what you enjoy occasionally. There may be no need for a dramatic life shift.

You may have squandered your enthusiasm in the past on what family and your peers expected or wanted for you. No more. You are here to achieve YOUR goals, YOUR dreams and to be who YOU want to be. You will have to hold onto this thought as well as there will be those who, as before, want you to fulfil their hopes and dreams. To effect creative recovery you must undergo a time of mourning as well. You are dealing with the abandonment of the "mediocre" self you have been making do with. The rebirth of the Phoenix in you can be as dramatic or as simple as necessary. It can be as minimal as you just feel happier with how things are and take some time for yourself. It could be a complete life change. That is for you to decide and discover.

OPENING THE GATE

The first step is to take the lock off of the gate which has been keeping you a prisoner. This is a lock that you put there yourself and it has been built up over the years like "Marley's Chains" in a Christmas Carol.

Please take a sheet of paper and write down one thing that you have wanted to do, could realistically do, would still like to do and have never done. Next write down three reasons why you haven't done it already and feel you cannot do it. Next write down all the ways you could overcome all the reasons you have just written down.

Are you thinking of all the reasons why you cannot achieve what you want to do or are you thinking of all the reasons why your excuses aren't valid?

I would like you to listen to the way that you speak for a while. Not to the point of being pedantic about it but just take note for a while.

Are you positive in the way that you speak? Do you use negatives more often than positives? When you are asking questions, do you first say "I don't suppose it is possible that..." or phrases such as that?

The next step is to realise that much more is possible for you than you may have first thought. Before you write any idea off, think of it as if it is already happening. Is it realistic? It is possible? That is the way to open that gate and believe that it can be possible. Then you are part way on the way towards making it possible.

I would like you to take all the junk mail that you can collect for a week or two and put it on the floor in front of you. Now I want you to think of all those things you usually say to yourself whenever you want to do something to stop yourself. Pick up the junk mail bit by bit and tear it up as you think of those excuses. Cut through those barriers you are putting up and rip them to pieces.

Now that you have an interesting pile of paper in front of you, pick out the pieces you like the look of. Perhaps you like the colour or the shape? Pick them up, take some glue and piece of paper and stick them onto the paper to make a collage. It doesn't matter how you do it, this is how YOU do it. This is how you like it and it is with the pieces that you personally like.

Now look at the colours and shapes in front of you. Are there any colours you have chosen more than any others? Colours are very important in our lives. We can effect our moods by what we wear, how we decorate our homes and the colours we have around us. This can be a very valuable tool, even when faced with having to wear a black or grey suit to work. If you have a choice of blouse, let that reflect the colour that you need. A coloured tie is the obvious way to express yourself. If you have to wear a white shirt then a little helper I was told about is wearing red knickers. It may sound daft but it actually works. Red is a very strong colour, the base chakra colour. It grounds us and gives us security and keeps us close to the earth. In that way it also helps with confidence. If you are interested in colour therapy then there is a whole world of colour to learn about and experiment with.

MAKING IT HAPPEN (MANIFESTATION)

You may have heard about MANIFESTATION. It involves wanting something to happen and by that wish somehow it does happen. This can be positive and negative. By thinking that something won't happen and by blocking yourself you are not only putting your own gate in the way, you are asking the universe to make sure it doesn't happen as well.

Manifestation and proclamation influence your waking world whether you like it or not. Take back control!

If you want to manifest something you have to want something. A simple journal or paper and pen can help. Grasped for the moment and the words creeping across the page and liberating themselves from your cluttered and life infested mind.

The so much that you have to do set aside in a blurt of feeling and freedom. Your request made to the Universe.

Manifesting is transforming thoughts, dreams and ideas into reality using intention and action. The power of positive thinking and actually knowing what you want so that you can think about them specifically, visualize them happening and being grateful for all you have been given in the past.

You would be bringing something into your life through attraction and belief.

FINDING YOUR CREATIVITY

We are all victims of our own inner critic. It is a loud little quiet voice. He is like an imp on your shoulder who keeps a constant stream of criticism and niggles of little fears. Just remember that it is that little

48

voice, it is not the truth.

If your critic is being a nuisance then take a piece of paper and write all over it how useless your critic is in stopping you and how you are going to prove your critic wrong. You will have this page when your critic is being particularly difficult.

You can let that little critic rattle on with its criticism and just keep writing across the page. That is your defiance. If it helps you can imagine this critic as the funniest creature you have ever seen or imagine it as an ugly goblin dressed in something very silly. You could also think of it as a serpent, keen to lure you into stepping away from what is important to you. What is important is to take away its importance in your life and realise that it is your enemy sometimes.

If it is chattering too much then draw it as a cartoon or a stick man in your Journal and put a big cross over it, crossing it out. By making it a "physical thing" you are taking its power away and by crossing it out you are again taking its power over you away.

It may be that you feel it was a parent who installed this critic in your life. The point is to stop the censor but keep the calm voice of reason. It is knowing the difference between the two. One will help to stop you doing something unsafe or really daft, the other will stop you doing something creative and wonderful. Learning the difference between them is the first step to walking through that gate safely.

LOGIC BRAIN AND CREATIVE BRAIN

There are plenty of books and studies about this subject. Logic brain is your survival brain. It thinks in a neat, linear fashion and sees the world in categories and well known principles. If anything is unknown it is seen as wrong and dangerous. It is the sensible one.

An original thought terrifies Logic Brain! So, stop listening to the ridicule and the doubts and fears and start listening to Creative Brain who wants you to have a bit of fun and who instinctively feels that something is possible.

You need both and they need to learn to work together. Creativity and the logic of science can work wonderfully in union.

THE RECLAIMED MOMENTS

Life can be very busy and in the past finding any time for yourself may have been difficult. With lockdown this may well have changed for you already. You may now have more time than you know what to do with! It doesn't mean that you can't have a Creative Date with yourself. You may well not have space for yourself even in lockdown with others at home and needing your time. Your Creative Date is your time. You have to defend it from all comers and make sure that you have that time. You can't include anyone in it. You can tell them about it as it may be quicker than them wondering and trying to find out. It is very simple, not selfish, just your time. It is your space and if there are challenges to it, you will have to make sure it happens.

This is quality time to spend with your creativity. It doesn't have to be expensive and it is just what you want to do. It costs time not money.

This is a weekly trip that you have to commit yourself to. It could be a walk to the end of the garden, time locked in your room. Wherever it is it is something that you "book" with yourself, and try to watch yourself trying to wriggle out of. The time will get encroached upon and other parties will try and get involved. You will have to learn to guard against these incursions. This time is valuable and essential to your discovery of self.

FANCY A CUPPA?

When you buy a jar of coffee you could be buying it for many reasons. Is it just as a wake up cuppa? Is it to have a chat with friends? Spoonful by spoonful you will work your way down the jar. Each cup being a memory of all the things you see and do while you are drinking that cup. That can be a meditation in itself as that space you are making for yourself in your day to drink your coffee is space which is yours to claim, to use or just to have breathing space from "doing".

Are you drinking the coffee (or tea) for taste or for the social aspect? There are whole rituals which revolve around making a cup of tea. They revolve around showing off the utensils. Does the cup matter? My mother always thought so. In these rushed days we grab a mug and get on with it.

What of the jar? Is it just a jar? It can be. It holds what you need it to hold, it goes into the glass recycling, is melted down and becomes another jar or bottle. Or, can it become something else? We'll get to that later.

CLEAR YOUR MIND

The mind is a wonderful thing and it can come up with some wonderful ideas.

Ideas in the mind clutter the mind and can be a stress in themselves. They flutter around and remind us of what we haven't managed to do or what we still have to do. If you want to get them out of your mind without losing them then write them down in your Thought Journal. Then you can come back to them when you need them rather than having to carry them around like luggage.

Downloading things from your mind is a good exercise and it provides a physical "list" where you can find information when you need it and cross jobs off when they are done. That gives a sense of satisfaction in itself. Also, ideas which come to you can be lost by other distractions and disappear like mists in the wind. Those great ideas will be "on hold" not lost forever.

I started carrying a small notebook and pencil or pen with me at all times and this can be both amusing and rewarding. People have kept journals and travel journals for years. They are invaluable for downloading all that information and thoughts that otherwise will clutter your hard drive (brain). The ideas are still there and you can revisit them when you want to and take them further but you don't have to hold onto them so tightly as they are already noted down.

The more you work your mind, the more it works. It needs to fire up and think and "be" and if you don't allow it to exercise itself it will find other ways to amuse itself, usually in the form of anxiety and depression as then it has your attention.

It may be that you feel that your job is "mundane" and your time is wasted by what you are doing. On the contrary you are in the very beneficial situation of having time to think and imagine other things while you are being paid to do it. Your mind is always free, particularly if you are doing something repetitive, as you don't need to really be there all the time emotionally as long as you concentrate enough to "get it right" and do your best and of course as long as it is safe to do so.

As part of my job in the past I had to sort out the law books. Their pages came in regularly as things changed and the pages had to be replaced. I was always happy to do that even though it was the Receptionist's job. She had enough to do, I had some spare time, so I didn't mind and my philosophy has always been "Ours is not to do or die, ours is just to pacify". So if the books weren't up to date there would be stress, I didn't want the stress, so I was happy to do the menial task of keeping them up to date.

I realized that during that repetitive time of taking one page out and replacing it with another I had time to think. It was a time when the body was busy and the mind could think through what I wanted to free of any need or responsibility to do anything else. It was "my time".

While at the farm this moved on to being the time when I was mucking out. It is a positive thing to do as you start with a big pile of animal poo and then little by little it can be shovelled into the wheelbarrow and wheeled somewhere else, then it becomes manure.

From the manure things can grow. Then of course we got the bigger barn and needed a skid steer to do it and all that was lost.

That is if you muck out alone. If you do it with others it is a lovely social time where you can chatter about anything you like as you don't have to concentrate.

Any time you have something to do which is repetitive and you don't need to concentrate on it then that is time for you.

It could be time to have that notebook with you to make those notes as you have no idea what ideas will come up and you don't want to lose them. Save them for later and then you can write them down in your journal properly and when you read them back perhaps they will be the seed of something great.

If you are having trouble thinking about what to do because the world is chattering too much then it is time to take half an hour a day to think about what you would like to do and do it. It can be simple things.

Keep a small plastic non-recyclable cup from a drink you have had. Put a hole in the bottom. Find some soil. Find a plant or a seed from something you have eaten (doesn't matter what it is, weeds are just plants out of place). Then plant it in the soil in the cup. You'll need to put something to hold water like an old saucer underneath it. Take time every day to give that plant a little bit of water. Take that time as your time, your little breathing space in the chaos of the day. That is your "happy time".

Take a short walk and look for "Nature out of Place". It can be a piece of grass growing in concrete, it can be a leaf which has blown from a tree. However much we create concrete boxes for ourselves nature will always find a way in. Make a note in your diary of what you have seen and how you felt.

Take time to feel the breeze on your face. When you are walking, take a moment to feel the air touching you, the breeze. Watch it blowing your hair (if you have long hair). Watch it blowing a leaf and focus on that leaf, how it moves and how something inanimate has suddenly become something moving. That moment in time will never happen again. Wind has always blown. It will blow long after you are gone. Not that particular wind, that is just that bit of air moving but a bit of air will be moving somewhere. Then focus on that breeze blowing your troubles away. Throw your problems into the air and imagine them blown away by that breeze. Then think about how you can be the breeze and make them gone!

If you have the opportunity take a moment to turn everything off which makes noise and sit and enjoy the peace. Focus on the silence or the other noises you can hear, ones you would miss normally.

Take a moment wherever you are (as long as it is safe to do so, not while driving please). Sit down or stand still. Take a deep breath in and let it out slowly. Imagine you are in a beautiful woodland or beside the sea or somewhere else you would like to be. This doesn't have to be a real place or a memory. Feel that you are there. Imagine the soil or sand under your feet, the breeze on your face. This is your place. Nobody else can go there or be there with you. It is somewhere you can escape to when you need to.

Look around and commit it to memory. What is on the floor at your feet?

Are there trees?

Are there birds?

This is your space and your escape. When you feel the world is getting you down you can call up this image and remember the peace and tranquility there is there.

.

3 MINDFULNESS AND CARE JARS

Time to take stock of your life! If you feel overwhelmed and don't know where to start why not start with an empty coffee jar?

HAPPY JAR

Take a jar with a lid. It doesn't have to be a special jar, any jar will do. Find yourself a piece of paper and a pen. That is all that you need. If you have time and a candle available then light a candle and perhaps put on some music which you really like and which makes you happy. The decision of this music in itself can be a step in the process. Then shut the door and keep everyone out. This works best if you find yourself a quiet place, a private place as these are your thoughts and should not be influenced by others. They may feel curious or intimidated by what you are doing. You may have to take a little time to explain that you just need a little bit of time to think.

Choose your time for doing this as well. A time when there are no other demands on your life. If there are chores to do, do them first. Clear your mind, clear your responsibilities and then take that time with a clear mind. This is your time of calm and your time to think.

When you have your space and you have your candle lit and your music playing take the piece of paper. On it write all the good things that have happened to you. One by one, as you remember them and they don't

55

have to be in any order. Don't worry about "getting them all". If you think of something later you can always add it in.

Write them as a list, one below the other, leaving enough space between them to cut them out.

Then take a pair of scissors and cut them out so that they lay on the table in front of you. There will hopefully be lots of slips of paper of all the happy times in your life.

Then, one by one, pick them up, fold them up so that the writing is on the inside, thank them and put them in the jar.

When you have put them into the jar cut some spare slips and keep them near the jar. When you think of more, add them in. If you don't feel there are enough then it is time to think about what would make you happy and go and do some things so that you can write them on the spare paper.

Take another piece of paper and write down all the things which would make you happy. Write them in the same way. Fold that paper and put it into the top of your jar uncut so you can get them out again.

Then it is time to go out into your life and make them happen. As they happen cut them out of the piece of paper and add them to the other slips of paper in the jar.

When you have a down day or the "black dog" of depression is nibbling at your ankles it is time to get your jar out, put it on the table, make yourself a drink and take out the bits of paper randomly and remember those happy times.

The Happy Jar can cost you very little but it may come to mean a lot.

You can decorate your jar or add things to it. If you go to the cinema or a show and enjoy it then you could put the ticket into the jar too. They are all happy memories there for you when you need them.

If you have anything that will fit in the jar that you want to keep safe that is a happy memory then put it in the jar. It is your jar, there are no "rules". Perhaps you have a ribbon from when your child was young, anything that is important to you is something for the jar.

That jar is there for when you feel down. You can reach into the jar, pull out a happy memory and remember.

TAKE A HIKE (THE MEMORY JAR)

That is exactly what you want your worries to do. They chitter, chatter and make things so much worse. There is no glory in them, let them go. They don't help and they won't solve anything. Only in the quiet moments when you can think will you think your way out of a problem and find solutions. It is oh so easy to focus on the problem and let it drag you down. That won't get rid of it.

Life around you probably doesn't help either. There are so many things you have to do and the more you worry about what isn't done the more this piles up both physically and emotionally. To be able to sort the problem you need clarity, time and space. It is up to you to make that space.

If you can then take a moment to plan a little trip. Just a short walk or a trip to the seaside, a park or a forest. There are places everywhere that you can do this. You can plan your trip or you can be spontaneous. Even if you are being spontaneous you should first look outside the window and make sure you have the right coat, the right boots or shoes and that you are dressed appropriately for the weather. It may seem obvious but anything that is going to distract you or be unpleasant is going to make what you are going to do more difficult.

You can do this any time. Of course make sure that you are safe and not walking where you are likely to be afraid or in danger. Your peace of mind is very important while taking this walk.

It may be that you are short of time, you are busy, you can make excuses. You can always make excuses but what about a lunch hour? You can plan ahead. If you buy your food every day then buy food for that day so that you save time and can have time spare for your walk rather than the shop queue. Perhaps you could take it with you like a picnic and have it in the park (weather permitting). It is one less excuse and a chance to get outside. You need to get anywhere that is away from your workplace or home.

You will be surprised where there are green spaces. I worked in London and even there you are never far from a square or bit of green.

This is your time but it isn't just a walk. It is a chance to focus. While you walk you can think, plan or just think of nothing. While you are on your walk take time to look around, to hunt down some treasure to take home with you. It can be a stone, perhaps a leaf, perhaps a flower. That one thing is the most important thing in the world. Focus on finding it above all other things you might be thinking about. You may find many things but you can only take one back with you.

When you find the special something and when it is safe to do so stand with both feet firmly placed on the ground. Then take a deep breath, breathe it in and then let it out slowly. Imagine that you are breathing out all your worries with that breath. Breathe in again, gather them up and breathe them out. In that moment all you should be doing is focusing on the thing you have found and breathing out your worries.

That one thing is beautiful. If it is a stone or something else it has taken many thousands of years to be that one thing in that one place in your hand. Bits of it have been part of many other things which have been part of many other things. For that moment in time what you are seeing is perfect. In the next moment it will be different but it will still be perfect. It cannot be any less than perfect because perfection is what it is supposed to be at that point in time, as it is, in your hand.

It is a part of a cycle of life and part of all that there is. In that one moment in the world everything is as it is. In the next moment everything will be different, that one moment will never be the same again. As it is with troubles. Every moment they are closer to being solved.

Problems are as they are now but it only takes a solution or being able to deal with them and life will move on.

When you walk on, watch the ground and see if you can find something else. Perhaps there is an acorn, a leaf, a stick and that is something else you can bring back with you. Now you have twice what you had before. You have your memories before and your memories after.

When you get home find a jar or buy one of our Memory Jars and put what you have found in it. As you take more trips add to your treasures in your jar. If you have the time you can decorate your jar. It is your jar, your space, your piece of the universe.

You probably won't remember which walk each piece is from or when you got it but as your jar gains its little collection of things you will know you had those walks and that is sometimes enough. If you would rather know then write what you found in your diary together with how you felt about it.

They are a reminder of the time and space you had and how easy it is to make that space and escape. You are never trapped and they are a reminder that you can physically see and touch. You can take them out of the jar, touch them and remember.

Problems mount up if they aren't dealt with and sometimes you just can't deal with them. This makes more problems and a feeling of helplessness and being trapped. You are never trapped. There is always an answer, you just have to think of what it is. Admitting that the situation has got the better of you is a start and if necessary call out for help. There are plenty of people who are trained to listen if you would rather your friends didn't know.

When you get back from your walk you can start planning how you are going to solve your problems.

JARRING EVENT

There comes a time in everyone's life when there is a major life event. It can be good or bad but one thing is certain, the memory will stay with you forever.

In time that memory will fade and in some ways, if it is a bad event, that can be exactly what you want it to do.

Here it is best to have a jar and a cardboard box.

For the jar you could write down on bits of paper all the happy bits of the memory. You could take a moment at any time and perhaps keep paper and pen with you. Perhaps a tiny version in your pocket, handbag or wallet. This is for you to write down your thoughts. Let them get out of your head so they don't run around in there can cause mayhem.

In a digital age there are more than likely no physical photographs for you to hold and "feel the moment". Images flicker on a screen but that doesn't have the same physical grounding as a photograph can have. So, perhaps you'd like to keep paper which has been "misprints" and then print out small versions of your photographs and put them in your jar to remember a specific event. If there are physical things you can keep from the event e.g. a twig from the ground at a wedding, some of the confetti after it is thrown, a shell, a feather, then put that in your jar as well. These things have no value monetarily but emotionally they are priceless because they were part of the day.

If the event is an unpleasant one then do the same thing but put everything into a cardboard box. That is a box you can throw into a bonfire to cleanse yourself of the feelings or bring them somewhere that you can safely burn the box. If you are burning garden rubbish then throw the box on the fire. Bless it and let those bad memories go into smoke and ash. You are finished with the memories, let them float into the ether.

AFFIRMATIONS JAR.

When you feel doubt or need a bit of guidance or reassurance then it could be time to turn to your Affirmations Jar.

This is something that only you can create and it is something you can do on a day when you are feeling positive.

There are a whole list of Affirmations you could put into the jar but these Affirmations have to be yours. When you have a quiet moment you can add to your jar.

If you have the time then sit somewhere quiet with a pen and paper and clear your mind. You are a unique person, everyone is different so the Affirmations you make should be personal to you.

In advance you could collect up bits of paper and make slips of paper to write your Affirmations on, to fold and to get them ready for a moment when you can sit and write them down. If you are particularly busy then put them in a place in your purse or wallet and write on them when you think of something.

EXAMPLES

You are special.

Today is yours.

Inspire someone today.

Smile a lot today.

Laugh a lot today.

Live Your Dreams.

If you have any ideas while you are reading this then why not write them down.

THE JAR LIST

This is like a "Bucket List" but in a jar and on a much smaller scale. This is a list of small things that you can do easily each day if you take the time.

There will be times in your life when you question "What have I done?" Well, what you do is up to you and if you want to do things you will have to make tie to do them.

You will also have to make your list realistic and things that you can do with little or no cost at all. What you are "spending" is your time and what you will get back is far more valuable. You may have to trade time you would spend doing something else but you can always do that "something else" another day if it is something you do regularly.

If you make your list simple achievable things like "Take a Walk", "Read a Book", "Watch a Film", "Listen to a Specific Song"

The list will be very personal to you and things that you will enjoy. Only put things on the list that you personally will enjoy, not just things that will make a good selfie and comment on social media!

Take a moment to sit and write this list when you are somewhere that is familiar to you. It could be on the train going to work, in a lunch hour etc. List the things on a piece of paper. You can then write them out again on slips of paper when you get home and put them in your jar. You can add to them any time that you want to or think of something else.

The list will be personal to you and it has to be things that you do by yourself that you will enjoy.

You are doing this for you. You can talk about them to others but while you are doing the you are doing them for you and you must do them alone and only because you want to.

If you get some time to yourself then you can go to your jar, pull out a piece of paper and "do that thing". Once you have done it you can put that piece of paper into your "Completed Jar". If you don't manage to complete the task then it can go back into the Jar List.

If you specifically enjoy doing something and you want to do it again then you can write it on a few bits of paper and add these to the Jar to give yourself more chances of doing it again.

That saves wasting time wondering what to do when you have some precious spare time.

4 CARE DOLLS

Care Dolls are simple dolls shaped like a "gingerbread man" who are stuffed with filling and then decorated. They can have an intent or just be decorative.

If you are giving one as a gift you can either make it yourself or you can buy one from us which is already made up. This can be either decorated or you can decorate it yourself.

The making of them starts with cutting the initial shape from felt. This can be to a set pattern or freehand. This can also be an animal or other shape if you prefer.

Dolls have been with us for many years, either made ourselves or bought from a shop. They can be handmade, knitted or mass produced. Some are collectable, some are toys.

Every Christmas many dolls are placed on the top of a Christmas Tree. They are a part of the Celebrations and taken from their box and brought out into the light for the duration of the holiday celebrations.

Either made as toys or for rituals the "effigy" of a human has been with us for millennia.

The dolls I am writing about here are specifically created to be Care Dolls.

They are a gift of love and something physical which can be given as a token.

They are also something you can make or buy for yourself. They are something you can physically hold and decorate with things which are important to you. In a minimalist world such meanings have been lost. In the rush to Feng Shui your home the articles which carried the memories of the love with which they were given have been swept away.

In "olden days" when people went on holiday they brought back "trinkets" for those left behind. These were gifts of love which were a physical reminder that while the friend or relative was travelling they were thinking of those they love. The gifts themselves were unimportant, it was the meaning and they each had an "energy" which could spark a thought of that person who had given the gift when they are seen.

These things do not necessarily fit with the modern age of clean lines. So, what we have come up with is a "Memory Jar" or a "Care Jar". This is a simple jar which can be filled with things and then sent to someone you care about. In this jar you can also put a small "Care Doll". This can either be made yourself, we can provide a pre-cut kit for you to sew or we can sew it for you.

As these things are personal we will have to build our collection of what is offered as we go along.

When I made the first doll I drew out various shapes onto a piece of paper and then cut that out. I pinned it to a double sheet of felt and then cut out the first doll. I then took a needle and embroidery thread (silk) and split the thread into three strands from the six strands there are in a thread. That is enough to sew the doll. Then there was a choice of stitches. It could be done on a sewing machine but that doesn't put the level of "care" into the doll. With each stitch there is a purpose and little by little the doll is built. Obviously this means that these cannot be mass produced and can only be made one by one.

The standard dolls which are made are about the length of a hand. They are a good size to be given as a gift on their own. I am now working on a design for a smaller one to be put into a Care Jar.

The main body will be small enough to fit into the jar with its decoration and allow space in the jar for other things. It would be possible to put a large one in but he or she would be a bit squashed! The Care Jar will keep the doll clean and safe and it also provides a jar which can be used for putting other keepsakes in.

You can make a doll yourself. As long as the basic shape you end up with looks like a doll you can use any medium that you like. Perhaps you could cut a shape from cardboard and then paint and decorate it. Perhaps you would like to use felt or another material. Then you can hand sew it and fill it with other bits of material, cotton wool or shredded non-recyclable plastic. It is up to you how creative you want to be.

When your doll is made he or she will need eyes and perhaps a mouth. Perhaps you will clothe your doll or perhaps you will decorate it as it is.

These dolls are a great way to use broken bits and pieces of jewellery, odd beads, odd buttons, bits of wool and other bits and pieces you may have around.

Perhaps your children have grown up and you have bits and pieces from when they were small. Old necklaces and beads they once played with but don't need anymore. Those little memories which could be sewn into or onto a doll and kept for the future.

It is the intent which is important when making a doll. Dolls can be made for all types of reasons. Perhaps for luck, perhaps just to show you care, perhaps as something you can hold when you are stressed or worried.

CARE DOLLS & CANDLES

(Herbs can also be added to candles)

LOVE

Gemstone:	Rose Quartz
Oils:	Orange Blossom, Jasmine, Rose
Colour:	Red, Pink, White
Timing:	New Moon, First Quarter Moon, Friday at Dawn
Verbal:	Oh Spirit of Love. Bring Joy, Happiness and Harmony into the life of the owner of this doll. All around you and all who touch you will experience the perfection of universal love. Blessings Upon You.
Herbs:	Aster, Basil, Birch, Bleeding Heart, Caraway, Cardamon, Catnip, Chamomile, Chestnut, Cinnamon, Cinquefoil, Clove, Clover, Coltsfoot, Cumin, Coriander, Cyclamen, Dairy, Dittany of Crete, Dock, Elm, Geranium, Ginger, Hawthorn, Hazel, Heather, Hyacinth, Iris, Ivy, Jasmine, Juniper, Lady's Mantle, Lavender, Crocus, Lemon Balm, Lilac, Lovage, Mallow, Mandrake, Marjoram, Meadowsweet, Mistletoe, Myrtle, Orchid, Pansy, Passion Flower, Periwinkle, Poppy, Primrose, Rose, Rosemary, Dill, Betony, Rowan, St John's Wort, Sandalwood, Sea Holly, Sorrel, Thyme, Tulip, Willow, Yarrow, Lemon Verbena, Mimosa, Peppermint, Rue.

DRIVING TEST

Herbs:	Mint, Sunflower, Elecampane, Marigold
Gemstone:	Red Jasper
Inclusion:	Magnet
Oil:	Cedar, Pine

Colour: Red, Orange, Yellow, Purple, White
Timing: New or Full Moon

GOOD LUCK

Gemstone: Jade, Calcite, Citrine
Oil: Orange, Mint
Inclusion: Magnet, Clover, Horseshoe
Colour: Gold, Red, Purple, Green
Timing: New Moon, First and Second Quarter
Spells: Bluebell, Clover, Daffodil, Fern, Heather, Holly, Moss, Myrtle, Strawberry.
Herbs: Angelica, Beech, Broom, Clover, Elm, Hazel, Heather, Holly, Marigold, Nutmeg, Oak, Peony, Poppy, Rose, Star Anise, Sunflower

Additional Shape: Black Cat Charm

HEALING DOLL & HEALING HARE

Herbs: Bay, Olive Leaf, Black Tea, Woodruff (not for Children), Chocolate Mint, Angelica, Ash, Bay, Burdock, Calamus, Cinnamon, Coltsfoot, Comfrey, Coriander, Cowslip, Dock, Echinacea, Elder, Eucalyptus, Fennel, Feverfew, Flax, Garlic, Hazel, Horehound, Hyssop, Juniper, Lemon Balm, Lungwort, Mallow, Marjoram, Mint, Mistletoe, Mugwort, Nettle, Oak, Pine, Plantain, Rose, Rosemary, Rowan, Rue, Sage, St John's Wort, Sorrel, Tansy, Thyme, Vervain, Willow, Agrimony, Bracken, Carnation, Cedar, Hops, Ivy, Myrrh, Peppermint.
Spells: Angelica, Bay, Blackberry, Cowslip, Cranberry, Fennel, Garlic, Hops, Lavender, Rosemary, Rowan, Sorrel, Violet

DREAM DOLL

Herbs: Ash, Catnip, Chamomile, Elder, Heather,
          Jasmine, Mugwort, Poppy, Rose, Star Anise, Yarrow

Prophetic Dreams: Cinquefoil, Marigold, Mimosa, Mugwort

SLEEP DOLL & SLEEP SHEEP

You could make a set of Chakra Coloured Sheep or sheep numbered 0 –
9 with the number on each sheep to act as a counting play tool as well.

Herbs: Agrimony, Cinquefoil, Peppermint, Poppy, Eyebright,
          Lavender, Aniseed, Calendula, Chamomile, Cloves,
          Hops, Lemon Balm, Passionflower, Marjoram, Mimosa,
          Mint, Mugwort, Lilac, Lemon Verbena, Lemongrass,
          Rose, Rosemary, Thyme
Gemstones: Selenite, Quarts, Rose Quartz, Moonstone, Jade,
          Dalmatian Jasper, Celestite.

MONEY CARE DOLL

Herbs: Peppermint, Lavender, Cinquefoil, Dill, Basil,
          Chamomile, Clove, Clover, Coriander, Cumin, Dandelion,
          Ginger, Honesty, Mint, Oak, Rose, Sage, Ash, Benzoin,
          Myrtle, Pine, Poppy, Bergamot, Calamus, Cedar,
          Comfrey, Dock, Elder, Flax, Gorse, Honeysuckle,
          Jasmine, Mandrake, Marjoram, Nutmeg, Periwinkle
Gemstone: Lodestone, Bloodstone, Moss Agate, Snowflake
          Obsidian
Inclusions: Paper Money or 3 Coins in growing denominations
Colour: Green for Growth, Brown for finding hidden, White for
          making
Alternative Shape: Prosperity Pig

Spell: Cinquefoil, Honest, Lemon Balm, Marigold, Moss, Orange, Rowan, St John's Wort, Snapdragon, Sunflower, Tulip

CONFIDENCE DOLL

Herbs: Birch, Carnation, Fennel, Ginger, Thyme, Yarrow, Sweetpea

WORRY BEADS

I found out about these in a magazine and set about making some. You can make them from any beads you have laying around and thread. If you prefer something a bit special you can of course buy beads on line and we have made lots to sell, it is just finding somewhere to sell them as with postage it makes them very expensive.

When you are stressed you can run them through your fingers and feel the stones etc.

5 HERBS, VEGETABLES AND PLANTS

WHAT ARE THEY ASSOCIATED WITH?

In our past we have relied on plants for food, medicine and they have been used for medical purposes. Historically those who needed plants could wander into the wild and pick what they wanted and needed to use. That isn't the case now. Even if they do grow there are laws in certain places about picking what is growing there. That keeps the plants safe as with the increased population they would soon be picked to extinction if the interest in them was great enough. That means that the more useful they are, the more likely it is that they would be wiped out.

It is not a huge jump in logic that it would be sensible for us to farm them and for people to include them in their gardens. Seed is available, either foraged or through places which sell it. Once we can get it established we can sell it too and these plants can be preserved for the future.

The next decision of course is to decide what to plant. That will greatly rely on whether it is useful or not. I knew I had to do research on this so rather than the vast pile of notes to stay in my cupboard I thought I'd put it all here. Then there will be a record of what it is claimed that the plants do and why we are growing them. Once they are grown they will be available, fresh in pots, fresh as cut herbs, dried, as seed and any other way that we may be able to package them for you.

The following list is intended for information and amusement. We in no way endorse using these herbs medicinally or make any claims about what they can do. We have collected information in one place about what these herbs are "reputed" to do. This in no way endorses them and we have not indicated whether they should be used internally or externally. If you wish to take this research further there are books written by experts who will be able to help you.

Nothing in this book is intended to take the place of your Family Practitioner and if you feel that you are unwell you should seek their advice immediately.

ADDER'S TONGUE (Ophioglossum vulgarum.

Erythronium americanum) American Adder's Tongue, Serpent's Tongue, Adder's Mouth, Yellow Snowdrop, Dog's Tooth Violet

Planet:	Moon in Cancer
Gender:	Female
Element:	Water
Powers:	Healing
Medicinal:	Cleansing, Astringent, Old Ulcerated Wounds, Wounds (Poultice "Green Oil of Charity"), Internal Wounds, Internal Bleeding, Bruises, Vomiting (Tea), Washing Sensitive Skin.

AGRIMONY (Agrimonia eupatoria) Roseacaeae, Rose Family.

Perennial Church Steeples, Tea Plant, Little Cockbur, Fur-burr, Catch-as-catch can, Liverwort, Sticklewort

Planet:	Jupiter
Gender:	Male
Element:	Air
Sign:	Cancer
Care Doll:	Protection, Sleep, Healing
Flowers:	June – September

Height:	2ft
Powers:	Protection, Sleep
Medicinal:	Indigestion, Heartburn, Diarrhea, Food Allergies, Bed Wetting, Cystitis, Cleansing Wounds, Cooled Infusion for Sore and Inflamed Eyes, Sores, Ulcers, Tonic, Blood Cleanser, Tea and Gargle for Sore Throat, Tea and Gargle for Laryngitis, Tea and Gargle for Mouth Inflammations, Poultice for Arthritic and Rheumatic Joints, Stomach Problems, Open Wounds, Liver Complaints.
Magical:	Repels negative energy. Protection against Goblins. Spiritual and Psychic Healing where person has dabbled in unwise areas. House cleansing. Temple cleansing.
Incense:	Cleanse the aura
	Cleanse a new house.
Herb Pillow:	Restful Sleep.
Uses:	Tannins, Bitters, Essential Oil.

ALFALFA (Medicago sativa) Lucerne, Purple Medic, Buffalo Herb

Pea Family. Nitrogen Binding

Planet:	Venus
Element:	Earth
Gender:	Female
Care Doll:	Prosperity, Money
Height:	2-3ft
Powers:	Prosperity, Anti-Hunger, Money
Growing:	Perennial, Pea Family. Blooms June and October.
Medicinal:	Improve appetite, Eliminate Water Retention, Help Peptic Ulcers and Jaundice. Animal fodder, Increases Milk Production, Lasts longer than most cattle plants, Stomach Ulcers, High in protein (50%), flour for bread, Leaves make a cereal, Improve the appetite, Eliminate Water Retention, Peptic Ulcers, Jaundice, Astringent, Detoxifying, Antifungal, Pituitary Gland Function, Blood Cholesterol, Detoxifier, Anemia, Ulcers, Colitis,

	Diabetes, Hemorrage, Arthritis, Sciatica, Rheumatism, Fluid Retention, Neutralise Carcinogens, Breath Freshener, Nitrogen Binding
Culinary:	Sprouted Alfalfa Seeds
Magical:	Fertility and Plenty. Grow in the home to protect against poverty.
	Burn and scatter ashes around the property for prosperity. Burn the herb and carry ashes in an amulet in pouches to easy money problems. Protection vs Poverty
	Fertility and plenty, material wealth and stability
Vitamins:	A, B1, B12, C, D, E, K
Incense:	Earth Incense with Patchouli Oil, Pine Wood and Salt
	Money Drawing with Cypress Wood and Patchouli Oil
Dogs:	Arthritis, Blood Disorders, Minerals, Vitamins, Proteins, Anti-Inflammatory, Anti toxicant, Diuretic, Rheumatism, Musculoskeletal System, Digestive Tract, Liver, Cancer Preventative, Bleeding Disorders, Anticoagulant, Absorption of fat soluble nutrients, Stimulates growth hormones, Acidic urine, Bladder irritation, Crystal formation, Change of diet, Mental vigour

ALKANET (Alkanna tinctoria) Dyer's Bugloss

Planet:	Venus
Gender:	Female
Element:	Water
Medicinal:	Treat Wounds, Ulcers, Rashes, Burns, Bed Sores, Jaundice, Spleen, Kidneys.
Dyes:	Root (Reddish)
Culinary:	Flowers and Young Leaves – raw in salads or cooked like Spinach.
Powers:	Purification, Prosperity
History:	Powdered root was used as rouge.
	Cultivated before late Sixteenth Century.

ALYSSUM

Care Doll: Protection, Moderating Anger

AMARANTH (Amaranthus hypochondriacus)

Planet: Saturn
Gender: Female
Element: Fire
Deity: Artemis
Care Doll: Healing, Protection

ANGELICA (Angelica Archangelica) Masterwort, Archangel, Garden Angelica, The Angel's Herb, Bellyache Root, Root of the Holy Ghost, Herba Angelica (Angel's Plant) DIABETICS SHOULD NOT TAKE INTERNALLY SHOULD NOT BE TAKEN IN LARGE DOSES OVER AN EXTENDED PERIOD

Planet: Sun in Leo, Venus
Element: Fire
Gender: Male
Deity: Venus, Michael, Sun Gods
Sign: Leo
Grown: Perennial
Flowers: July and August of the Second Year
Height: 6ft (1.8m)
Care Doll: Protection, Good Luck, Healing
Powers: Exorcism, Protection, Healing, Visions
Medicinal: Known as cure all, Moisturising, Stimulant, Expectorant, Tonic, Antibacterial, Diuretic, Tea Strengthens Digestion, Menstrual Cramps, Pre Menstrual Stress, Amenorrhea, Colds, Flu, Bronchitis, Digestive Aid, Eyebath for Tired Eyes, Scabies, Itching, Wounds, Leaves as compresses for Inflammations, Crushed leaves for Travel sickness as acts as Car Air Freshener, Hiccups, Heartburn, Flatulence, Digestive Problems, Tea for

Stomach Ache, Anemia, Headaches, Arthritis, Rheumatism, Poor Circulation, Adrenal Excess, Poor Blood Clotting, Poor Liver Function, Anaphrodisiac, Coughs, Stimulate Appetite, Tonic for Colds and Flu Skin lotion for scabies, itching, wounds and rheumatism. .

Culinary: Flavouring stewed fruit, Candied stems, Flavouring Gin and Liqueurs, Salads.

History: Cultivated in Britain since Sixteenth Century. Name derives from the Greek Angelos which means "a messenger".

Magical: Banishment, Divination, Exorcism, Visions. Remedy against enchantments and evil potions. Add to bath water to remove curses or spells against the individual. Powdered root sprinkled around home to ward off evil. Protection against evil and plague. Purification, energy of the Sun, cleansing power of Fire (Person, Sacred & Personal Space and fumigation during Exorcism). Worn as garlands or used as decorations. Invoke the Archangel Michael.

Circle: South, Fire, Quarter of the Summer Solstice (Coamhain).

Incense: Offering, thrown into bonfire.

TEA: Aids Digestion, Ease Stomach Ache and Intestinal Problems, Relieve Toothache and Counter Flatulence.

APPLE (Malus pumila, Pyrus malus, Malus domestica) SEEDS IN LARGE AMOUNTS ARE POISONOUS

Planet:	Venus
Element:	Water
Gender:	Female
Totem Bird:	Wren
Colour:	Green
Gemstone:	Amethyst
Runes:	Ing, Peorth, Cweorth
Day:	Friday
Ogham:	Quert

Powers:	Love, Healing, Garden Magic, Immortality
Deities:	Aphrodite, Apollo, King Arthur, Athene, Cerridwen, Diana, Dionysus, Eve, Flora, Godiva, Grannos, Hera, Herakles, Hermes, The Hesperides, Iduna, Mabon, Modron, Olwen, Titaea, The Triple Goddess, Venus, Vishnu, Zeus
Medicinal:	Cure all, Constipation, Acid Stomach, Digestion, Rotten Fruit as Poultice for sore eyes
Culinary:	Cooked or Raw, Cider, Chutneys, Sauces, Jams, Jellies
Magical:	Symbol associated with the Goddess. Wands. Symbolises the Sun.
Incense:	Love and Beltane

ARCHANGEL, White (Lamium album) Dead Nettle, Blind Nettle

Colour:	White
Planet:	Venus
Medicinal:	Internal Disorders, Menstrual Problems, Open Wounds, Staunch Bleeding, Reduce Inflammation
Culinary:	Young leaves in Salads, Soups, Cooked as Vegetable. Sugared flowers "Heart Merry Flowers".

ASH (Fraxinus excelsior) Norse Tree of the World

Planet:	Sun
Gender:	Male
Element:	Water and Fire
Totem Bird:	Snipe and Common Tern
Totem Animal:	Horse
Colour:	Grass Green
Deities:	Uranus, Poseidon, Thor, Woden, Neptune, Mars, Gwydion
Gemstone:	Sea Green Beryl, Coral and Garnet
Runes:	As, Gyfu, Hagal, Ebwaz, Os,
Powers:	Protection, Prosperity, Sea Rituals, Health
Medicinal:	Tonic for Liver Complaints, Rheumatism, Fever,

Flatulence, Mild Laxative.

Culinary: Ash Keys Pickle
History: Making Spears, Snake Repellent
Magical: Burn Logs to drive away evil
Incense: Horned God Incense
              Axis Mundi Incense

ASPARAGUS (Asparagus offinalis)

Medicinal: Diruetic, Liver tonic, Aids Digestion, Urinary Complaints,
              Arthritis, Rheumatism, Tonify the Liver, Hepatitis,
              Elimination of Urine, Pre Menstrual Syndrome

ASPEN (Populus tremula) White Poplar

Planet: Saturn in Capricorn, Sun
Element: Fire
Gender: Male
Totem Bird: Swan
Colour: Red
Gemstone: Amber
Rune: Peorth
Ogham: Eadha
Powers: Eloquence, Anti-Theft
Deities: Apollo, Death Goddess, Hercules, Jupiter, Mut, Nun, The
              Valkyries, White Goddess
Medicinal: Lower Fever, Digestive Problems, Coughs, Sore Throat,
              Burns, Inflammation, Chapped Skin, Scratches
Magical: Shields made from Aspen so wood could offer
              protection from death and disease. Hercules crowned
              himself with aspen after killing the giant Cacus. It is the
              tree of the Underworld and grants access to it. A char
              against death and disease for the ancients.
Festival: Samhain. Aspen heralds the winter at the festival and
              the rebirth of the sun at Yule.

ASTER (Aster alpinus albis) Michaelmas Daisy, Starwort

Planet:	Venus
Gender:	Female
Sign:	Libra
Element:	Water
Care Doll:	Love

BALM Lemon (Melissa officinalis) Lemon Balm, Sweet Balm, Honey Balm, Sweet Melissa

Planet:	Moon
Element:	Water
Gender:	Female
Sign:	Cancer
Deities:	Artemis, Diana, Moon Goddess
Growing:	Perennial
Powers:	Love, Success, Healing
Medicinal:	Healing and Refreshing, Bleeding, Nervous Troubles, Dressing Wounds, Menstrual irregularities, Clearing the Mind, Sharpening the Understanding, Increasing the Memory, Spots, Boils, Sores, Catarrh, Headaches, Lower Temperature, Ease Tension, Indigestion caused by Anxiety and Depression, Stress and Depression.
Culinary:	Petals in Salads, syrup, jam, wine, vinegar, dessert
History:	Greece, root said to cure bite from Rabid Dog.
Tea:	Balm Tea,
Uses:	Lemon Balm Bath, Rinse for Greasy Hair, Insect Bites.

BARLEY (Hordeum vulgare)

Planet:	Saturn, Venus
Gender:	Female
Element:	Earth
Powers:	Love, Healing, Protection
Medicinal:	Digestive Disorders, Bronchitis, Gastro Intestinal Inflammations, Skin Sores.

Culinary:	Ale – Malted Barley, Soups and Stews – Husk Removed, Malt Extract
Plant:	When the moon is Middle Waxing

BASIL (Ocimum basilicum), ANNUAL, Sweet Basil, Witches Herb, St Joseph's Wort, Albahaca, American Dittany, Our Herb, Kiss me Nicholas

Family:	Mint
Planet:	Mars in Scorpio
Gender:	Male
Element:	Fire
Sign:	Scorpio
Deities:	Vishnu, Erzulie, Krishna, Lakishmi
Totem Animal:	Scorpion, Basilisk
Tarot:	Death
Station:	South West, West
Festival:	Lughnasa, Herfest
Care Doll:	Protection, Love, Money
Powers:	Love, Exorcism, Wealth, Flying, Protection
Medicinal:	Expectorant, Antiseptic, Antibacterial, Antifungal, Stimulating, Antidepressant, Antispasmodic, Carminative, Tonic, Diaphoretic, Fever Reducing, Immune System, Mental Fatigue, Clears the Mind, Concentration, Emotions, Fear, Sadness, Chest Infections, Congested Sinuses, Chronic Colds, Head Colds, Abdominal Pain, Indigestion, Vomiting, Tired Muscles, Arthritis, Rheumatism, Gout, Intestinal Parasites, Ringworm, Acne, Fly Repellant, Gastro Intestinal Complaints, Soothe Nerves, Snuff for Headaches and Nasal Colds
Culinary:	Sauces, Soups and Drinks
History:	From Roman Times.
Magical:	Banishment, Happiness, Exorcism, Peace, Strewing Herb

BAY (Laurus nobilus) Sweet Laurel, Grecian Laurel, Sweet Bay, Sweetleaf, Hero's Crown, Indian Bay, Baie Daphne, Laurier D'Apollon, Lorbeer, Laurier Sauce

Planet:	Sun in Leo
Element:	Fire
Gender:	Male
Sign:	Leo
Rune:	Peorth, Sigel, Sol
Festival:	Summer Solstice
Tool:	Wand
Tarot:	Sun
Station:	South
Deities:	Adonis, Apollo, Aesculapius, Ceres, Cerridwen, Cupid, Daphne, Eros, Faunus, Ra, Vishnu
Care Doll:	Protection, Healing
Powers:	Protection, Psychic Powers, Healing, Purification, Strength
Medicinal:	Bruises, Rheumatism, Improve Appetite, Reduce Fever, Aches and Pains, Antiseptic.
Culinary:	Soups, Stews, Sauces
Use:	Insect Repellent
History:	Greece & Rome – wreath to honour heroes and Poets
Magical:	Dedicated to Apollo and his son Aesculapuis, the god of
Medicine.	Psychic Powers, Purification, Strength
Incense:	Healing and Purification

BEAN (Vicia faba) Broad Bean

Planet:	Venus
Gender:	Male
Element:	Air
Deities:	Demeter, Cardea
Powers:	Protection, Exorcism, Wart Charming, Reconciliations, Potency, Love
Medicinal:	Inflammation, Swellings, Kidney Stones, Provoke Urine.

Culinary: Dried Vegetable, Pottage

BEECH (Fagus sylvatica) One of Largest British Trees, Queen of the

Woods, Mother of the Woods, Bok, Boke, Buche, Buk, Buke, Faggio,
Fagos, Faya, Haya, Hetre

Planet:	Mars, Saturn
Rune:	Nyd, Peorth, Eweorth
Ogham:	Phagos
Gender:	Female
Deities:	Artemis, Diana
Powers:	Wishes
History:	Many animals forage on masts.
Magical:	Tablets for Amulets and permanent magical scripts. Suitable for Rune Pieces.
Uses:	Firewood, Bright and Clear. Tablets used for writing.

BEET (Beta) White Beet (Beta vulgaris) Red Beet (Beta hortensis)

Mangel, Mangold

Planet:	Jupiter (White Beet), Saturn (Red Beet)
Gender:	Female
Element:	Earth
Power:	Love
Medicinal:	Cleansing, Digestive, Provoke Urine, Headaches, Giddiness, Jaundice, Menstrual Problems.
Culinary:	Leaves like Spinach, Porray (thick vegetable soup), Flavouring, Roots
History:	From Anglo Saxon times

BERGAMOT (Monarda didyma) Bergamot Orange (Mentha

citrata) Citrus Plant (Citrus Bergamia) Perennial Bee Balm, Oswego Tea,
Monarda, Indian's Plume, Scarlet Mop

Planet:	Mercury, Sun
Element:	Air
Gender:	Male
Sign:	Gemini, Virgo

Care Doll:	Banishment, Money
Medicinal:	Antidepressant, Antiseptic, Antiviral, Repels Insects, Joyous, Uplifting, Acne, Boils, Oily Skin, Eczema, Psoriasis, Cuts, Insect Bites, Cold Sores, Chicken Pox, Shingles, Expels Worms, Cystitis, Thrush, Vaginal Itching, Discharge, Stimulant, Nausea, Digestive Flatulence, Menstrual Pains, Headaches, Insomnia, Regulate the Appetite, Chest Complaints, Catarrh, Sore Throats, Draw out Infection, Cold Sores, Chicken Pox and Shingles.
Culinary:	Bergamot Oil used to flavour Earl Grey Tea comes from Citrus Bergamia (Planet: Sun, Element: Fire).
History:	First grown in Britain in 1745 when seed was sent from Lake Ontario. Wild Bergamot used by the Oswega Indians as a drink and the flowers were boiled by the Omaha and Ponca Indians to make hair oil.
Magical:	Carry in purse to attract money.
Incense:	Meditation, Clairvoyance and Vision
Tea:	Meditation
Pillow:	Restful Sleep
Essential Oil:	Friendship, Happiness, Depression

BETONY (Stachys officinalis/Stachys betonica) Woundwort,

Bishop's Wort, Wood Betony, Sentinel of the Woods, Herb St Fraiid, Lousewort, Betayne, Bidney, Wild Hop, Vetoyu, Bitney, Perennial

Planet:	Jupiter, Gemini, Sagittarius, Aries
Element:	Fire
Gender:	Male
Sign:	Aries
Deities:	Cerunnos, Herne
Care Doll:	Protection, Purification, Love
Dye:	Yellow
Medicinal:	Cure All, Migraine, Indigestion, Nervous Complaints, Staunching Bleeding, Healing Wounds, Sores, Ulcers, Boils. Culinary: Dry leaves – Tea, Conserve
History:	Native to Britain. Grown in Monastery Gardens and

Graveyards.

Magical:	Protection from Witchcraft and evil spirits. Protection of the soul and body if worn. Beneath a pillow protects the sleeper from visions and bad dreams. Planted in garden to protect the house from evil. Scattered near doors and windows to prevent evil from entering.

BETONY, Water (Betonica aquatica)

Planet:	Jupiter in Cancer
Medicinal:	Poultices, Ointments, Infusions to treat wounds and speed healing process.

BETONY, Wood (Betonica officinalis, Stachys betonica, Stachys,

Officinalis) Bishopswort, Lousewort, Purple Betony

Planet:	Jupiter in Aries
Gender:	Male
Element	Fire
Powers:	Protection, Purification, Love
Medicinal:	Dressing Wounds

BINDWEED Greater (Convolvulus sepium) Lesser Bindweed

(Convolvulus arvensis) Dwarf/Garden Bindweed (Convolvulus tricolor)
PURGATIVE ACTION IS UNPREDICTABLE NOT SUITABLE FOR SELF
MEDICATION Hedge Bindweed, Lady's Nightcap, Lesser Bindweed or
Cornbine (Convolvulus arvensis), Scammony (Convolvulus sepium),
Bellbine, Old Man's Nightcap, Hooded Bindweed, Bearbind, Hedge
Convolvulus

Planet:	Moon in Cancer, Saturn
Element:	Water
Gender:	Female
Tool:	Cup
Deities:	Mother Goddesses, Virgin Mary
Growing:	Perennial Climber
Medicinal:	Laxative, Purgative, Boils.
History:	Native to Britain.

Magical: Used as a wash, added to Incense: consecrate ritual cup

SILVER BIRCH (Betula pendula, Betula alba)   Lady of the
Woods, Birk, Beithe, Bereza, Berke, Bouleau

Planet:	Venus
Element:	Water
Gender:	Female
Totem Bird:	Pheasant, Golden Eagle
Colour:	White
Gemstone:	Topaz, Rock Crystal, Red Sard
Ogham:	Beith
Festival:	Beltane
Tool:	Staff
Station:	South East
Rune:	Beorc
Deities:	Brigantia, Brighid, Earth Mother, The Lady of the Woods, The Summer Goddess, Thor
Powers:	Protection, Exorcism, Purification
Medicinal:	Mouthwash, Kidney Stones, Bladder, Skin Disorders, Eczema, Gout, Rheumatism, Arthritis.
Culinary:	Sugar, Fermented (Wine, Spirits, Vinegar)
History:	Bark as writing material. Used in tanning.
Magical:	Sacred to Celts to drive out evil spirits (birching of wrongdoers and the insane), Twigs made into Broomsticks.

BLACKTHORN (Prunus spinosa), Rose Family Sloe, Slae, La
Merre du Bois (the Mother of the Woods)

Planet:	Saturn
Element:	Earth, Fire
Gender:	Female
Sign:	Scorpio
Gemstone:	Mother of Pearl, Dark Green Malachite
Totem Bird:	Thrush, Rook
Colour:	Blood Red, Purple

Deity:	Cerridwen
Care Doll:	Protection
Dye:	Red
Medicinal:	Tonic, Mild Laxative, Mouth Wash, Stimulate Appetite, Reduce Fever, Bladder, Kidney, Digestive Disorders.
Culinary:	Jellies, Syrups, Jams, Wines, Verjuice, Gin, Fruit Cheeses
History:	Purple/black juice of raw sloe used as marking ink on linen and cloth.
Magical:	Tree of cursing. Used to summon the Wild Hunt. Banishment. Divination.
Festivals:	Spring Equinox: Blossoms appear. Samhain: Berries ripen, used to make wine for the festival. Winter Solstice: Wood is offering to the Underworld powers for the return of the sun.
Uses:	Weapons and clubs, Staves.

BLUEBELL (Hyacinthoides non-scripta) Wild Hyacinth (Endymion non-scriptus) POISON when fresh Harebell

Planet:	Venus in Libra
Powers:	Luck, Truth
Medicinal:	Bleeding, Increase Urine.

BORAGE (Borago officinalis) Borage Family, Annual Bee Bread, Bugloss, Cool Tankard, Herb of Gladness

Flowers:	May - September
Colour:	Blue
Planet:	Jupiter in Leo
Element:	Air
Gender:	Male
Sign:	Leo
Festival:	Lughnasa
Tarot:	Hierophant
Station:	South West
Deities:	Llew, Lugh, Warrior Gods
Care Doll:	Happiness, Courage

Powers:	Courage, Psychic Powers
Medicinal:	Milk Production, Expectorant, Astringent, Anti Inflammatory, Diuretic, Calming Nerves, Adrenal Stimulant, Liver, Cardiovascular, Metabolic, Eczema, Diabetes, Bruises, Fevers, Dry Skin, Bronchial Infections, Kidney, Bladder, Bowel, Arthritis, Nervous Disorders, Comforts heart, removes Melancholy, and calms.
Culinary:	Like Spinach, in salads, Cucumber flavour to wine and cold drinks
History:	Stirrup cup for the Crusaders
Magical:	Courage, Psychic Powers
Uses:	Mucilage, Starch, Tannins, Saponins, Flavonoids, Mineral Salts.
Dogs:	Borage Seed Oil. Dull Coat, Itchy Skin, Excessive Shedding, Metabolic Functions, Breakdown of Carbohydrates and Fats, Heart, Uterus, Vascular System. Leaf: Adrenal function, After Steroid Therapies.

BUGLOSS (Lycopsis arvensis, Anchusa arvensis) Borage, Alkanet

Planet:	Jupiter in Leo
Element:	Water
Care Doll:	Prosperity, Purification
Medicinal:	Inoffensive extra bulk, comfort the heart, drive away melancholy
Culinary:	Pot Herb with Meat, Cordials. Young leaves and flowers in salads

BOX (Buxus sempervirens) Boxwood POISONOUS

Planet:	Mars in Scorpio
Dye:	Auburn Hair Dye Medicinal: Rheumatism.
History:	Hedging, Topiary, shelter for other plants, making small boxes, printing blocks, engraving plates and musical instruments.

BRACKEN, FERN (Pteridium aquilinum) Bracken Fern aka

Female Fern (Pteris aquilina) Male Fern (Dryopteris felix-mas) Royal Fern (Osmonda regalis) Maidenhair Fern (Adiantum capillus veneris)
CAN CAUSE ABORTIONS

Planet:	Bracken and Maidenhair Fern: Mercury
	Male Fern: Mars
	Royal Fern: Saturn
Element:	Air
Gender:	Male
Totem Animal:	Snake
Totem Bird:	Nightjar
Ogham:	Ngetal
Festival:	Coamhain, Yule
Deities:	Hades, Pluto, The Sidhe
Care Doll:	Protection, Healing
Dye:	Young Fronds, Yellowish Green
Powers:	Healing, Rain Magic, Prophetic Dreams
Medicinal:	Intestinal worms, reduce swellings, wounds, ulcers.
Culinary:	Young unfoiled fronts as vegetable or brewing beer.
History:	Burnt Bracken ashes in glassmaking, substitute for soap, fertilizer.
Magical:	Riches, Hidden Treasure. Prophetic Dreams. Fern Seed gathered on Midsummer Eve will give Protection from Evil. If collected Midnight until 1am it will give prophetic dreams. Three grains can be used to summon. The Elder Branch can be used to draw a circle to demand magic fern seed for physical strength. A char made on Midsummer Eve will Protect the Home (Hardened Hand Frond) On the Winter Solstice if seeds are carried it may be possible to find Underground Treasure.

BRAMBLE (Rubus fruticosus) Blackberry

Planet: Venus in Aries
Dye: Fruit (Blue-Grey), Root (Orange)
Medicinal: Astringent, Tonic, Dysentery, Diarrhoea, Haemorrhoids, Burns, Swellings, Ulcers, Stomach Disorders, Mouthwash, Sore Throat, Gum Inflammation, Sores, Gout, Scratches.
Culinary: Fresh or Cooked fruit, Jams, Jellies, Syrups, Cordials, Vinegar, Wine,
Tea: Herbal Tea
History: Since Neolithic times, harvested from wild

BRIAR, DOG ROSE (Rosa canina) Wild Rose, Wild Briar, Brimmle, Canker, Cat-whin, Choop-rose, Cockbramble, Dike-rose, Hip-tree, Horse-bramble, Humack, Lawyers, Heddygrinnel, Pigs Rose

Planet: Venus, Moon
Element: Water
Gender: Female
Gemstone: Emerald
Tarot: Seven of Cups
Deities: Adonis, Aphrodite, Cupid, Demeter, Eros, Hathor, Hulda, Venus
Care Doll: Love, Protection, Good Luck, Healing
Medicinal: Vitamin C, Cough, Flavour Medicines, Tonic, Mild Laxative, Astringent, Healing Wounds, Antiseptic Tonic, Sore and Sensitive Skin, Aphrodisiac, Sedative,   Tonic, Antidepressant, Detoxifying, Digestive.
Culinary: Petals in Salads, syrup, jam, wine, vinegar, dessert
History: Greece, root said to cure bite from Rabid Dog.
Perfume: Rose Water
Magical: Love, Protection, Good Luck, Healing, Dreams, Sleep, Money, Psychic Powers, Divination

BROOM, Common (Sarothamnus scoparius, Cytisus scoparius)

DANGEROUS IN LARGE DOSES POISONOUS

Planet:	Mars
Element:	Air
Care Doll:	Protection, Good Luck
Dye:	Green
Medicinal:	Heart, Circulatory Disorders, Kidney and Bladder Complaints, Dropsy, Gout, Sciatica, Pains of the Hips and Joints, Head and Body Lice, Slightly Narcotic.
Culinary:	Pickled flowers and buds for flavouring savoury sauces
History:	Badge of the Plantagenet Kings. Stalks and branches used to make brooms, Bark used to make paper and cloth.
Tanning:	Leaves
Magical:	Purification, Divination

BROOM, Butcher's (Ruscus aculeatus) Box Holly

Planet:	Mars
Medicinal:	Kidney Stones, Hemorrhoids, Gout, Jaundice, Inflammation, Perspiration and Mild Laxative.
Culinary:	Like Asparagus
History:	Used by butchers to clean chopping boards, decoration on meat

BRYONY Red (Bryonia dioica) White Bryony (Bryonia alba)

POISONOUS Wild Vine, Ladies' Seal, Wood Vine, Tatterberry, Tamus, Wild Hops, Cowbind, Cow's Lick, Felon-berry, Hedge Grape, Snake-berry, Tetter Berry, Wild Wood Vine, English Mandrake, Snake Grape, Gout Root, Mad Root

Planet:	Mars
Element:	Earth
Gender:	Male
Growing:	Perennial
Medicinal:	Leprosy, Old Sores, Gangrene, Skin Ailments.

Magical:	Substitute for Mandrake for making poppets.
Incense:	Underworld Journeys

BURDOCK Lesser (Arctium minus) Greater (Arctium lappa) Daisy

Family, Biennial Beggar's Buttons, Cockle-bur-plant, Sweethearts, Happy Major, Cuckoo Button, Cockle-burr, Bardona, Bardana, Burr Seed, Clotbur, Grass Burdock, Hardock, Hurr-burr, Turkey Burrseed, Bachelor's Buttons, Bazzies, Butter-dock, Cleavers, Clite, Cloud-burr, Clog-weed, Cockles, Cuckold Buttons, Donkeys, Eddick, Flapper-bags, Gypsy comb, Kisses, Loppy Major, Pig's Rhubarb, Sticky Jacks, Touch-me-Not, Tuzzy-muzzy, Wild Rhubarb, Personata, Happy Major, Burr-top.

Flowers:	July - September
Planet:	Venus
Element:	Water
Gender:	Female
Deity:	Blodeuwedd
Care Doll:	Healing, Protection
Medicinal:	Blood purifier, colds, flu, fevers, leprosy, eczema, psoriasis, boils, skin complaints, bruises, ulcers, swellings, sciatica, Diuretic, Lymphatic Cleanser, Acne, Spots, Rashes, Psoriasis, Eczema, Liver Problems, Rheumatism, Gout, Chronic Cystitis, Loss of Appetite.
Culinary:	Salads, boiled as vegetable, candied, drinks
Magical:	Wear a necklace of dried burdock to protect against magic. Incense. Spread around house or temple. Burdock Beer for rituals of Purification and Protection. Water Incenses and Venus Planetary Incenses.
Uses:	Essential Oil, Fatty Oil, Tannins, Polyacetylene, Mucilage, Inulin.
Dog:	Seborrhea, Pyoderma, Rheumatoid Diseases

CABBAGE (Brassica Oleracea capitata)

Planet:	Moon
Gender:	Female
Element:	Water
Powers:	Luck
Medicinal:	Inflammations, sores, scabs, inhibit bacteria, detoxify liver, adder bite.
Culinary:	Staple food
History:	Romans and Anglo Saxons

CALENDULA (Calendula officinalis) Marigold, Pot Marigold,

Mary Buds, Summer's Bride, Husbandman's Dial, Holigold, Bride of the Sun, Spousa Solis, Golds, Gold, The Sun's Gold, Bees-love, Oculis Christi, Drunkard, Marygold, Mary Gowles, Ruddles.

Planet:	Sun
Element:	Fire
Gender:	Male
Sign:	Leo
Deities:	Sun Gods
Care Doll:	Protection, Good Luck
Dye:	Yellow
Powers:	Protection, Prophetic Dreams, Legal Matters, Psychic Powers
Medicinal:	Anti Fungal, Burns, Wounds, Conjunctivitis, Varicose Veins, Bed Sores, Ulcers, Bruises, Gum Inflammations, Corns, Warts and Skin Rashes, Painful Periods, Aid Digestion, After Tooth Extraction, Scalds, Insect Bites, Stings, Stop Bleeding of Deep Cuts, Cracked Skin, Cuts, Chilblains, Catarrh, Sunburn, Acne, Tired Feet, Haemorrhoids, Inflammations, Antispasmodic, Antiseptic, Antifungal, Healing, Anti-Inflammatory, Digestive (Colic), Stomach and Duodenal Ulcers, Children's Infections, Children's Fevers, Sore Eyes, Itchy Skin Rashes, Grazes, Broken Chilblains, Eczema, Fungal

Infections, Thrush, Vaginal Infections, Cradle Cap, Dry Skin, Wound Healing, Cuts, Grazes, Insect Bites.

Magical: Used in all Festival Rites particularly the Solstices and Equinoxes to honour the sun. Petals used in incense, a bathing herb and thrown into bonfire. Petals added to water, infused in oil and added to incense used in rituals of divination or consecration of divinatory tools. Protection, Good Luck, Happiness, Prophetic Dreams, Legal Matters, Psychic Powers.

CARAWAY (Carum carvi) Carrot Family.

Flower: May – July. Biennial
Planet: Sun, Mercury
Gender: Male
Element: Air
Care Doll: Protection, Love, Lust, Health, Anti-Theft, Mental Powers
Powers: Protection, Lust, Health, Anti-theft, Mental Powers
Medicinal: Wound Healing, Blood Staunching, Malaria, Facial Blemishes, Stimulant, Carmative, Antispasmodic, Muscle Relaxant, Relaxes Uterine Tissues, Menstrual Cramps, Indigestion, Gas, Colic, Flatulence, Accumulation of Toxins and Fluids, Colicky Children, Scalp Treatment, Internal Parasites
Culinary: Herbal Teas, Wines and Liqueurs
Uses: Essential Oils

CARROT Wild (Daucus carota) Garden (Daucus carota sativus)

Bird's Nest, Philtron, Gizri, Queen Ann's Lace
Planet: Mercury, Mars
Element: Fire
Gender: Male
Care Doll: Fertility
Powers: Fertility, Lust
Medicinal: Anaemia, kidney complaints, liver, bowel disorders,

intestinal worms, itchy skin, sores, ulcers, eyes, night vision, Energizing, Cleansing, Anti-inflammatory, Antiseptic, Antibacterial, Cleanse the Body, Stress, Fatigue, After Illness, Eye Problems, Infant Diarrhea, Bowel, Slows Bacterial Growth, Wounds, Cuts, Inflammation, Abscesses, Infection, Glandular Problems, Headaches, Joint Problems, Menstrual Cycle, Skin Disorders.

Culinary:	Raw in salads, cooked as vegetable, drink.
History:	Not cultivated in Britain until Medieval times. Carrots were purple, almost black.
Magical:	Lust, Impotence
Uses:	Beta Carotene, Antioxidant

CATNIP (Nepeta cataria) Catnep, Catmint, Cat's Wort, Field Balm, Cat, Catrup, Nepeta, Nip, Cat's Delight

Planet:	Venus
Element:	Water
Gender:	Female
Totem Animal:	Cat
Tarot:	Strength
Humour:	Cold
Growing:	Perennial
Deities:	Bast, Cerridwen, Freya, Sekhmet
Care Doll:	Love, Dreams, Happiness
Medicinal:	Nightmares, Bruises, Colds, Fevers, Inducing Sweating, Reducing Temperature, Headaches of a Nervous Origin, Relaxing, Stomach Upsets, Dyspepsia, Colic in Young Children, Flatulence, Menstruation, Scalp Irritations.
Culinary:	Conserve
Magical:	Attracts good spirits and luck. Can be smoked or tea drunk to help with shape shifting work or invoke a bond with a cat totem animal. Gift for pet to build psychic relationship. Used in incense to invoke the Goddess Bast and Sekhmet and the cat forms of Freya and

Cerridwen. Cat Magic. Beauty.

Incense:	Love
Essential Oil:	Cats, Luck, Love

CELANDINE Lesser (Ranunculus ficaria)

Ranunculus, Pilewort, Goldy Knob, Fig-wort, Smallwort, Foalfoot, Crain, Grian, Filding Cup, Golden Guineas, Celydoyne, Chelidonium, Devil's Milk, Garden Celandine, Greater Celandine, Kenning Wort, Swallow Herb, Swallow-Wort, Tetterwort.

Planet:	Sun
Element:	Fire
Gender:	Male
Festival:	Ostara
Deities:	Artemis, Diana, Hecate, Sun Gods
Growing:	Perennial
Care Doll:	Happiness
Powers:	Protection, Escape, Happiness, Legal Matters
Medicinal:	Haemorrhoids, Varicose Veins,
History:	Native to Britain
Magical:	Thrown into the fire to celebrate Ostara. Put in Incense. Visionary herb used as an infusion to bathe the third eye chakra, wash crystal ball or scrying mirror.
Incense:	Sun

CELERY (Apium graveolens)

Planet:	Mercury
Element:	Fire
Gender:	Male
Care Doll:	Mental Powers, Sleep
Powers:	Mental Powers, Lust, Psychic Powers
Medicinal:	Wound Healing, Blood Staunching, Malaria, Facial Blemishes, Moisturising, Diuretic, Sedative, Expectorant, Antispasmodic, Fluid Retention, Premenstrual, Syndrome, Irregular Menstruation, Insomnia, Colds, Coughs, Sinus Congestion, Respiratory

Infection, Bronchitis, Laryngitis, Arthritis, Gout, Rheumatic Disorders, Swollen Glands, High Blood Pressure, Liver Tonic, Sciatica, Appetite Suppressant, Digestive.

Culinary: Herbal Teas, Wines and Liqueurs
Magical: Lust, Psychic Powers, Sleep, Concentration

CENTUARY (Centaurium erythraea) Febrifuga, Feverwort,

Gentian, Century, Filwort, Centory, Bloodwort, Banwort, Bitter Herb, Hurdreve, Sanctuary

Planet: Sun
Element: Fire
Gender: Male
Totem Animal: Horse
Powers: Snake Removing
Deities: Chiron (Patron of Herbalists)
Medicinal: Wound healing, Blood Staunching, Malaria, Gastric and Digestive Stimulant, Anorexia, Dyspepsia, Liver Complaints.
Magical: Communion with plant spirits. Dedicatory drink of the Herbalist. Commune with Chiron.
Culinary: Herbal Teas, Wines and Liqueurs
History: Native to Britain. Named after Chiron the Centaur who used the herb to heal a wound contaminated by Hydra.

CHAMOMILE (Anthemis nobilis) Roman Chamomile

(Matricaria chamomilla) German Chamomile Chamomile, Whig Plant, Plant Physician, Scented Mayweed

Planet: Sun
Element: Water
Gender: Hot
Festival: Midsummer
Deities: Cernunnos, Ra, St Anne, Sun Gods
Care Doll: Love, Dreams, Sleep, Money
Medicinal: Sedative, Stress, Anxiety, Insomnia, Gastritis,

Indigestion, Inflammations of the Mouth, Eye Bath for
Inflamed and Sore Eyes, Sore Throat, Healing of
Wounds and to reduce Inflammation,   Calming, Sleep,
Anti-Inflammatory, Antiseptic,   Antispasmodic,
Digestive, Antidepressant, Stress Relieving, Anxiety,
Tension, Headaches, Insomnia, Toothache, Menstrual
Cramps, Arthritis, Neuralgia, Digestive Upset, Acidity,
Heartburn, Wind, Colic, Itchy Skin, Rashes,
Inflammation, Cuts, Boils, Allergies, Insect Bites,
Chilblains, Menstrual Cycle, Fluid Retention, Restless
and Overexcited Children, Children's Fevers and
Teething, Colicky Babies.

Magical:	Herb of the Sun, Regeneration, Healing, Protection. Planted on graves. Ritual Bath. Incenses to connect with the Sun and invoke Sun Gods. Include in Magical Amulets to boost their power.
Festival:	Midsummer. Thrown into Festival Fire, Used in Incenses and Garlands and added to Ritual Cup. Oil for magical barrier to prevent negativity entering. Planted in garden as Guardian Herb.
Incense:	Relaxation and Sleep
Pillow:	Sleep
Dogs:	Dyspepsia, Flatulence, Colic
Essential Oil:	Health, Healing, Calmness, Balance

CHERRY Sweet (Prunus avium)

Planet:	Venus
Gender:	Female
Element:	Water
Powers:	Love, Divination
Medicinal:	Coughs, Bronchial Complaints, Improve Digestion, Refresh Tired Skin, Relieve Migraines, Cold, Horseness, Eyesight, Appetite, Kidney Stones.
Culinary:	Cooked, Eaten Raw, Wine
History:	Introduced by the Romans. Grafted onto the rootstock

of wild cherry. Wood for wood carving and turning.

CHERVIL (Anthriscus cerefolium) Carefolium, Chervel, Sweet Chervil

Planet:	Jupiter
Element:	Air, Water
Gender:	Female
Tool:	Cauldron
Deities:	Cerridwen
Medicinal:	Cleansing tonic for liver, kidney and stomach complaints. Aching Joints, Swellings, Haemorrhoids, Conjunctivitis, Sore Eyes, Reduce Fevers, Jaundice, Gout, Stimulate Digestion, Restorative, Blood Cleansing. Culinary: Salads, sauces, soups History: Introduced to Britain by Romans.

CHESTNUT (Castanea sativa) Sweet Chestnut

Planet:	Jupiter
Gender:	Male
Element:	Fire
Powers:	Love
Medicinal:	Coughing, Fevers, Agues, Cough, Spitting Blood.
Culinary:	Roasted, boiled as vegetable, stuffings, soups and puddings, porridge "Pollenta", ground into flour.
History:	Introduced into Britain by the Romans but fruit seldom ripens in cool climate. Timber used for fencing, beams and paneling. Nut meal used to whiten linen and make starch.

CHICKWEED WINTERGREEN (Trientalis europaea) CHICKWEED (Stellaria media) –

Planet:	Moon
Gender:	Female
Element:	Water
Powers:	Fidelity, Love

| Medicinal: | Heal Wounds, Cure Blood Poisoning, Haemorrhages, Ulcers in the Kidneys or Bladder. |
| History: | Food for birds and domestic fowl. |

CHICORY (Chicorium intybus) Wild Succory, Bunk, Monks Beard,
Goats Beard, Hawks Beard, Watcher of the Road, Succory, Wild Cherry

Planet:	Jupiter, Sun
Element:	Air
Gender:	Male
Deity:	The Corn Lord
Growing:	Perennial
Dye:	Blue
Powers:	Removing Obstacles, Invisibility, Favors, Frugality
Medicinal:	Liver disorders, Gallstones, Kidney Stones, Inflammations of the Urinary Tract, Rich in Calcium, Copper and Iron, Jaundice, Spleen, Liver, Cleansing Digestive and Urinary Systems, Skin Problems, Boils Eczema, Inflammations.
Magical:	Incenses to mark Lughnasa and Autumn Equinox

Divination. Flowers to in infusion to consecrate divinatory tools. Used to bathe the third eye chakra and to wash crystal ball or scrying mirror.

| Incense: | Jupiter Planetary Incense |

CHILI PEPPER (Capsicum spp) Red Pepper

Gender:	Male
Planet:	Mars
Element:	Fire
Powers:	Fidelity, Love

CHRYSANTHEMUM (Chrysanthemum sinsense) POISON

Gender:	Male
Planet:	Sun
Element:	Fire
Power:	Protection

CINQUEFOIL (Potentilla canadensis) Silverweed (Potentilla anserina) Creeping Tormentil (Potentilla reptans) SILVERWEED IS MORE ASTRINGENT, TAKE INTERNALLY WITH CARE

Five Finger Grass, Sunfield, Five Fingers, Crampweed, Five Finger Blossom, Goosegrass, Goose Tansy, Moor Grass, Silver Cinquefoil, Pentaphyllon, Silverweed, Synkefoyle.

Planet: Silverweed Jupiter, Tormentil Sun

Element:	Fire
Gender:	Male
Totem Bird:	Goose
Deities:	The Mother Goddess
Care Doll:	Love, Money, Protection
Dye:	Red
Powers:	Money, Protection, Prophetic Dreams, Sleep
Medicinal:	Cuts and Wounds, Sore Throats, Mouth Ulcers, Diarrhoea, Aid to Digestion, Haemorrhages, Inflammations, Fevers.
Culinary:	Silverweed Eaten raw or cooked. Ground to make porridge and bread.
Magical:	Pre Ritual Bath. Protection, Prophetic Dreams, Sleep
Ritual:	Beltane (Cast into the Fire, Incense or Ritual Cup)

CLARY SAGE (Salvia sclarea) SAGE SHOULD NOT BE TAKEN OVER AN EXTENDED PERIOD OF TIME Muscatel Sage, Clear Eye, Christ's Eye, Eyeseed, Oculus-Christi, Officinalis Christi

Planet:	Mercury, Moon
Element:	Air
Rune:	Dag
Medicinal:	Eye Problems, Swellings, Boils, Ulcers, Splinters
Culinary:	Wine
Animals:	Yes
Essential Oil:	Purification, Stress, Healing, Strength, Dream Magic

CLEAVERS (Galium aparine) Goosegrass, Clives, Catchweed,

Bed Straw, Little Sweethearts, Hayriff, Robin-run-in-the-hedge, Mutton
Chops, Everlasting Friendship, Sticky
Buds, Scratch-Weed, Grip-grass

Planet:	Moon, Saturn (conflict of information)
Element:	Water, Fire (conflict of information)
Gender:	Female
Festival:	Ostara
Dye:	Red (Roots with alum)
Powers:	Relationships, Commitment, Protection, Tenacity
Medicinal:	Tonic, Lymphatic System, Swollen Glands, Tonsillitis, Adenoid Trouble, Ulcers and Tumours
Culinary:	Tea. Young leaves eaten as vegetable or added to soups, salads and stews. Seeds as coffee substitute.
Magical:	Ritual cup for Ostara Rites. Divination

CLOVE-PINK (Dianthus caryophyllus) Gilly-Flower, Carnation

Planet:	Jupiter (Pink or Stock), Moon (Wallflower)
Element:	Fire
Deity:	Jupiter
Care Doll:	Confidence, Courage
Medicinal:	Fainting, Headaches, Nervous Disorders, Mouth Ulcers, Cleanse the Blood, Relieve Inflammations, Gout, Aches and Pains in Joints and Sinews, Malignant Fevers, Promote Perspiration, Quench Raging Thirsts.
Culinary:	Flavour Soups, Sauces, Jams, Cordials, Wines, Vinegar, Syrup, Crystallized.
History:	Oils used in Soaps and Perfumery.
Magical:	Protection, Strength, Healing

CLOVER (Trifolium repens) White Clover, Red Clover (Trifolium

pratense) Dogs: Yes. Trefoil, Honeysuckle

Planet:	White Clover (Mercury), Red Clover (Venus)
Element:	All four

Gender:	Male
Festival:	Beltane
Tool:	Pentacle
Metal:	Copper
Humour:	Hot
Deities:	Aprhodite, Freya, Hathor, The Triple Goddess, Venus, Rowen
Care Doll:	Love, Protection, Good Luck, Money, Success
Powers:	Protection, Money, Love, Fidelity, Exorcism, Success
Medicinal:	Skin Complaints, Exzema, Psoriasis, Liver, Gall Bladder, Improve Appetite, Cure Indigestion, Bronchitis, Whooping Cough, Inflammations, Rheumatic Aches and Pains, Cancerous Growths, Bites of Venomous Creatures, Heal Wounds and Sores.
Culinary:	Salads and Soups, Wine.
History:	Forage Crop, Ploughed Back as Green Compost, Makes Superior Honey.
Magical:	Good Luck, Clairvoyant Powers. Amulet, Love, Protection, Money, Banishment, Success, Fidelity, Exorcism, Success.
Dog:	Tumors, Blood Disorders, Cysts, Skin Tumors, Swollen Lymph Nodes

COLEWORT (Brassica oleracea) Kale

Planet:	Moon
Medicinal:	Liver, Spleen, Kidney Stones, Hoarsness, Voice Loss, Muscle Aches, Reducing Swellings, Skin Eruptions.
Culinary:	Pot Vegetable, Porray

COLTSFOOT (Tussilago farfara)

Planet:	Venus
Element:	Water
Gender:	Female
Powers:	Love, Visions
Medicinal:	Coughs, Colds, Shortness of Breath, Irritation, Reduce

Swellings, Heal Skin Ulcers, Bronchitis, Laryngitis, Asthma.

Culinary: Salads, Soups, Vegetable. Flowers make wine.

History: Flower painted on doorpost indicated Apothecary's Shop. White hairs on leaves scraped and dried as tinder and stuffing pillows.

Uses: Tea, Lozenges

COLUMBINE (Aquilegia vulgaris) POISONOUS Culverwort,

Granny's Bonnet, Lion's Herb, Granny Bonnets, Aquilegia

Planet: Venus

Element: Water

Gender: Female

Totem Birds: Eagle, Dove

Deities: Aphrodite, Venus

Powers: Courage, Love

Medicinal: Antiseptic, Ulcers, Common Skin Diseases, Sedative, The Plague.

History: Symbolised the Holy Spirit and Holy Ghost. Mostly grown for decoration.

COMFREY (Symphytum officinale) Blackwort, Assear, Slippery

Root, Healing Herb, Gooseberry Pie, Salsify, Church Bells, Pigweed, Sweet Suckers, Consound, All-Heal, Consolida, Knit Back, Gum Plant, Wallwort, Yullac, Saracen's Root, Knitbone, Boneset, Bruisewort

Planet: Saturn in Capricorn

Element: Air, Water

Gender: Female

Sign: Capricorn

Care Doll: Protection, Healing, Money, Travel Safety

Dye: Yellow

Powers: Safety during Travel, Money

Medicinal: Bruises, Wounds, Sprains, Broken Limb (sets like plaster), Colds, Bronchitis, Stomach Ulcers, Back Pain,

Healing, Mucilaginous, Cuts, Cracked Skin, Dry Skin, Arthritis, Bunions, Aches, Pains, Hiatus Hernia, Stomach Ulcers.

Culinary:	Root is edible. Vegetable. Excessive eating can be dangerous.
History:	Brought to Britain by the Crusaders from the Holy Land.
Uses:	Compost and Mulch

CORIANDER (Coriandrum sativum) Cilentro, Chinese Parsley, Culantro

Planet:	Mars
Element:	Fire
Gender:	Male
Humour:	Hot
Deities:	Aphrodite, Venus
Care Doll:	Healing, Money, Love
Powers:	Love, Health, Healing
Medicinal:	Moisturising, Stimulant, Diuretic, Aphrodisiac, Respiratory Problems, Allergies, Hay Fever, Urinary Infections, Cystitis, Rashes, Hives, Burns, Digestive Disorders, Gas Pains, Vomiting, Indigestion, Purifies the Blood, Decongests Liver, Reduces Heat and Fever, Anti-Inflammatory, Arthritis, Cuts, Scrapes, Tired Muscles.
Magical:	Love Charms and Incenses. Herb of Immortality. Ritual Cup and Handfastings. Soul Bindings. Used to anoint candles in love magic. Herb of peace and protection.

CORN (Zea Mays) Seed, Silk Giver of life, Maize, Sacred Mother, Seed of Seeds

Gender:	Female
Planet:	Venus
Element:	Earth
Powers:	Protection, Luck, Divination

CORNFLOWER (Centaurea cyanus) Bluebottle, Blue-blow, Hurt-Sickle, Cyanus

Planet:	Saturn
Element:	Water
Gender:	Female
Gemstone:	Moonstone
Deities:	Flora, The Harvest Mother
Care Doll:	Fertility
Medicinal:	Digestive and Gastric Disorders, Lotion for Sore and Tired Eyes, Wounds, Ulcers, Mouth Sores.
Culinary:	Fresh in salads.
Uses:	Colour Ink, Cosmetics and Medicines.

COWSLIP (Primula veris) Paigle, Palsywort, Bunch of Keys

Planet:	Venus in Aries
Element:	Water
Gender:	Female
Deity:	Freya
Care Doll:	Healing
Powers:	Healing, Youth, Treasure-Finding
Medicinal:	Healing Wounds, Mild Sedative, Headaches, Insomnia, Nervous Tension, Arthritis (radix arthritica), Whooping Cough, Bronchitis, Palsy.
Culinary:	Salads, Cowslip Wine, Syrup, Pickle, Conserve, Vinegar, Mead. Crystallized or sugared.
History:	Wrinkle removing cosmetic.
Magical:	Youth. Treasure Finding.

CRAB APPLE (Malus sylvestris) Wild Apple

Planet:	Venus
Medicinal:	Scalds, Sprains, Sore Throats, Mouth Disorders.
Culinary:	Jelly, Jam and Wine. Verjuice added like Lemon Juice.
History:	Ancestor of all cultivated apples. Wood for carving and

	wood engraving. "Crab" from Norse word for Scrubby.
Magical:	Love and Marriage. Throwing pips into the fire while
	reciting lover's name (if pip explodes the love will last).

CROCUS (Crocus vemus)

Gender:	Female
Planet:	Venus
Element:	Water
Powers:	Love, Visions

CUCUMBER (Cucumis sativus) Cowcucumber, Agurk, Haswey,

Kheyar, Lekiti, Gurka

Gender:	Female
Planet:	Moon
Element:	Water
Powers:	Chastity, Healing, Fertility

CUMIN (Cumimum cyminum) Cumino, Cumino Aigro, Sanoot,

Kimoon

Gender:	Male
Planet:	Mars
Element:	Fire
Powers:	Protection, Fidelity, Exorcism, Anti-Theft

CYCLAMEN (Cyclamen) Groundbread, Pain-dePorceau, Sow

Bread, Swine Bread

Gender:	Female
Planet:	Venus
Element:	Water
Deity:	Hecate
Powers:	Fertility, Protection, Happiness, Lust

DAFFODIL (Narcissus) Asphodel, Daffy-Down-Dilly, Fleur de

Coucou, Goose Leek, Lent Lily, Narcissus, Porillon

Gender:	Female
Planet:	Venus
Element:	Water
Powers:	Love, Fertility, Luck

DAISY (Bellis perennis/Chrysanthemum leucanthemum) POISON

Flower of Spring, Gowan, Open Eye, Day's Eye, Banwood, Banewort,
Ewe-gowan, Little Star, Silver Pennies, Billy Button, Measure of Love,
Herb Margaret, Bainswort, Bruisewort, Child's Flower, Field Daisy,
Llygay Dydd (Welsh – Eye of the Day), Maudlinwort, Moon Daisy

Planet:	Venus in Cancer
Element:	Water
Gender:	Female
Sign:	Cancer
Festival:	The Equinoxes
Deities:	Alcestis, Aphrodite, Apollo, Artemis, Belenos, The Dryad Belidis, Christ, Freya, Thor, Venus, Virgin Mary
Care Doll:	Love, Happiness
Powers:	Lust, Love
Medicinal:	Ointment: Bruises, Wounds, Stiff Neck, Swellings, Lumbago, Aches and Pains, Fevers, Coughs, Catarrh, Inflammatory Disorders of the Liver, Skin Tonic, Mouth Ulcers.
Culinary:	Salads, Cooked as Vegetable to serve with meat
History:	Symbol of Innocence. Used on the battlefield as a wound herb. Closes at night. Measuring love by pulling the petals off "He loves me, he loves me not". Flowers in pot pourri.
Magical:	Lust

DAMIANA (Turnera diffusa/Turnera aphrodisiaca)

LONG TERM EXCESSIVE USE CAN DAMAGE THE LIVER

Mexican Damiana

Planet:	Pluto
Element:	Water
Gender:	Female
Gemstone:	Clear Quartz
Deities:	Artemis, Diana, Ganesha, Vishnu, Zeus Medicinal: Aphrodisiac, Nervous System, Hormonal System, Depression, Anxiety.
Powers:	Lust, Love, Visions
Magical:	Sexual magic. Incense to increase levels of energy during a ritual. Tea can aid divination and improve psychic power.

DAMSON (Prunus Institia or Prunus domestica) Bullace

Planet:	Venus
Medicinal:	Mild Purgative, Bleeding, Fevers, Diarrhoea.
Culinary:	Stewed, Bottled, Jams, Jellies, Preserves, Bullace Wine.
History:	Named after Damascus in Syria. Wood for turning and cabinet making.

DANDELION (Taraxacum officinale) Witch Gowan, Devil's

Milk Plant, Lion's Teeth, Golden Suns, Clocks and Watches, Piss-a-bed, Stink Davie, Heart Fever Grass, Dog Posy, Blowball, Peasant's Clock, Cankerwort, Crow-parsnip, Irish Daisy, Doon-headclock, Fortune Teller, One O'clocks, Swinesnout, Wet-a-bed, Shit-a-bed, Bum-pie, Burning Fire, Clocks, Combs and Hairpins, Conquer More, Devil's Milk Pail, Fairy Clocks, Farmer's Clocks, Horse Gowan, Lay-a-bed, Male, Mess-a-bed, Pisamoolag, Pissimire, Pittle Bed, Priest's Crown, Schoolboy's Clocks, Shepherd's Clock, Stink Davine, Tell-time, Time Flower, Timeteller, Twelve O'Clock, Wishes, Wet-weed, White Endive, Wild Endive

Planet:	Jupiter
Element:	Air

Gender:	Male
Sign:	Sagittarius
Totem Bird:	Falcon
Gemstone:	Opal
Festival:	Beltane
Deities:	Hecate, St George, Theseus
Care Doll:	Money
Powers:	Divination, Wishes, Calling Spirits
Medicinal:	Diuretic, Nourishing, Digestive, Water Retention, Edema, Swollen Ankles due to Circulatory Probles, Cystitis, Vitamins A and C, Potassium, Liver Tonic, Digestive, Diruetic, Liver Problems, Gall Bladder, Indigestion, Loss of Appetite, Constipation, Arthritis, Skin Disease, Chronic and Wasting Diseases, After Strong Chemical Drugs
Magical:	Divination, Wishes, Calling Spirits
Dog:	Diuretic, Minerals, Potassium, Vitamins, Proteins.

DILL (Anethum graveolens or Peucedanum graveolens) Dillweed, Dillseed, Aneton, Dilly Garden Dill, Chebbit, Sowa, Keper, Hulwa, Buzzalchippet

Planet:	Mercury
Element:	Fire
Care Doll:	Protection, Money
Powers:	Protection, Money, Lust, Love
Medicinal:	Digestive Problems, Flatulence, Stomach Cramps, Headaches, Insomnia, Colic in babies, Hiccups, Bad Breath, Allay Hunger Pains, Promote flow of milk.
History:	Introduced into Britain by the Romans.
Magical:	Love Potions. Protection vs Evil Eye. Lust, Love
Uses:	Perfume Soap and Cosmetics

DITTANY (Dictamnus albus) DITTANY OF CRETE (Dictamus

origanoides) Burning Bush, White Dittany, Fraxinella

Planet:	Venus
Element:	Water
Care Doll:	Love
Powers:	Manifestations, Astral Projection
Medicinal:	Pains, Cramp, Rheumatism, Kidney Stones, Fevers, Nervous Complaints, Epilepsy,
Culinary:	Scented Tea, Flavouring Liqueurs and Wines.
History:	Produces a volatile vapour which can be ignited. Distilled dittany water probably used as cosmetic.
Magical:	Manifestation, Astral Projection

DOCK Common (Rumex abrustifolius) Broad Leaved Dock, Butter

Dock, Yellow or Curled Dock (Rumex crispus)

Planet:	Jupiter
Element:	Air
Gender:	Male
Care Doll:	Love, Healing, Money
Dye:	Greenish Yellow
Powers:	Healing, Fertility, Money
Medicinal:	Skin Complaints, liver disorders, respiratory problems, laxative, anaemia, nettle stings.
Culinary:	Vegetable, Pot Herb
History:	Wrap butter

DOG ROSE (Rosa canina) See BRIAR

ELDER (Sambucus nigra) Devil's Eye, Lady Elder, Frau Holle, Tree of

Doom, Old Lady, Lady Ellhorn, Whistle Tree, Pipe Tree, Elderflower

Planet:	Venus
Element:	Air, Water
Gender:	Female
Totem Bird:	Rook, Owl

Totem Animal:	Badger
Gemstone:	Malachite, Green Jasper
Ogham:	Ruis
Colour:	Red
Rune:	Feoh
Deities:	Crone aspects of the Goddess, Dryads, Earth Goddesses, Fairies, Holda, Hulda, Venus
Care Doll:	Protection, Healing
Medicinal:	Diaphoretic, Diuretic, Anti-Inflammatory, Sinusitis, Colds, Hay Fever, Flu, Fever, Hot dry skin, Bring down Temperature, Protect Kidneys, Rashes, Sore eyes, Runny eyes, Eyestrain, Sunburn, Chapped Skin, Discoloured Skin, Colds (infants) .
Culinary:	Elderflower Tea and Wine.
History:	Sabucus comes from Greek Sambucu, a musical instrument. Panpipes made from stems.
Magical:	Exorcism, Prosperity

ELECAMPANE (Inula helenium, Enula campana) Elfwort, Elfdock, Horse Heal, Scabwort, Nurse-heal, Alycompaine, Enula, Alantwurzel, Wild Sunflower, Velvet Dock, Aunee, Elfwort, Horseheal
PERENNIAL

Colour:	Yellow
Planet:	Mercury
Element:	Air
Gender:	Male
Tarot:	All the Eights
Festival:	Coamhain Summer Solistice – Nature Spirits, Attune to Vibrations, throw into fires, offering to Wildfolk.
Humour:	Hot
Deities:	Elves, Helen of Troy
Care Doll:	Protection, Attract New Lover
Powers:	Love, Protection, Psychic Powers
Medicinal:	Appetite Stimulant, Counteract Rich Diet, Asthma, Indigestion, Sweeten the Breath, Horse Medicine, Sheep

Scab, Cough, Sore Throat, Bronchial Complaints, Chest
Infections, Whooping Cough, Digestive, General Tonic,
Antiseptic, Cleansing Properties, Acne, Itchy Skin,
Herpes, Minor Cuts, Bruises, .

Culinary:	Elizabethan Marzipan, Candied Roots
Magical:	Used by Druids. Herb of High Summer.
Uses:	Incense, Drinks, Decoctions

ELEGANTINE (Rosa rubiginosa or Rosa eglanteria)

Sweet Briar or Briar Rose

Planet:	Jupiter
Medicinal:	Skin, Scar Tissue, Burns, Scalds, Digestion, Sharpen Appetite, Colic, Diarrhoea
History:	Native to Britain.

ELM English (Ulmus procera) Elven Elm, Elven Tree

Planet:	Saturn
Element:	Earth
Gender:	Female
Totem Bird:	Rook
Deities:	Elves, Hoenin, Lodr, Odin, Orpheus
Powers:	Love
Medicinal:	Burns, Wounds, Haemorrhoids, Skin Inflammation, Baldness, Scurf, Leprosy, Broken Bones.
History:	Native to Britain. Wych Elm (Ulmus glabra) hardiest of the species. Used for underground water pipes, Boats, Coffins, Bridges, Groynes and Waterfronts. Hubs of Cartwheels. Norse myth claims Embla the first woman was created from the elm.

EYEBRIGHT (Euphrasia Officinalis/Euphrasia rostkoviana)

Red Eyebright, Euphrosyne ANNUAL

Planet:	Sun
Element:	Air
Gender:	Male

Sign:	Leo
Totem Bird:	Linnet
Deity:	Euphrosyne
Care Doll:	Sleep
Powers:	Mental Powers, Psychic Powers
Medicinal:	Hayfever, Eye Inflammations, Eyestrain, Digestive Tonic, Head Colds
Magical:	Tea or Incense to see the positive side of life, inspiration and joy.
Uses:	Tea (Fasting, Study), Incense (Positivity, Inspiration, Joy)

FENNEL (Foeniculum vulgare) Sweet Fennel, Finkle, Seaside,

Ferny-plant PERENNIAL

Planet:	Mercury
Element:	Fire
Gender:	Male
Festival:	Coamhain
Deities:	Apollo, Dionysus, Prometheus
Care Doll:	Protection, Healing, Confidence, Courage
Dye:	Yellow
Powers:	Protection, Healing, Purification
Medicinal:	Flatulence, Stomach Aches, Constipation, Gripe Water, Eyewash for Bad Eyesight, Digestive Aid, Sore Throats, Alleviate Hunger, Antidote against poisonous herbs and mushrooms and snake bites, Improve Memory, stimulate milk flow, Aphrodisiac, Warming, Carminative, Antispasmodic, Antidepressant, Lactagogue, Balances Hormones, Diuretic, Antimicrobal, Wind, Nausea, Stomach Cramps, Irritable Bowel, Infant Colic, Milk Flow, Reduce Colic, Blepharitis, Tired Eyes, Anemia, Anxiety, Depression, Disturbed Spirits, Arthritis, Water Retention, Edema, Gum Disease, Infection, Fast Hunger, Menopause, Antiseptic, Premenstrual Water Retention, Urinary Tract Infections, Flatulence.
Culinary:	Herbal Teas, Salads, Garnish on Vegetables, Soups,

	Stuffing, Sauces, Pot Herb in Meat Stews, Pastries, Bread, Liqueurs.
History:	One of the nine herbs held sacred by Anglo Saxons. Valued by the Ancient Greeks and Romans. Medieval Monasteries used it as a strewing herb to sweeten the air.
Magical:	Hung over doors and inserted in keyholes to ward off Evil Spirits. Healing, Confidence, Courage, Purification.
Uses:	Used to scent soaps and perfumes.
Dogs:	Dyspepsia, Flatulence, Colic.
Animals:	Yes
Dogs:	Yes
Essential Oil:	Courage, Energy

FENUGREEK (Trigonella foenum-graecum) Bird's Foot, Greek Hay Seed, Classical Greek Clover, Methi

Planet:	Mercury
Element:	Air
Gender:	Male
Tarot:	The Magician
Deity:	Apollo
Powers:	Money
Medicinal:	Milk production, Digestive Problems, Bronchitis, Coughs, Cleansing the Body, Removing Toxins, Infectious Diseases, Anaemia, Sore Throats, Mouth Ulcers, Chapped Lips.
History:	Used in Embalming Fluid by the Egyptians. Also for culinary, cosmetic and medicinal purposes.
Uses:	Hair treatment (Dandruff)

FERN

Gender:	Male
Planet:	Mercury
Element:	Air
Deities:	Laka, Puck

Powers: Rain Making, Protection, Luck, Riches, Eternal Youth,
            Health, Exorcism.

FEVERFEW (Tanacetum parthenium/Chrysanthemum

parthenium) Febrifuge Plant, Featherfew, Bachelor's Buttons,
Nosebleed, Midsummer Daisy AVOID DURING PREGNANCY   PERENNIAL

Planet:	Venus
Element:	Water
Gender:	Female
Festival:	Midsummer (Incense, Ritual Cup, Flowers on Altar)
Care Doll:	Protection, Healing
Medicinal:	Fevers, Anti-Inflammatory, Antispasmodic, Emmanagogue, Analgesic, Migraine, Arthritis, Headaches, Fevers, Tonic, Melancholy, Vertigo, Nervous Complaints, Hysterical Complaints, Skin Problems, Insect Repellent, Inflamed Gums, After Tooth Extraction, Mild Laxative, Bruises, Bites, Stings, Acne, Restful Sleep, Relaxation
Culinary:	Tea (Stress)
Magical:	Incense (Protection, Restful Atmosphere, Meditation)

FIG (Ficus carica) Common Fig, Fico, Mhawa, Chagareltin

Planet:	Jupiter
Gender:	Male
Element:	Fire
Deities:	Dionysus, Juno, Isis
Powers:	Divination, Fertility, Love
Medicinal:	Sore throats, bronchial complaints, constipation, boils, small tumours, haemorrhoids, warts, mad dog bite, Dropsy
Culinary:	Fresh or dried eaten raw or stewed. Jam
History:	Sacred to the Romans as it sheltered the she wolf who suckled Romulus and Remus. Said to be the tree that Judus Iscariot hanged himself after betraying Christ.

FIGWORT (Scrophularia nodosa) Throatwort, Carpenter's
Square, Rosenoble

Planet:	Venus
Gender:	Female
Element:	Water
Powers:	Protection, Health
Medicinal:	Scrofula, Haemorrhoids, Mild Laxative, Heart Stimulant, Pain Reliever, Blood Cleansing Tonic, Sores, Ulcers, Scratches, Minor Wounds, Skin Diseases, Eczema, Fungal Infections.

FLAX (Linum usitatissumum) Perennial Flax (Linum perenne)
Purging Flax (Linum catharticum) Linseed, Linen Eating seeds in
quantity can be poisonous

Flowers:	June and July
Planet:	Mercury
Element:	Fire
Gender:	Male
Rune:	Wyn
Deities:	Arachne, Arianrhod, Brighid, Hulda, Inanna, Neith, Uttu
Care Doll:	Healing, Money, Protection, Good Fortune
Powers:	Money, Protection, Beauty, Psychic Powers, Healing
Medicinal:	Urinary Infections, Constipation, Respiratory Disorders, Gallstones, Coughs, Sore Throats, Swellings, Burns, Boils, Abscesses, Ulcers, Aches, Pains, Horse Cough, Catarrh, Bronchitis, Urinary Infections, Pulmonary Infections, Cuts, Inflammation, Pleurisy, Pulmonary Conditions.
Culinary:	Linseed Oil used in Cooking, roasted seeds, Bread from corn mixed with flax seeds.
History:	Cultivated since Prehistoric times
Magical:	Healing, Money, Protection, Beauty, Good Fortune
Uses:	Fibers woven into linen, ropes, nets, sacks, sails and bowstrings, napkins, cloths, wimples, tow used as lamp

wicks, stuffing to prevent draughts. Linseed Oil paint, varnish, printer's ink and soap, lubricate cart wheels. Waste from pulped seed fed to cattle.

FORGET ME NOT (Myosotis sylvatica) Scorpion Grass

PERENNIAL

Planet:	Venus
Element:	Water
Gender:	Female
Festival:	Ostara (Decorations)
Totem Animal:	Mouse
Deities:	Persephone
Care Doll:	Remembrance, Death
Uses:	Incense, Bathing Herb

FOXGLOVE (Digitalis purpurea) Fox-fingers, Lady's Thimble,

Witches Fingers, Witches Bells, Bluidy Man's Fingers, Flowater-leaves, Fairy's Glove, Fairy's Cap, Fairy's Thimbles, Witches Gloves, Bloody Fingers, Dead Man's Bells, Cow-flop, Digitalis, Fairy Petticoats, Fairy Weed, Floppy-dock, Floptop, Folk's Gloves, Fox Bells, Foxes Glofa, The Great Herb, Lion's Mouth, Lusmore, Lus Na Mbau Side, Our Lady's Gloves POISONOUS

Planet:	Venus
Element:	Water
Gender:	Female
Totem Animal:	Fox
Deities:	Fairies
Powers:	Protection
Magical:	Used to make a thick black dye to paint crossed lines on stone floors to prevent evil entering. Associations with the Fairies. How you use the plant will make them friends or enemies. Incense to contact the Fairies. Used with Fox Totems. Cords may be dyed black with Foxglove.
History:	Native to Britain

FUMITORY (Fumaria officinalis) Beggary, Earth Smoke,

Fumiterry, Fumus, Fumus Terrae, Kaphnos, Nidor, Scheiteregi,
Taubenkropp, Vapor, Wax Dolls

Gender:	Female
Planet:	Saturn
Element:	Earth
Powers:	Money, Exorcism

GALANGAL (Alpina offinalum) Chewing John, China Root, Colic

Root, East India Catarrh Root, Galingal, Galingale, Gargaut, India Root,
Kaempferia Galanga, Low John the Conqueror, Rhizoma Galangae

Element:	Fire
Planet:	Mars
Gender:	Male
Powers:	Protection, Lust, Health, Money, Psychic Powers, Hex Breaking

GARDENIA (Gardenia jasminoides)

Planet:	Moon
Element:	Water
Gender:	Female
Powers:	Love, Peace, Heating, Spirituality

GARLIC (Allium sativum) Poor Man's Treacle, Stinkweed

PERENNIAL

Planet:	Sun, Mars
Element:	Fire
Gender:	Male
Deity:	Hecate
Rune:	Gar
Care Doll:	Protection, Purification, Healing
Powers:	Protection, Healing, Exorcism, Lust, Anti-Theft
Medicinal:	Wound Healing, Blood Staunching, Malaria, Facial Blemishes, Lower Serum Cholesterol, LDL Cholesterol,

High Blood Pressure, Heart Disease, Atherosclerosis, Infected Wounds, Infections of Stomach, Intestinal Worms, Stomach Acid, Bronchitis, Lung Infection, Antifungal, Athlete's Foot, Antiseptic, Open Wounds, Lower Blood Pressure, Asthma, Flu, Colds, Ear Infections, Antibiotic, Boost Immune System, Fever, Diabetes, Cancer, Respiratory Ailments, Ear Inflammation, Coughs, Blood Tonic, Reduce Cholesterol, Arthritis, Rheumatism, Underactive Thyroid

Culinary:	Herbal Teas, Wines and Liqueurs
Magic:	Protection against Black Magic and Evil, Under Pillows to protect children. Rope of it in Kitchen to bring Health and Protection. Incense. Used during the Waning or Dark Moon.

GENTIAN (Gentiana verna)

Planet:	Mars
Element:	Fire
Gender:	Male
Powers:	Love, Power
Medicinal:	Stomach Complaints, Digestive Disorders, Ulcers, Skin Complaints, Digestive Disorders, Ulcers, Skin Complaints, Reduce Fever, Stimulate Appetite, Promote Digestive Juices and Bile, Cleansing Wounds.
Culinary:	Bitter Liqueurs and Aperatifs
History:	Named after Gentius, King if Illyria.

GERANIUM Erodium (Heron's Bill), Pelargonium (Stork's Bill), Geranium (Crane's Bill)   Herb Robert (Geranium robertianum)

PERENNIAL

Planet:	Venus
Element:	Water
Gender:	Female
Deities:	Aphrodite, Athene, Isis, Menthu, Minerva, Shiva, Venus
Care Doll:	Love, Protection, Fertility, Health

Powers:	Fertility, Health, Love, Protection
Medicinal:	Uplifting, Refreshing, Balancing, Anti-Inflammatory, Soothing, Astringent, Antiseptic, Diuretic, Insect Repellant, Apathy, Anxiety, Stress, Hyperactivity, Depression, Arthritis, Acne, Diaper/Nappy Rash, Burns, Blisters, Eczema, Cuts, Congested Pores, Infections, Sore Throats, Mouth Ulcers, Swollen Breasts, Fluid Retention, Lymph Circulation, Blood Circulation, Premenstrual Pain, Premenstrual Tension, Menopausal Problems, Balancing Effect.
Magical:	Protective and Healing Incenses, Incense (Invoke Venus, Aphrodite and Isis, Love and Harmony)
Essential Oil:	Harmony, Friendship, Calmness, Positive Energy, Addictions

GINGER (Zingiber offinale)

Planet:	Mars
Element:	Fire
Gender:	Male
Care Doll:	Love, Protection, Money, Confidence, Courage, Success, Power
Powers:	Love, Money, Success, Power
Medicinal:	Warm the stomach, promote perspiration, treat colds, flu, lung infections, improve blood circulation to peripheral parts, stimulate digestion, improve liver function, relax muscle spasms, ease flatulence, colic and nausea, stimulate circulation, relieve muscular and rheumatic aches and pains. Reducing motion sickness.
Culinary:	Fresh, Dried, Pickled, preserved in syrup, stems were crystallized, spice to cakes, confectionery, gingerbread, ginger beer.
History:	Romans brought it to Britain.
Magical:	Love, Protection, Money, Confidence, Courage, Success, Power
Uses:	Used in perfumes

GOLDENROD (Solidago odora) Aaron's Rod, Blue Mountain

Tea, Goldruthe, Gonea Tea, Sweet Scented
Goldenrod, Solidago, Verg d'Or, Wound Weed, Woundwort

Planet:	Venus
Element:	Air
Gender:	Female
Powers:	Money, Divination

GOOSE GRASS (Galium aparine) Cleavers, Clivers,

Catchweed

Planet:	Moon
Dye:	Red
Medicinal:	Cleansing Tonic, Glandular and Urinary Problems, Skin Disorders, Lymphatic Swellings, Burns, Ulcers, Skin Inflammations, Grazes, Wounds, Sores, Staunch Bleeding, Blood Cleansing, Strengthen Liver,
Culinary:	Young shoots cooked as a vegetable, added to soups. Seeds as coffee substitute.
History:	Native to Britain. Favourite food of Geese. Used to strain hair out of milk. Used as pin heads by lace makers.

GOOSEBERRY (Ribes uva-crispa)

Planet:	Venus
Medicinal:	Cooling Astringent, Appetite, Quenching Thirst, Cool hot swellings and inflammations, breaking up stones in the kidneys or bladder, dressing to heal wounds. Culinary: Bottled, stewed, used to flavour wine, jellies, jams, pickles, sauces, broth.
History:	Native to Britain

GORSE (Ulex eurpaeus) Furze, Whin, Broom, Frey, Fyrs, Gorst, Goss, Prickly Broom, Ruffet, Whin

Planet:	Mars, Sun
Element:	Fire
Gender:	Male
Gemstone:	Emerald
Colour:	Yellow gold
Totem Animal:	Hare
Ogham:	Onn
Deities:	Jupiter, Onniona, Spring Goddess, The Sun Lord, Thor
Care Doll:	Protection, Money
Festival:	Midsummer (Burned for Health and Good Luck)
Dye:	Yellow
Powers:	Protection, Money
Medicinal:	Jaundice and Kidney Problems,
Culinary:	Buds pickled, substitute for tea. Flowers Gorse Wine. Gorse Flower Tea.
History:	Native to Britain. Used for fuel, hedging plant, hanging washing over.
Magical:	Considered unlucky if allowed into the house. Welsh (Protection against Witches), Hope, Positivity, Reconnect with Soul, Depression, Finding true path, Positive Action.

GRAPEVINE (Vitis vinifera) Vine

Planet:	Sun
Element:	Water
Gender:	Female
Deities:	Dionysus, Bacchus, Hathor
Powers:	Fertility, Garden Magic, Mental Powers, Money
Medicinal:	Headaches, Inflammations, Heartburn, Diseases of the Joints, Staunch Bleeding, Heal Wounds, Settle the Stomach, Check looseness of the bowels,
Culinary:	Raw, Dried: Currants, Raisins, Sultanas, Pressed for

Juice, Jelly, Fermented, Wine and Verjuice (grape vinegar)

History: Introduced to Britain by the Romans.

GROUND IVY (Glechoma hederacea/Nepeta glechoma)

Alehoof, Cat's Foot, Gill-go-by-the-ground, Turn-hoof, Hay-maids, Tun Hoof, Gill Ale, Gill-over-the-ground, Gill, Gill Hen, Hedge Maids, Jenny Run-ith Ground, Jill, Hayfole, Heihow, Heyhove, Devil's Candlestick, Creeping Charlie, Field Balm, Hedgemaids, Lizzy-run-up-the-hedge, Robin-run-in-the-hedge

Planet: Venus
Gender: Female
Festival: Ostara
Powers: Divination
Culinary: Brewing beer.
Magical: Incense, Ritual Cup.

GROMWELL Blue (Lithospermum purpurocaeruleum)

Creeping Gromwell

Dye: Red colouring agent
Medicinal: Urinary Disorders, Colic, Kidney Stones, Oral Contraceptive, Irritant Skin Conditions

GROUNDSEL Common (Senecio vulgaris) Ground Glutton,

Groundeswelge, Grundy Swallow, Sention, Simson
Taken in large quantities can damage the liver

Planet: Venus
Element: Water
Gender: Female
Powers: Health, Healing
Medicinal: Toothache, Inflammation, Haemorrhoids,   Gout, Menstruation problems, Staunch Bleeding, Provokes Urine, Kidney Stones
History: Native to Britain.

HAREBELL (Capanula rotundifolia) Scottish Bluebell

Planet:	Venus
Medicinal:	Heal Wounds, Staunch Bleeding, Reduce Inflammation
Magical:	Associated with Witches who were said to transform themselves into Hares, Fairies, Goblins and other Supernatural beings.

HAWTHORN (Crataegus monogyna/Crataegus oxacantha)

May, Quickthorn, Bread and Cheese, Hagthorn, Moon Flower, Whitethorn, Tree of Fairies

Planet:	Mars
Element:	Fire
Gender:	Male
Totem Bird:	Crow
Colour:	Purple
Gestone:	Topaz, Lapis Lazuli
Rune:	Thorn, Odal
Ogham:	Uath
Festival:	Beltane
Deities:	Blodeuwedd, Cardea, Creiddylad, Fairies, Flora, Hymen, Olwen, Thor
Care Doll:	Love, Protection, Fertility, Happiness, Chastity, Fishing
Medicinal:	Heart Disorders, Circulatory Disorders, Kidney Stones, Dropsy, Pains, Strengthens the Heart, Lowers Blood Pressure, Relaxes Arteries, Heart Failure, Irregular Heartbeat, Angina, High Blood Pressure, Anxiety with Palpitations, Sore Throat
Culinary:	Jellies, Wines, Liqueurs and Sauces
History:	Joseph of Aramathea brought the first Hawthorn to England in 63AD. The Holy Thorn. Greece and Rome a symbol of Hope and Protection. Hedging plant to protect livestock.
Magical:	Solitary Hawthorn near spring is a marker to the world of the Fairies. Strips of Cloth tied to Hawthorn in the

Spring.

Dog: Strengthens Cardiac Output, Moderates Blood Pressure, Increases Circulation

HAZEL (Corylus avellana) Cobnut, Hale, Woodnut

Planet:	Mercury
Element:	Air
Gender:	Male
Totem Bird:	Crane, Robin
Totem Animal:	Salmon, Salamander
Colour:	Brown
Gemstone:	Red Banded Agate, Opal, Magnetite, Amethyst
Festival:	Herfest
Tool:	Wand
Deities:	Aengus, Artemis, Diana, Chandra, Connla, Fionn, Hecate, Lleu, Mac Coll, Manannan, Mercury, Ogma, Taliesin, Thor
Powers:	Luck, Fertility, Anti-Lightning, Protection, Wishes
Medicinal:	Varicose Veins, Circulatory Disorders, Menstrual Problems, Haemorrhoids, Slow Healing Wounds.
Culinary:	Nuts or cobs eaten raw, used in cakes, bread, confectionery, liqueurs. Oil used in cooking
History:	Native to Britain. Coppice Tree. Bind Bundles, Weave Baskets, Make Hurdles, Build Coracles. Wattle in Buildings.
Magical:	Sacred. Symbol of Fertility, Immortality. Wands, Forked Twigs for Dowsing and Divining. Nuts carried to repel evil spirits or ward off rheumatism. Associated with Halloween "Nutcrack Night".
Uses:	Oil used for Soap and Cosmetics.

HEATHER (Calluna vulgaris) Ling, Common Heather, Heath,
Scottish Heather

Planet:	Venus
Element:	Water
Gender:	Female
Gemstone:	Peridot, Amethyst
Totem Animal:	Lizard, Bee
Totem Bird:	Lark
Colour:	Purple
Ogham:	Ura
Humour:	Cold
Deities:	Attis, Butes, Cybele, Isis, Osiris, Uroica, Venus
Dye:	Yellow and Orange
Powers:	Protection, Rain-Making, Luck
Medicinal:	Urinary and Kidney Problems, Rheumatic and Arthritic Pain, Mild Sedative.
Culinary:	Young shoots flavour beer.
History:	Used as fuel "Ling". Used for thatching, bedding and basket weaving. Heather Honey.
Magical:	Lucky White Heather.
Uses:	Tanning

HELLEBORE (Helleborus niger) Black Hellebore, Christmas
Rose, Melampode, Fetterwort, Fetter-grass, Bear's Foot, Christmas
Herb, Christmas Flower

Planet:	Saturn
Element:	Water
Gender:	Female
Gemstone:	Onyx
Deities:	Athene, Hecate

HENNA (Lawsonia inermis)

Powers:	Healing
Uses:	Hair Dye

HERB ROBERT, GERANIUM (Geranium

robertianum)   Bloodwort, Dragon's Blood, Fox Geranium, Fox Grass,
Knife and Fork, Robin Flower, Stinking Bob

Planet:	Venus
Element:	Water
Gender:	Female
Deity:	Robin (The Woodland Lord)
Medicinal:	Fractures, Ulcers, Wounds, Insecticide, Haeorrhoids, Diabetes, Gout, Blood Tonic, Lowers Blood Sugar Level, Eye Inflammation, Mouth Wash, Mouth Ulcers, Sore Throat,
Magical:	Incense (Commune)

HIBISCUS (Hibiscus sabdariffa) Kharkady, Graxa, Gumamela,

Shoeflower, Tulipan

Planet:	Venus
Element:	Water
Gender:	Female
Powers:	Lust, Love, Divination

HOLLY (Ilex aquifolium)

Planet:	Mars/Saturn
Element:	Fire
Gender:	Male
Gemstone:	Topaz, Red Carnelian
Totem Bird:	Robin,
Animal:	Dog
Colour:	Dark Grey
Rune:	Man
Ogham:	Tinne
Festival:	Yule
Tool:	Spear
Deities:	Holly King, Jesus, Lleu, Lugh, Mars, Saturn, Tannus,

Taran, Thor

Care Doll: Protection, Good Luck

Powers: Protection, Anti-Lightning, Luck, Dream Magic

HOLLYHOCK (Alcea rosea)

Planet: Venus
Element: Earth
Gender: Female
Deities: Plant Devas
Dye: Colouring for Red Wine
Medicinal: Inflammation of mucus membranes, Coughs, Asthma,
                Sore Throat, Chronic Gastric Gastritis, Enteritis,
                Constipation, Nausea, Headaches, Diarrhoea, Insomnia.
Magical: Incense (Protection, Healing, Meditation, Contact Plant
                Spirits, Soothing and Relaxing, Atmosphere). Shelter to
                Fey Folk
Uses: Bath Infusion (Skin problems, cuts, bruises)

HONESTY (Lunaria) Lunary, Money Plant, Silver Dollar

Planet: Moon
Element: Earth
Gender: Female
Powers: Money, Repelling Monsters

HONEYSUCKLE Garden Honeysuckle (Lonicera
periclymenum) Wild Honeysuckle (Lonicera caprifolium)   Woodbine,
Woodbind, Suckling, Caprifoly, Goatl-leaf, Dutch Honeysuckle,
Mother of the Wood, Luscius Woodbine, Evening Pride
Berries are poisonous IN LARGE DOSES IT CAN INDUCE VOMITING

Planet: Jupiter
Element: Earth
Gender: Male
Sign: Cancer
Totem Animal: Bee, Goat
Ogham: Uillean

Deities:	Cerridwen, Fairies, Pan
Festival:	Beltane (Wine), Midsummer & Lughnasa (Flowers), Harvest Rite (Incense), Samhain (Incense: Underworld Entrance)
Care Doll:	Protection, Fidelity, Money
Powers:	Money, Psychic Powers, Protection
Medicinal:	Warming, Bee Stings, Coughs, Catarrh, Asthma, Chilblains, Bad Circulation.
Culinary:	Flowers for salads, substitute tea
History:	Emblem of Fidelity and Affection.
Magical:	Protection, Fidelity, Money, Psychic Powers, Luck, Cycles of Life, Accepting Change, Flow of Energy. Tea (Higher Guidance, Wider Perspective, Letting go of the past and unnecessary)
Uses:	Pot Pourri and Perfumes
Incense:	Pan, Goat Totems

HOPS (Humulus lupulus) Beer Flower PERENNIAL

Planet:	Mars
Element:	Air
Gender:	Male
Totem Animal:	Wolf
Deities:	Brighid, Leto
Festivals:	Beer and Ale for Ritual Cup
Care Doll:	Sleep, Healing
Powers:	Healing, Sleep
Medicinal:	Appetite Stimulant, Digestive Problems, Jaundice, Menstrual Cramps, Flow of Milk, Neuralgia, Arthritis, Rheumatism, Boils, Rashes, Bruises, Colic, Irritable Bowel, Nervous Tension.
Magical:	Infusion (Connect with Animal Energy within, particularly Wolf Totems)
Uses:	Tea (Sedative, Calming), Sleep Pillow (Natural Sleep, Toothache, Earache)

HOREHOUND (Marrubium vulgare) White Horehound, Seed
of Horus, Bull's Blood, Eye of the Star, White Horehound, Hoarhound,
Maruil, Soldier's Tea, Marrubium, Haran Haran, Huran, Llywd y Cwn

Planet:	Mercury
Element:	Air
Gender:	Male
Tarot:	The Magician Cabala: Hod
Deities:	Horus, Isis, Osiris
Care Doll:	Healing, Protection
Powers:	Protection, Mental Powers, Exorcism, Healing
Medicinal:	Cough, Catarrh, Asthma, Respiratory Complaints, snake bite, chest pains, pains in the side, chronic cough, maladies of the male genitals, heart, liver, digestive problems, malaria, worms and dog bites. Horehound candy as cough sweets.
Culinary:	Leaves make liqueurs, ales and wine.
Magical:	Healing, Protection, Mental Powers, Exorcism

HORSERADISH (Amoracia rusticana/Cochlearia armoracia)

AVOID IF PREGNANT OR KIDNEY PROBLEMS PERENNIAL

Planet:	Mars
Element:	Fire
Gender:	Male
Dye:	Yellow
Powers:	Purification, Exorcism
Medicinal:	Diuretic, Stimulant, Clears Nasal Passages, Antiseptic, Stimulates Blood Flow, Aids Digestion, Clean Teeth, Kill Bacteria, Control Mouth Ulcers, Acne, Sinus Infections, Rheumatism, Chilblains, Stiff Muscles, Rheumatism, Sciatica, Skin Lotion.
Magical:	Incense (Protection), Powder (Wards off Evil), Fire Incense, Mars Planetary Incense, Banishment, Purification, Exorcism

HOUND'S TONGUE (Cynoglossum officinale)

Rats and Mice, Gypsy Flower, Dog Bur, Dog's Tongue, Sheep Lice,
Tongue of Dog, Woolmat

Planet:	Mercury
Element:	Fire
Gender:	Male
Powers:	Tying Dog's Tongues
Medicinal:	Soothing, Healing, Painkilling, Cuts, Bruises, Burns, Sores, Skin Diseases, Coughs, Colds, Mad Dog Bite, Baldness, Venereal Disease. Insect Bites.
Culinary:	Native of Britain.
Magical:	Dogs would be silenced and unable to bark at a person who placed a leaf under their big toe.

HOUSELEEK (Sempervivum tectorum) Thunderflower,

Thunder-plant, Homewort, Ever Living, Plant of the Roof, Fouet, Fow,
Hockerie-topner, House-green, Huslock, Imbrake, Jobarbe, Jubarb,
Jupiter's Beard, Sungreen, Suphelt, Seagreen, Hen and Chickens, Live
For Ever, Jupiter's Eye, Thor's Beard, Sengren

Planet:	Jupiter
Element:	Air
Gender:	Male
Rune:	Thorn
Deities:	Jupiter
Powers:	Luck, Protection, Love
Medicinal:	Ulcers, Burns, Scalds, Inflammations, Skin Rashes, Stings, Insect Bites, Warts and Corns, Toothache.
Culinary:	Salads or Vegetable
History:	Introduced to Britain by the Romans. Grown on the roof in Greece and Rome.
Magical:	Dedicated to Thunder Gods, Roman Jupiter and Scandinavian Thor. Charlemagne ordered that it be grown throughout the Empire for magical properties including keeping witches and evil spirits away.

HYACINTH (Hyacinth orientalis)

Planet: Venus
Element: Water
Gender: Female
Powers: Love, Protection, Happiness

HYDRANGEA (Hydrangea arborescens)

Seven Barks
Powers: Hex Breaking

HYSSOP (Hyssopus officinalise)   Ysopo, Isopo

Planet: Jupiter
Element: Fire
Gender: Male
Sign: Cancer
Gemstone: Amethyst, Lapis Lazuli
Tarot: The Kings
Deities: King David, Moses, Pluto, Solomon, Zeus
Care Doll: Healing, Dispels Negativity
Powers: Purification, Protection
Medicinal: Expectorant, Antispasmodic, Bactericidal, Antiseptic,
               Hypertensive, Emmenagogue, Digestive, Tonic,
               Sedative, Coughs, Colds, Catarrh, Sore Throat, Chest
               Infection, Bites, Cuts, Stings, Bruises, Inflammation, Low
               Blood Pressure, Tonic, Circulation, Indigestion, Colicky
               Cramps, Stress, Anxiety, Fatigue, Increasing Alertness,
               Lice, Rheumatism, Digestive Aid, Lung Complaints, Poor
               Appetite, Ear Infection, Eye Infection.
History: Mixed with Lamb's Blood to protect from the seven
               plagues of Egypt. Used in Solomon's Sprinkler for Holy
               Water.
Magical: Healing, Dispels Negativity, Purification, Protection
Essential Oil: Grief

INDIGO (Indigofera tinctoria)

Planet:	Saturn
Element:	Water
Gender:	Female
Grow:	True Indigo (Polytunnel), Wild Indigo (Outside)
Dye:	Blue
Medicinal:	Used by Native American Indians but can cause Vomiting
Magical:	Dye used to dye robes

IRIS, Yellow Flag (Iris pseudacorus) Florentine Iris (Iris Florentina/Iris germanica) Fleur-de-luce, Fleur-de-lys, Orris Root, Queen Elizabeth Root. Can Cause Reactions

Planet:	Venus
Element:	Water
Gender:	Female
Deities:	Aphrodite, Hera, Iris, Isis, Juno, Osiris, Venus
Dye:	Flowers: Yellow. Roots: Black used as ink
Powers:	Purification, Wisdom
Medicinal:	Root. Chest Complaints, Purgative, Clears the Brain,
Culinary:	Roots used as a spice. Added to liqueurs and beers. Roasted seeds as coffee substitute.
History:	Named after the Greek Goddess of the Rainbow and the messenger of the Gods. As Fleurl-de-lys adopted by King Louis VII of France in the Second Crusade against the Saracens. Strewn on floors, used to cover chairs and repair thatched roofs.
Magical:	Pliny said that a libation should be offered pre digging of the root to appease the earth. Draw three circles round it with the point of a sword. Pull it up and raise it to the heavens. Those who gather it should be chaste. Churches hung about the door to ward off evil spirits.
Use:	Perfumery and cosmetics since Egyptian times. Put in wardrobes. Pot Pourri. Hair Powder or dry shampoo.

IVY, Common (Hedera helix) Climbing Ivy

All Parts are Poisonous DO NOT USE INTERNALLY

Planet:	Saturn
Element:	Water
Gender:	Female
Gemstone:	Jasper
Totem Animal:	Goat
Totem Bird:	Mute Swan
Colour:	Sky Blue
Rune:	Ior
Ogham:	Gort
Deities:	Ariadne, Arianrhod, Bacchus, Cerridwen, Dionysus, Gorgopa, Hymen, Isis, Kundalini, Lakshmi, Osiris, Persephone, Psyche, Saturn, The White Goddess
Festival:	Winter Solstice
Care Doll:	Love, Fidelity, Protection, Healing
Powers:	Protection, Healing
Medicinal:	Rheumatic Pains, Bronchial Complaints, Whooping Cough, Burns, Scalds, Sores, Wounds, Painful Swellings, Bruises, Neuralgia and Sciatica, Hangover, Tired Muscles, Sunburn, Skin Tonic, Cellulite, Headaches.
History:	Ivy Bush seen as the sign of a Tavern. Crown of Ivy presented to Winners of the first Eisteddfods.
Magical:	Sacred. Used in Festivals to decorate the wands of fertility god "Father Liber" (Dionysus or Bacchus). Wine drunk out of ivy wood cups. Protective Magical Plant. Change of Consciousness. Altered state of mind. Last sheaf of harvest bound with Ivy (Ivy Girl). Life and Rebirth. The Life Maze. Resurrection. Immortality of the Spirit. Wand entwined with Ivy topped with fir cone. Prophecy, Vision, Sacrifice.

IVY, Ground (Glechoma hederacea) Alehoof, Gill-Go-Over-The-Ground

Planet:	Venus
Medicinal:	Inflamed eyes, failing eyesight, colds, chest complaints, digestive troubles, menstrual pains, bladder and kidney infections, boils, ulcers, wounds, skin irritations, cough medicine, nasal congestion, headaches.
Culinary:	Clarifying of ale, salads, soups, gruels, spinach.
History:	Native since prehistoric times. Varnish made from the resin.

JASMINE Common (Jasminum officinalis/Jasminium grandiflorum) Jessamine, Moonlight on the Grove

Planet:	Jupiter in Cancer, Moon
Element:	Water
Gender:	Female
Humour:	Cold
Gemstone:	Quartz
Number:	Nine
Deities:	Artemis, Diana, Ganesha, Maternal Aspects of the Goddess, Quan Yin, Virgin Mary, Vishnu, Zeus Care Doll: Love, Dreams, Money
Powers:	Love, Money, Prophetic Dreams
Medicinal:	Depression, chest and respiratory complaints, nervous tension, menstrual problems, general tiredness. Cold and Catarrhous conditions, aphrodisiac, cure for frigidity. Mild sedative, remedy for headache, Uterine tonic, Male Sex Organs, Anti Depressant, Antiseptic, Expectorant, Anti- inflammatory, Analgesic, Impotence, Menstrual Cramp, Uterus, Childbirth, Prostrate Problems, Postnatal Depression, Stress, Lethargy, Joints, Wry wrinkled and ageing skin, Catarrh, Chest Infection, Throat Infection.
History:	Grown in England from the Sixteenth Century.

Magical:	Meditation, Psychic Dreams
Uses:	Perfumery. Flowers in Pot Pourri, Incense (Relaxed romantic or sexual atmosphere, Aura Boost, Psychic Protection)
Essential OIl:	Balance, Confidence, Dreams, Sensuality, Relaxation, Protection

JUNIPER (Juniperis communis) Mountain Yew, Melmot Berry,

Horse Saver, Bastard Killer, Enebro,
Gemeiner Wachholder, Geneva, Gin Berry, Ginepro, Gin Plant Should
not be taken during pregnancy or by those with kidney problems

Planet:	Mars, Sun
Element:	Fire
Gender:	Male
Sign:	Aries
Ogham:	Aiteal
Deities:	The Furies, Pan
Festivals:	Samhain, Yule
Care Doll:	Love, Protection, Healing
Dye:	Brown
Powers:	Protection, Anti-Theft, Love, Exorcism, Health
Medicinal:	Warming and relieves symptoms, Stomach Pains, Chest Pains, Side Pains, Flatulence, Coughs, Colds, Tumours, Disorders of the Uterus, Antidote to poisons, defense against the plague, strengthen the brain, curing wind, eating berries could cause abortion, Cleansing, Diuretic, Tonic, Astringent, Antiseptic, Healing, Stimulates Appetite, Soothing, Detox, Rheumatoid Arthritis, Cellulite, Confusion, Exhaustion, Cystitis, Weepy Eczema, Acne, Cuts, Scrapes, Hemorrhoids, Hair Loss, Nervous Tension,
Culinary:	Oil of Juniper used to flavour liqueurs e.g. gin, Marinades, Stews, Sauces, Meat Dishes. Smoke preserved meats.
History:	Native of Britain. Slow growing tree. Strewn on floors

to sweeten smell of rooms. Burned to clear the air of infection especially during epidemics. Used in embalming.

Magical: Branches burnt as a purifying herb in temples. Protection against witches, devils and evil spirits. Love, Protection, Healing, Banishment, Exorcism, Health, Purification, Justice, Truth. Healing Rituals. Banishes Negativity. Attracts Healthy Energies. Berries in Amulets. Tea. Incense (Fresh Needles).

Incense: Drive Away Evil Spirits, Deter Diseases

LADY'S MANTLE (Alchemilla vulgaris) Dewcup, Bear's Foot, A Woman's Best Friend, Breakstone, Piercestone, Lion's Foot, Leontopodium, Nine Monks, Stellaria   PERENNIAL

Planet: Venus

Element: Water

Gender: Female

Rune: Beorc

Deities: Earth Goddess

Care Doll: Love, To Attract Love

Dye: Green

Powers: Love

Medicinal: Female Ailments (vaginal discharges, itching and menstrual disorders),   Ruptures,   Wounds, Staunch Bleeding, Inflammations, Bruises, Boils, sores and Burns, digestive tonic, diarrhoea, Astringent, Menstrual Bleeding, Cramps, PMS, Thrush, Vaginal Discharges, Infertility, Children's Diarrhea, Menopausal Discomfort, Post Childbirth, Kidney Stones, Digestive Complaints, Gastroenteritis, Flatulence, Diarrhoea, Wounds, Inflammation, Skin Problems, Eye Inflammations, Conjunctivitis, Ache, Mouth Sores, Ulcers, Laryngitis.

Culinary: Salads

Magical: Leaves produced shining peals of water used by

medieval alchemists' experiments to turn metal into gold. Dedicated to the Virgin Mary. Tea (Connect with Goddess within, Accepting Femininity, Men who want to connect with feminine side). Dewcup (Dew from leaves). Philosopher's Stone

Uses: Cattle feed to increase milk production. Horse & sheep fodder. Used in Cosmetics.

LAVENDER Common or English (Lavendula augustifolia,
Lavendula offinalis, Lavendula vera, Lavendula spica, Lavendula stoechas, Lavendula latifolia, Lavendula intermedia) Spike, Elf, Nard, Nardus, Elf Leaf

Planet:	Mercury
Element:	Air
Gender:	Male
Deities:	Cernunnos, Circe, Hecate, Medea, Saturn, Serpent Goddesses.
Festival:	Midsummer Fire for Old Ones
Care Doll:	Love, Protection
Powers:	Love, Protection, Sleep, Chastity, Longevity, Purification, Happiness, Peace
Medicinal:	A strong antiseptic with antibacterial properties. Lavender Oil treats cuts, bites, stings, burns, coughs, colds, chest infections, rheumatic aches, giddiness, flatulence. Tonic for nervous and digestive disorders. Herb for tension, insomnia and depression. Headaches, Soothing, Antidepressant, Antiseptic, Antibacterial, Analgesic, Decongestant, Antispasmodic, Tonic, Wounds, Bruises, Spots, Insect Bites, Flu, Respiratory Problems, Tonsilitis, High TemperatureOral Thrush, Throat Infections, Catarrh, Digestive Spasms, Nausea, Indigestion, Rheumatism, Depression, Insomnia, Headaches, Stress, Hypertension, Nervous Debility, Aches and Pains, Exhaustion, Dizziness, Halitosis, Flatulence, Colic.

Culinary:	Salads, jellies, jams, vinegars, pottages, stews. Crystallised flowers.
History:	Introduced to Britain by the Romans. Latin for "to wash".
	Scented additive to bath water. Strewing Herb. Insect Repellant. Lavender in POSIES to newly Married Couples for luck for the future.
Magical:	Love, Protection, Dreams, Sleep, Money, Happiness, Chastity, Purification, Peace, Evil Eye Protection. Strewing herb. Carrying or Inhaling to see ghosts.
Uses:	Lavender Water and Tea. Pot Pourri, Herb Cushions, Sachets for freshening and keeping moths away from linen. Oil used in varnishes, perfumes, soaps and cosmetics.
Incense:	Inner Stillness, Peace, Harmony, Intellect, Logical Thought
Essential Oil:	Balance, Clarity, Forgiveness, Healing

LEEK (Allium porrum)

Planet:	Mars
Element:	Fire
Gender:	Male
Care Doll:	Love, Protection
Powers:	Love, Protection, Exorcism

LEMONGRASS (Cymbopogon citratus)

Planet:	Mercury
Element:	Air
Gender:	Male
Powers:	Repel Snakes, Lust, Psychic Powers

LEMON VERBENA (Lippia cirtiodora) Yerba Louisa,

Cedron, Herb Louisa EXTENDED USE COULD IRRITATE STOMACH

Planet:	Venus, Mercury
Element:	Air

Gender:	Male
Festival:	Ostara (Altar Candles, Incense)
Station:	East
Care Doll:	Sleep
Powers:	Purification, Love
Medicinal:	Indigestion, Flatulence, Stomach Cramps, Nausea, Asthma, Neuralgia, Migraine, Vertigo, Palpitations, Heartburn, Combat Depression, Lethargy.
Magical:	Purification, Love, Prevention of Dreams
Uses:	Candles (Leaves infused in candle wax), Incense (Raise vibrations, Peaceful and joyous atmosphere, Invoke East), Handmade Herbal Paper.

LETTUCE (Lactuca sativa) Garden Lettuce, Wild Lettuce or Great Prickly Lettuce

Planet:	Moon (Garden Lettuce), Mars (Wild Lettuce)
Element:	Water
Gender:	Female
Care Doll:	Protection, Love, Sleep
Protection:	Chastity, Protection, Love, Divination, Sleep
Medicinal:	Sedative (wild lettuce) most potent when it goes to seed (narcotic effect, helps to induce sleep, calm anxiety and ease pain. The milky sap or latex in wild lettuce known as poor man's opium. Mania, Nervous Disorders, Coughs, Respiratory Problems, Aching Muscles and Joints, Liver Complaints, Digestive Complaints. Overdosing can cause poisoning
Culinary:	Cooked as vegetable, added to porrays and soups.
History:	Greeks and Romans believed it to be a protection against drunkenness as well as an aphrodisiac. Aphrodite was reputed t ohave laid the dead body of her beloved Adonis on a bed of lettuce leaves. Leaves pickled in honey vinegar. Lactuca derived from the Latin for milk in reference to milky sap.
Magical:	Chastity, Protection, Love, Divination, Sleep

LICHEN (Fungus and algae) Lungwort (Lobaria pulmonaria)

Planet:	Jupiter
Dye:	Cudbear lichen (Ochroelchia tartarea) which grows on Birch trees yields a crimson dye.
Medicinal:	Lungwort (Lobaria pulmonaria) and Ancient Scribbler (Graphis scripta) antibiotic properties. Throat infections and lung complaints including tuberculosis. Lungwort for diseases of the lungs and for coughs, wheezings, and shortness of breath, yellow jaundice and inward bleeding
History:	In Anglo Saxon charters trees were called har or "hoar" trees which had beard like lichens growing on them. Some landmarks in Wales and Cornwall were known as Maen mellyn or yellow stone referring to a rock covered with the yellow lichen Xanthoria.

LILAC (Syringa vulgaris)

Planet:	Venus
Element:	Water
Gender:	Female
Care Doll:	Love, Sleep
Powers:	Exorcism, Protection
Medicinal:	Fevers, Malaria, Intestinal Worms, Rheumatic Pain in Joints, Cause Nausea
History:	Introduced in Sixteenth Century.
Magical:	In parts of the country the white flowered variety was supposed to be unlucky. Clover whose flowers have five petals were said to bestow luck. Lilac symbolized the first emotions of Love. Love, Sleep, Exorcism, Protection.
Used:	In perfumery.

LILY Madonna (Lilium candidum) Garden Lily, White Lily

Planet:	Moon (Lily), Mercury (Lily of the Valley)
Element:	Water
Gender:	Female
Deities:	Adonis, Attis, Athene, Ceres, The Angel Gabriel, Isis, Jupiter, Kundalini, Lakshmi, Maiden Goddesses, Osiris, Psyche, St Anthony, St Catherine, Venus, Virgin Mary
Powers:	Protection, Breaking Love Spells
Medicinal:	Bruises, Boils, Corns, Burns, Ulcers, Inflammations, Softening Hard Skin. Lily of the Valley is potentially poisonous but used to treat gout, sore eyes, poor memory, loss of speech, heart disease. Dried and powdered root used as snuff to clear the nasal mucous and relieve headaches.
Culinary:	Bulbs of Madonna Lily were cooked and eaten.
History:	Sacred to Juno, wife and sister of Jupiter and queen of the heaven. Native to the Holy Land and brought to Britain by the Crusaders. Associated with the Virgin Mary. Used at funerals to symbolize restored innocence of the soul after death.
Magical:	In some parts of the country it was said that it was used as ladders by the fairies. Spells to counter Witchcraft and Protection against Evil. Considered an unlucky plant especially if brought into the house.
Uses:	Perfume and Cosmetics.

LILY OF THE VALLEY (Convalleria Magalis) Conval Lily, Lily Convally, Lilly Constancy, Liriconfrancis, Lady's Tears, Mary's Tears, May Lily, Ladder-to-heaven, Convalleria, Jacob's Ladder, Male Lily

Planet:	Mercury
Element:	Fire
Gender:	Male
Totem Bird:	Nightingale
Deities:	Aesculapius, Apollo, Hermes, Maia, Mercury, St

Leonard, Virgin Mary

Powers: Mental Powers, Happiness

LOBELIA (Lobelia inflata) POISON Asthma Weed, Bladderpod,

Gagroot, Indian Tobacco, Pukeweed

Planet: Saturn
Element: Water
Gender: Female
Powers: Halting Storms, Love

LOVAGE (Levisticum officinale)   Love Root, Sea Parsley, Italian

Parsley, Loving Herbs, Love Parsley, Lubestico, Levisticum, Chinese
Lovage, Cornish Parsley, Love Herbs
DON'T USE IF PREGNANT OR HAVE KIDNEY PROBLEMS

Planet: Sun
Element: Fire
Gender: Male
Sign: Taurus
Tarot: The World
Care Doll: Love
Powers: Love
Medicinal: Colic, Indigestion, Flatulence, Stimulant, Removal of
               Toxins, Gargle.
Magical: Wash and Clean Magical Tools and Working Space

MADDER (Rubia tinctorum) Wild Madder (Rubia peregrenia)

Dyer's Madder, Krapp, Robbia   PERENNIAL

Planet: Mars
Element: Fire
Gender: Male
Festival: Lughnasa (Ale for Gatherings)
Dye: Red and whole range of colours
Medicinal: Jaundice, Sciatica, Paralysis, Healing Wounds, Bruises,
               Urinary Problems, Kidney Complaints, Bladder
               Complaints, Constipation, Palsy, Dropsy.

Magical: Warrior Spirit, Strength, Courage

MAGNOLIA (Magnolia grandifolia)

Blue Magnolia, Cucumber Tree, Swamp Sassafras

Planet: Venus
Element: Earth
Gender: Female
Powers: Fidelity

MALLOW (Malva sylvestris) Common Mallow, (Malva

Maschata) Musk Mallow

Planet: Venus
Element: Water
Gender: Female
Gemstone: Topaz
Deities: Osiris, Shiva, Venus
Care Doll: Love, Healing, Protection
Powers: Love, Protection, Exorcism

MALLOW, MARSH (Althaea officinalis) Velvet Leaf,

Mallards, Schloss Tea, Mortification Root

Planet: Venus, Moon
Element: Water
Gender: Female
Sign: Sagittarius
Gemstone: Topaz
Deities: Aphrodite, Venus
Care Doll: Love, Healing, Protection
Medicinal: Wounds, Bruises, Sprains, Inflammations, Stings, Insect
                 Bites, Coughs, Chest Complaints, Lung Complaints,
                 Diarrhoea, Insomnia, Cystitis, Gastric Ulcers, Acid
                 Stomach, Heartburn, Ulcers, Hiatus Hernia, Irritable
                 Bowel, Non-productive and dry cough, Irritable Bladder,
                 Dry Skin, Insect Bites, Wheeping Eczema, Impotency,
                 Aphrodisiac, Dry Hands, Sunburn, Dry Hair, Coughs,

	Vomiting, Sinus Headaches, Chest Complaints, Diarrhoea, Insomnia, Burns, Inflammations, Teething Babies, Boils, Abscesses.
Culinary:	Leaves eaten as vegetable, Salads, Soups and Stews. Unripe seed capsules "Cheeses" eaten raw with salads. In barley soup, stuff suckling pig. Original source of Marshmallow.
History:	Native to Britain. Comes from the Greek for "to cure". Mallow comes from the Greek for "to soften". Eaten to reduce sexual desire to counteract aphrodisiacs and love potions.
Magical:	Love, Healing, Protection, Exorcism. Steep leaves in vegetable oil to rub onto skin to cast out devils and protect against black magic. Incense (Exorcism, Protection, Otherworld Journeying, Handfasting). Ritual Cup for Handfasting.
Uses:	In cosmetics. Soap (Skin problems inc Psoriasis).
Dog:	Low grade infections, Respiratory, Digestive, Urinary Infections

MARJORAM Common (Origanum vulgare) Wild Marjoram,

Oregano, Sweet Marjoram, Knotted Marjoram (Origanum marjorana), Oregano, Origane, Origanum, Eastward Marjoram, Grove Marjoram, Joy of the Mountain, Knotted Marjorane, Marjorlaine, Mountain Mint, Winter Sweet, Sweet Margerone

Planet:	Mercury in Aries
Element:	Air
Gender:	Male
Sign:	Aries
Tarot:	The Cups
Deities:	Aphrodite, Jupiter, Osiris, Thor, Venus
Care Doll:	Love, Protection, Healing, Sleep, Happiness, Health, Money
Dye:	Reddish Purple
Powers:	Protection, Love, Happiness, Health, Money

Medicinal:	Cure all, Indigestion, Insomnia, Earache, Loss of Appetite, Dropsy and many other ailments. Digestion, Flatulence, Soothe Nerves, Cure Colds, Headaches, Promote Menstruation. Snuff to clear nasal congestion. Relieve pain, stings, bruises, rheumatic, Swellings, Warming, Analgesic, Antispasmodic, Sedative, Tonic, Antiviral, Antibacterial, Expectorant, Vasodilator, Digestive, Muscular Spasms, Strains, Nervous tension, Restful Sleep, Headaches, Migraine, Colds, Infections, Asthma, Tonsilitis, Coughs, High Blood Pressure, Improving Circulation, Calms Digestion, Eases Menstrual Cramps, Reduces Sexual Desire, Long Life, Bronchitis, Oral Thrush, Mouth Infection
Culinary:	Sweet and savoury pot herb with wide range of flavouring uses. Salads, Soups, Sauces, Stuffings, Stews, Meat Dishes, Flavour Beer and other alcoholic drinks.
Tea:	Leaves and Flowers
History:	Introduced into Britain by the Romans signifying peace and happiness. Worn by bridal couples, used to scent winding sheets, planted on graves to ensure the dead rest in peace. Strewing Herb.
Uses:	Pot Pourri, Cosmetics and Perfumes. Disinfectant, Preservative, Nosegay, Sweet Bag, Washing Water, Pomander, Furniture Polish for Oak, Keeps away woodworm.

MEADOWSWEET (Filipendula ulmaria/Spiraea ulmaria)

Queen of the Meadow, Bridewort, Little Queen, Gravel Root, Trumpet Weed, Lady of the Meadow, Steeplebush, Bride of the Meadow, Meadsweet, Mead Wort, Pride of the Meadow, Meadow Maid, Honeysweet, Dollor, Meadow Wort, Bridgewort, Dollof, Lace-makers-herb

Planet:	Venus
Element:	Water

Gender:	Female
Sign:	Gemini
Festival:	Coamhain (Flowers, Garlands and Decorations)
Deities:	Aine, Blodeuwedd, Gwena, Venus
Care Doll:	Love, Happiness
Powers:	Love, Divination, Peace, Happiness
Medicinal:	Antacid, Digestive, Astringent, Anti-Inflammatory, Diuretic, Acid Stomach, Heartburn, Ulcers, Hiatus Hernia, Indigestion, Diverticulitis, Wind, Rheumatism, Arthritis, Summer diarrhoea, Fevers, Upset Children's Stomach, Pain Relief, Head Colds, Gastritis, Peptic Ulcer, Diarrhoea, Rheumatism, Gout, Flu, Kidney and Bladder Complaints, Insomnia, Skin Tonic, Sores, Ulcers.
Culinary:	Tea from Flowers sweetened with honey
Magical:	Love, Happiness, Divination, Peace. Sacred to Druids. Bridal garland. Posies for Bridesmaids. Strew on path and home of newlyweds. Bridal Bouquet for happiness and special joy if oil is then made from the blossoms and used nightly before bed. Love, Marriage, Fertility, Plenty.
Uses:	Incense (Love). Flowers (Garlands, Bouquets, Incense, Decorations at Handfastings).

MIMOSA (Acacia dealbata) Mimosa Pudica, Albizzialebbeck

Planet:	Saturn
Element:	Water
Gender:	Female
Powers:	Protection, Love, Prophetic Dreams, Purification

MINT Spearmint (Mentha spicata) Pennyroyal (Mentha pulegium)

Peppermint (Mentha piperita) Watermint (Mentha aquatica)
Pennyroyal (Mentha pulegium) SHOULD NOT BE USED WHILE
PREGNANT AS IT MAY CAUSE ABORTION Woolly Mint (Bowles Mint),
Monk's Herb, Garden Mint, Pea Mint, Fish Mint, Green Lamb Mint, Our

Lady's Mint, Sage of Bethlehem, Lamb Mint, Cradlewort, Bishop's Wort, Churchwort

Planet:	Venus
Element:	Air
Gender:	Female
Festival:	Midsummer (Thrown on Bonfire, Used as Incense)
Deities:	Hecate, Mintha, Pluto, Zeus
Care Doll:	Protection, Healing, Sleep, Money
Powers:	Money, Lust, Healing, Travel, Exorcism, Protection
Medicinal:	Antiseptic, antibacterial, antispasmodic, anti-inflammatory, digestive problems, nervous headaches, fevers, colds, flatulence, colic and other ailments. Restorative, Watering Eyes. Pennyroyal to drive away fleas. Tonic, Anaesthetic, Sedative, Stimulant, Colds, Coughs, Catarrh, Insomnia, Dyspepsia, Calming the Nerves, Insomnia, Anxiety, Indigestion, Flatulence, Nausea, Bronchial Problems, Influenza, Asthma, Sluggish Bowels, Sore Throat, Mouth Ulcers, Toothache, Cuts, Bruises, Wounds, Hiccups, Hair Rinse, Footbath, Chapped Hands
Culinary:	Garnishing dishes and flavouring drinks, confectionery and sauces.
History:	Pharisees collected tithes in mint, dill and cumin. Named after Minthe a nymph in Greek Mythology who was changed into the herb by Persephone, the jealous wife of Hades.
Magical:	Watermint sacred to the Druids. Protection, Healing, Sleep, Money, Banishment, Lust, Travel, Exorcism, Prosperity, Concentration
Uses:	Stuffing cushions. Strewing Herb. Insect Repellant. Perfumery. Deters Rats and Mice.
Essential Oil:	Disenchantment
	Peppermint: Dreams, Calming, Soothing

MISTLETOE (Viscum album) Druid's Herb POISONOUS

Planet:	Sun
Element:	Air
Gender:	Male
Deities:	Apollo, Freya, Frigga, Venus, Odin
Powers:	Protection, Love, Hunting, Fertility, Health, Exorcism
Medicinal:	Seizures, Heart Disease, High Blood Pressure, Rheumatism, Gout, Nervous Disorders, Tumours, Falling Sickness, Apoplexy, Palsy.
History:	Grows on Apple, Hawthorn and Willow.
Magical:	Kissing underneath it.

MONEYWORT (Lysimachia nummularia) Creeping Jenny, Herb Twopence, String of Sovereigns

Planet:	Venus
Medicinal:	Astringent, Antiseptic, Wound Herb, Stomach Disorders, Intestinal Disorders, Slow Healing Wounds, Ulcers, Skin Complaints, Rheumatic Aches and Pains, Bleeding

MONK'S HOOD (Aconitum napellus) Aconite, Wolfsbane, Blue Rocket, Helmet Flower, Old Wife's Hood, The Queen Mother of Poisons, Chariot of Venus, Storm Hat, King's Coach, Friar's Cap, Friar's Cowl, Cupid's Car POISONOUS

Planet:	Saturn
Element:	Water
Gender:	Female
Deities:	Cerberus, Hecate, Medea, St Dunstan
Height:	2-3ft
Growing:	Hardy Perennial
Medicinal:	Painkiller, Sedative, Fever
History:	Classical fable is that it fell from the mouth of Cerebrus which Hercules dragged him from the underworld.
Magical:	Used by Witches. Traditional ingredient in Flying Ointment. Malevolent Magic. Elf Bolts – Chips of flint

coated with Aconite to throw at victim. A scratch will
kill. Said to kill Werewolves.

Uses: Extracts used to poison tips of arrows. Tips arrows to
kill wolves.

MORNING GLORY (Ipomoea) POISON Bindweed

Planet: Saturn
Element: Water
Gender: Male
Powers: Happiness, Peace

MOSS

Powers: Luck, Money

MUGWORT (Artemisia vulgaris) Artemisia, Witch Herb, Old

Man, Old Uncle Harry, Artemis Herb, Muggons, Sailor's Tobacco, Apple-
pie, Mugger, Smotherwort, Felon Herb, St John's
Plant, Cingulum Scanti, Johannis, Mother's Wort, Maiden Wort,
Muggins   NOT DURING PREGNANCY

Planet: Moon, Venus
Element: Water, Earth (Conflict of information)
Gender: Female
Gemstone: Moonstone, Pearl
Sign: Taurus, Libra
Festival: Midsummer (Garlands and Girdles, Thrown into Fire)
Deities: Artemis, Chandra, Diana, Hecate
Care Doll: Protection, Healing, Dreams, Sleep
Powers: Strength, Psychic Powers, Protection, Prophetic Dreams,
Healing, Astral Projection
Medicinal: Women's Problems, Indigestion, Upset
Stomach, Depression, Nerves, Hysteria, Tension,
Rheumatism, Anti Epileptic.
Magical: Protection, Healing, Dreams, Sleep, Banishment,
Strength, Psychic Powers, Prophetic Dreams, Astral
Projection. Root kept over door as protective charm.

Uses: Dream Pillow (Prophetic Dreams)
Bath Teabag (Refresh and Revive)

MULBERRY (Morus nigra) Black Mulberry

Planet: Mercury
Element: Air
Gender: Male
Deities: Athene, Lady Horse-head, Minerva, Pyramis, Sien-tsan, Singarmati
Powers: Protection, Strength
Medicinal: Colds, Fevers, Headaches, Staunch Bleeding, Kill Intestinal Worms, Mouth Ulcers, Sore Throats, Constipation, Snake Bite, Antidote to Aconite.
Culinary: Eaten raw or cooked. Pottage "Murrey" reinforced with pulped meat. Jams, Jellies, Syrup, Wine.
History: White Mulberry (Morus alba) food for silk worms.

MULLEIN Great (Verbascum thapsus) Aaron's Rod, Hag's Taper,

Bullock's Lungwort. White Mullein (Verbascum lychnitis) Black Mullein (Verbascum nigrum) POISONOUS Hag Taper, Bullock's Lungwort, Pig's Taper, Candlewick Plant, Aaron's Rod, Blanket Weed, Beggar's Blanket, Blanket Leaf, Velvet Dock, Feltwort, Flannel Weed, Our Lord's Flannel, Fluffweed, Hare's Bear, Old Man's Flannel, Rag Paper, Cow Lungwort, Jacob's Staff, Jupiter's Staff, Peter's Staff, Shepherd's Staff, Clot, Doffle, Graveyard Dust, Hedge Taper, Lady's Foxglove, Old Man's Fennel, Shepherd's Herb, Torches, Velvetback, Velvet Plant, Duffle, Cuddy, Hare's Beard, Blanket Herb

Planet: Saturn
Element: Water
Gender: Female
Deities: Circe, Odysseus, Jupiter, St Fiacre
Dye: Flowers infused with lye make blonde hair dye.
Powers: Courage, Protection, Health, Love, Divination, Exorcism
Medicinal: Coughs, Respiratory Disorders, Inflammatory Ailments, Burns, Wounds, Ulcers, Skin Diseases, Haemorrhoids,

151

Rheumatic Aches and Pains, Asthma, Sedative, Pain
Killer, Cattle Diseases, Soothing Expectorant, Healing,
Demulcent, Emollient, Astringent, Deep and Ticklish
Coughs, Asthma, Bronchitis, Diarrhoea, Itchy Eyelids,
Acute Earache, Bedwetting.

Culinary:	Flowers flavour Liqueurs
History:	Native to Britain. Used to wrap figs, dipping stems in wax and tallow for candles,
Magical:	Mythical herb "moly" given to Ulysses by Hermes as protection against the sorcery of Circe. Test of fidelity the plant is bent towards the lover's house and if it dies the lover is unfaithful.

MUSHROOM Field (Agaricus campestris) Garden Mushroom

Horse Mushroom (Agaricus arvensis) Giant Puffball (Lycoperdon
giganteum) Fairy-Ring Champignon (Maramius oreadus) Jew's Ear
(Auricularis auricula-judae)

Planet:	Mercury in Aries
Medicinal:	Jew's Ear Inflammations and soreness of the throat, boiled in milk, steeped in beer, vinegar or liqueurs. Boils, Abscesses
Culinary:	Cooked as a vegetable, soups, sauces, pickles, meat dishes. Dried over winter on strings.
History:	Hebrews considered mushrooms holy and only priests could eat them. Fly Agaric (Amanita muscaria) principle ingredient of Ambrosia, food of the Olympian Gods.

MUSTARD Hedge (Sisymbrium officinale) Black Mustard

(Brassica nigra or Sinapis negra) White Mustard (Sinapis alba, Brassica
alba, Brassica hirta) Wild Mustard (Sinapis arvensis) Black Mustard
(Brassica nigra) Gold dust, Singers Plant

Planet:	Mars
Element:	Fire
Gender:	Male

Sign:	Aries
Deities:	Aesculapius
Care Doll:	Protection
Powers:	Fertility, Protection, Mental Powers
Medicinal:	Circulation, Respiratory Infections, Stomach Complaints, Emetic, Muscular and Rheumatic Aches, Cold and Flu Symptoms, Poultice or Plaster for inflammations or ease pain, Toothache, Snuff to cure headaches. Hedge Mustard to treat failing voices and improve vocal performance. Overuse may blister sensitive skins. Antiseptic, Warming, Antibacterial, Antiseptic, Antiviral, Aids Digestion, Emetic, Laxative, Irritant, Expectorant, Chest Colds, Coughs, Constipation, Digestive Upsets, Hiccups, Backache, Joint Pain, Muscle Stiffness, Rheumatism, Neuralgia, Sciatica, Antiseptic, Deodorizer, Healing, Vitamin A, Iron, Zinc.
Culinary:	Young leaves and flowers in salads. Ground seeds mixed with water, vinegar, wine or Verjuice to make Mustards e.g. English. Food Preservative in pickles and chutneys. Mustard (and cress) (Sinapis alba) few days after Cress (Lepidum sativum)
History:	Cultivated by ancient Greeks, Romans and Egyptians. Introduced into Britain by the Romans. In medieval times it was produced in the Vale of Gloucester. Seeds made into balls for sale in shops and market places.
Uses:	Animal fodder and green manure.

MYRTLE (Myrtus communis)   Candleberry, Waxberry, Wax Myrtle, Bayberry

Planet:	Venus
Element:	Water
Gender:	Female
Totem Animal:	Dolphin
Deities:	Aphrodite, Artemis, Astarte, Ashtoreth, Freya, Hathor,

Marian, Venus

Care Doll:	Love
Powers:	Love, Fertility, Youth, Peace, Money

NASTURTIUM (Tropaeolum majus) Indian Cress

Planet:	Sun
Element:	Fire
Gender:	Male

NETTLE Common or Stinging (Urtica dioica) Roman Nettle (Urtica pilulifera) Devil's Apron, Naughty Man's Plaything, Scaddie, Tanging Nettle, Hokypoky, Jenny-nettle, Stilkng-leaf, Devil's Leaf, Heg-beg, Devil's Plaything

Planet:	Mars
Element:	Fire
Gender:	Male
Totem Animal:	Serpent
Gemstones:	Ruby, Fire Opal
Ogham:	Nin, Deanntag
Rune:	Feoh
Tool:	Nettle
Deities:	Agni, Blodeuwedd, Cernunnos, Hades, Horus, Jupiter, Osiris, Pcuvus (Earth Fairies), Pluto, The Lightning Serpent Lord, Thor, Vishnu, Vulcan, Yama
Care Doll:	Protection, Healing
Dye:	Green from leaves, Yellow from roots.
Powers:	Exorcism, Protection, Healing, Lust
Medicinal:	Keeps diseases away, Rheumatism, Gout, Arthritis, Anemia, Hemorrhages, Skin Diseases, Eczema, Wounds, Ulcers, Staunch Bleeding, Circulation, Milk in Nursing Mothers, Hair Loss.
Culinary:	Young nettle rich in vitamins and minerals, cooked as vegetable, added to soups and stews, nettle dumplings, nettle pudding, nettle porridge, nettle beer, nettle wine.

History:	Native to Britain since prehistoric times. Romans rubbed it on their bodies to keep them warm. One of the nine sacred herbs of the Anglo-Saxons. Stems used to make fibre or thread. Woven into coarse cloth, spun into rope, used to flagellate bare backs of Monks. Hens fed nettle seeds to get them to lay.
Magical:	Protection against Witches, Demons, Lightning, Protection, Healing, Banishment, Exorcism, Lust

OAK, English (Quercus robur)

Planet:	Jupiter, Sun
Element:	Fire
Gender:	Male
Colour:	Dark Brown or Black
Totem Bird:	Wren, Swallow, Eagle, Nightjar, Woodpecker
Totem Animal:	Bull
Gemstone:	Amethyst, Moonstone, White Carnelian, Lapis Lazuli
Deities:	Allah, Arianrhod, Artemis, Balder, Blodeuwedd, Brighid, Ceirddylad, Cernunnos, Cerridwen, Cybele, The Dagda, Dianus, Donar, Dryads, Erato, The Erinyes, Hades, Hecate, Hercules, Herne, Horus, Indra, Janicot, Janus, Jehovah, Jupiter, Kirke, Llyr, Nephthys, Odin, Pan, Pluto, Rhea, Tannus, Taran, Thor, Ukho, Vishnu, Zeus
Care Doll:	Protection, Good Luck, Healing
Powers:	Protection, Health, Money, Healing, Potency, Fertility, Luck
Medicinal:	Diarrhoea, Varicose Veins, Haemorrhoids, Enteritis, Sore Throats, Heal Wounds, Staunch Bleeding, Bleeding Gums, Scabs.
Culinary:	Acorns as food. Roasted and ground to make substitute coffee.
History:	Held sacred by pre Christian cultures including Greeks, Romans, Norse or Celts.
Magical:	Protection, Good Luck, Healing, Money, Fertility, Health

OATS Cultivated (Avena sativa)   Groats, Oatmeal, Joulaf

Planet:	Venus
Element:	Earth
Gender:	Female
Powers:	Money
Medicinal:	Insomnia, Depression, Loss of Appetite, Nervous Exhaustion, Thyroid Complaints, Debility after Illness, Lumbago, Stitches in the Side, Sciatica, Skin Problems, Itch, Leprosy, Laxative, Haemorrhoids, Constipation, Rheumatic Aches and Pains.
Culinary:	Staple food of monasteries, Gruel, Oatcakes, Oatmeal Pastries and Porridge
History:	Introduced to Britain during the Iron Age. Musical flute "oaten pipe" made from oat straw.

ONION Common (Allium cepa) Ever Useful Onion (Allium cepa perutile)   ONION, Wild (Allium ampeloprasm)

Planet:	Mars
Element:	Fire
Deity:	Isis
Care Doll:	Protection
Dye:	Skins produce Yellow to Golden Brown
Powers:	Protection, Exorcism, Healing, Money, Prophetic Dreams, Lust
Medicinal:	Antibiotic, Coughs, Colds, Respiratory Infections, Insomnia, Indigestion, Lethargy, Strengthen the Heart, Restore Sexual Potency, Insect Stings, Promote Hair Growth, Cold Watery Humours, Tooth Abscess, Boil, Bronchitis, Gastric Infection, Burnt Skin, Bites, Stings, Bruises, Unbroken Chilblains, Joint Problems, Arthritis, Fluid Retention, Intestinal Cleansing, Antibiotic Treatment, Heart Disease, Circulatory Disorders,
Culinary:	Raw, Cooked as a vegetable, salads, soups, stews, sauces, many other dishes, Dried or Pickled.

History:	One of the earliest plants to be cultivated valued by Indians, Chinese, Sumerians, Egyptians, Greeks and Romans.
Magical:	Ward off Snakes and Witches. Protection, Exorcism, Healing, Money, Prophetic Dreams, Lust

ORCHID
Early Purple Orchid (Orchis mascula) Spotted Bird's Orchis (Orchis ornithophora folio maculoso) Fox-Stones, Spotted Bird's Orchis

Planet:	Venus
Element:	Water
Gender:	Female
Care Doll:	Love Powers: Love
Medicinal:	Killing worms in children, strengthening genital parts and helping conception
Culinary:	"Salep" for people who travel long distances
History:	"Salep" is the same as "Sahlep" a nutritious drink extracted from the tubers. English salep reputed to be an aphrodisiac and energizing tonic made in Oxfordshire with tubers imported from the East.

ORPINE
(Sedum telephium) Livelong, Midsummer Men or Herbe aux charpentiers

Planet:	Moon
Medicinal:	Astringent, Wounds, Burns, Scalds, Haemorrhoids, Diarrhoea, Internal Ulcers, Sore Throats, Quinsy
History:	Used in France to heal wounds made by Carpenter's Tools. The botanical name Telephium comes from Telephus the mythical son of Hercules who was reputedly healed of a spear wound by the plant.
Magical:	Hang on the wall of a house on Midsummer's Eve it was said to ward off lightning and disease for as long as the leaves remained green. Two plants planted side by side for lovers, if they grow together that is a good sign.

ORRIS (Iris Garmanica) Florentine Iris, Queen Elizabeth Root

Planet:	Venus
Element:	Water
Gender:	Female
Deities:	Aphrodite, Isis, Osiris, Hera, Iris
Powers:	Love, Protection, Divination

OX-EYE DAISY (Crysanthemum leucanthemum) Marguerite,
Dun Daisy, Gowan, Golding, Gool, Maudlinwort, Guld, Great Ox-Eye,
Goldens, Moon Daisy, Horse Gowan, Field Daisy, Butter Daisy,
Horse Daisy, White Weed, Baldur's Brow

Planet:	Moon
Element:	Water
Gender:	Female
Deities:	Artemis, Jupiter, Mary Magdalene, St John, Thor, Zeus

PANSY (Viola tricolor) Banewort, Banwort, Bird's Eye, Bonewort,
Bouncing Bet, Garden Violet, Heart's Ease, Horse Violet, Johnny Jumper,
Johnny Jump-Ups, Kiss-Me-At-The Garden-Gate, Little Stepmother, Love
Idol, Love-In-Idleness, LoveLies Bleeding, Loving Idol, Meet-Me-In-The-
Entry, Pensee, Stepmother, Tittle-My-Fancy

Planet:	Saturn
Element:	Water
Gender:	Female
Powers:	Love, Rain Magic, Love Divination

PARSLEY Curled (Petroselinum crispum) Percil, Percelle, Perseli,
Persee, Perserely, Devil's Oatmeal, Percely, Persil, Petersilie,
Petroselinum, Rock Parsley DON'T TAKE DURING PREGNANCY

Planet:	Mercury
Element:	Air
Gender:	Male
Tarot:	Temperance
Deities:	Aphrodite, Archemorus, Persephone, Venus

Care Doll:	Protection
Dye:	Green
Powers:	Lust, Protection, Purification
Medicinal:	Menstrual problems, Urinary Infections, Gout, Asthma, Coughs, Jaundice, Dropsy, Eye Complaints, Stimulate Appetite, Encourage Milk Flow in Nursing Mothers, Breath Freshener especially after eating garlic, Cuts, Sprains, Insect Bites, Swellings, Wind, Diuretic, Antiseptic, Stimulates Appetite, Digestive, Mildly Laxative, AntiRheumatic, Fluid Retention, Premenstrual Syndrome, Cellulite, Cystitis, Piles, Broken or Thread Veins, Bruising, Flatulence, Stomach Cramps, Indigestion.
Culinary:	Sauces, Salads, Soups, Pickles, Pottages, many other dishes. Garnish. Roots grated raw or boiled as a vegetable.
History:	Sacred to Ancient Greeks, included in wreaths to crown victors of Isthmian Games. Decorate Graves. Devil supposed to take a portion of the sown seeds. When parsley grows in the garden the woman is dominant in the house.
Magical:	Protection, Fertility, Happiness, Lust, Purification

PASSION FLOWER (Passiflora incarnata) Grandilla, Maracoc, Maypops, Passion Vine

Planet:	Venus
Element:	Water
Gender:	Feminine
Powers:	Peace, Sleep, Friendships

PEA (Pisum sativum) Pease

Planet:	Jupiter in Aries, Venus
Element:	Earth
Gender:	Female
Care Doll:	Money, Love

Powers:	Money, Love
Medicinal:	Measles, Inflammation
Culinary:	Staple food of Medieval England, Soups, Pottages, Porreys, many other dishes. Dried and stored for winter use.
History:	Cultivated in Roman times.
Magical:	Good Fortune especially if one pea is found in a pod. Pod with nine peas inside was said to cure warts or determine future marriage partner.
Use:	Fatten Pigs and Pigeons

PEAR Common (Pyrus communis) Wild Pear (Pyrus pyraster)

Planet:	Venus
Element:	Water
Gender:	Feminine
Powers:	Lust, Love
Medicinal:	Wild for healing wounds and reducing inflammations
Culinary:	Raw or cooked, preserves, jams, puddings, comfits. Perry from fruit.
History:	Introduced to Britain by the Normans. Fine grained wood used for musical instruments, carving, turning and wood engraving.

PENNYROYAL (Mentha pulegium)

European Pennyroyal, Lurk-In-The-Ditch, Mosquito Plant, Organ Broth, Organs, Organ Tea, Piliolerian, Pudding Grass, Run-by-the-Ground, Squaw Mint, Tickweed

Planet:	Mars
Element:	Fire
Gender:	Male
Deity:	Demeter
Powers:	Strength, Protection, Peace

PEONY Common (Paeonia officinalis) Roman Peony, Male Peony
(Paeonia mascula) POISONOUS

Planet:	Sun in Leo, Moon
Element:	Fire
Gender:	Male
Sign:	Leo
Totem Bird:	Woodpecker
Deities:	Aesculapius, Apollo, Leto, Paeon
Care Doll:	Good Luck
Powers:	Protection, Exorcism
Medicinal:	Insomnia, Kidney Complaints, Bladder Complaints, Nervous Diseases, Epilepsy, Madness, Menstrual Discharge, Healing the Uterus,
Culinary:	Seeds as a spice, substitute for hot pepper
History:	Oldest of all cultivated flowers. Named after Paeon, physician to the Greek Gods, considered the plant of the Moon. The Peonia mascula was brought across the Channel by the Augustinians who established a priory on Steep Holm island, in the Bristol Channel. Only place where it grows in the wild.
Magical:	Only uprooted at night or the Woodpecker of Mars will attack the eyes in defense. A string of beads carved from dried Peony roots once worn as a protective charm against evil. Good Luck, Happiness, Protection, Exorcism
Uses:	Petals in Pot Pourri

PEPPER (Piper nigrum) Black Pepper

Planet:	Mars
Element:	Fire
Gender:	Male
Powers:	Protection, Exorcism

PEPPERMINT (Mentha piperita) Brandy Mint, Lammint

Planet: Mercury
Element: Fire
Gender: Male
Deity: Pluto
Powers: Purification, Sleep, Love, Healing, Psychic Powers

PERIWINKLE Greater (Vinca major) Sorceror's Violet, Flower of
Death.
Lesser Periwinkle (Vinca minor) POISONOUS Sorcerer's Violet, Blue
Buttons, Hundred Eyes, Devil's Eye, Joy on the
Ground

Planet: Venus
Element: Water
Gender: Female
Tarot: Heirophant
Deity: The Mother Goddess
Care Doll: Love
Powers: Love, Lust, Mental Powers, Money, Protection
Medicinal: Internal Bleeding, Sores, Wounds, Ulcers, Soothe
                 Inflammations, Relieve Cramps, Reduce Blood Pressure,
                 Nervous Tension, Mouth Bleeding, Nose Bleeding,
                 Diabetes, Constipation.
History: Symbol of Immortality. Linked with Death. Worn by
                 those about to be Executed.
Magical: Love, Lust, Mental Powers, Money, Protection

PINE, Scots (Pinus sylvestris)

Planet: Mars
Element: Earth, Air
Gender: Male
Tool: Wand
Festival: Ostara
Direction: East

Deities:	Astarte, Attis, Dionysus, Cernunnos, Cybele, The Great Mother, Herne, Osiris, Pan, Pitys, Poseidon, Rhea, Sun Gods, Sylvanus, Venus Care Doll: Protection, Healing
Dyes:	Cones yield a reddish yellow dye
Powers:	Healing, Fertility, Protection, Exorcism, Money Medicinal: Wounds, Skin Irritations, Muscular Aches and Pains, Urinary Disorders, Respiratory Infections, Gall Bladder Problems, Colds, Bronchitis, Aches and Pains
Culinary:	Ground inner bark makes bread, mix with oats to make griddle cakes. Cones flavour beer and wine.
History:	Native to Britain. Wood is soft yet strong and used for construction, joinery, waterwheels, ship's masts. Turpentine, resin, tar.
Magical:	Protection, Healing, Fertility, Exorcism, Money
Uses:	Soaps and Perfumery

PLANTAIN (Plantago lanceolata) Cuckoo's Bread, Englishman's Foot, The Leaf of Patrick, Patrick's Dock, Ripple Grass, St Patrick's Leaf, Slan-lus, Snakebite, Snakeweed, Waybread, Waybroad, Weybroed, White Man's Foot

Planet:	Venus
Element:	Earth
Gender:	Female
Powers:	Healing, Strength, Protection, Snake Repelling

PLUM (Prunus domestica)

Planet:	Venus
Element:	Water
Gender:	Female
Medicinal:	Constipation, Stimulate Digestion, Strengthen the Stomach, Kidney Stones, Skin Disease and Ringworm Culinary: Raw, Cooked, Pulped into a "Murrey", Jams, Preserves, stews, stuffing, sauces, desserts, cakes. Preserved in Brandy or Vinegar.
History:	Introduced into Britain by the Romans. Grafted onto

other fruit. Plentiful in the wild.

POPPY, Red (Papaver rhoeas) Corn Rose, Field Poppy, Cockrose, Soldiers, Canker, Canker Rose, Headache, Redweed, Blind Buff, Blindeyes, Headwaak, Corn Rose

Planet:	Moon
Element:	Water
Gender:	Female
Gemstone:	Fire Opal
Festival:	Herfest, Lughnasa
Tool:	Cup
Deities:	Agni, Ceres, Demeter, Hades, Harvest, Hypnos, Jupiter, Harvest Goddess, Harvest Mother, Mother Goddesses, Persephone, Pluto, Prosperine, Somnus, Vulcan, Yama
Care Doll:	Love, Good Luck
Powers:	Fertility, Love, Sleep, Money, Luck, Invisibility
Medicinal:	Syrup for coughs, throat infections, chest complaints, insomnia, whooping cough, Inflammations, pains and relieve migraines
Culinary:	Bread and Cakes. Oil used in cooking. Flowers used to colour wines.
History:	Discovered in Egyptian tomb dated from 2500 BC. Symbol of Remembrance, associated with fertility.
Magical:	Sacred to Ceres, the Roman Goddess of Corn, depicted wearing a wreath of the flowers. Potion containing poppies reputed to be an antidote for those bewitched into love. Love, Good Luck, Dreams, Fertility, Sleep

POTATO (Solanum tuberosum)

Planet:	Moon
Element:	Earth
Gender:	Female
Care Doll:	Healing
Powers:	Image Magic, Healing
Medicinal:	Detox, Antiulcer, Anti-inflammatory, Analgesic,

Stimulates Circulation, Stomach Ulcers, Arthritis, Bruise, Sprain, Burn, Tennis Elbow, Joint Pain, Inflammation of Prostrate, Premature Ageing, Heart Disease, Constipation, Irritable Bowel Syndrome

PRIMROSE (Primla vulgaris) Butter Rose, Password, Early Rose, First Rose, Easter Rose, Darling of April, First Rose

Planet:	Venus
Element:	Earth
Gender:	Female
Deities:	Blodeuwedd, Freya, Spring Goddesses
Care Doll:	Love, Protection Powers: Protection, Love
Medicinal:	Bronchitis, Insomnia, Inflammations, Nervous Tension, Rheumatism, Gout, Purify the Blood, Coughs, Sore Throats, Mild Sedative, Antispasmodic, Minor Wounds, Pains in the Joints, Blemishes, Migraine.
Culinary:	Flowers and young leaves added to salads, leaves boiled as vegetable, Primrose Pottage, Crystallized, Jams and Wine.
History:	Native of Britain. Herald of spring. Derived from Latin meaning first rose.
Magical:	Flowers eaten by children so they can see fairies. Included in love potions, charms against evil. Six petals seen as lucky. Lucky to bring thirteen primroses into the house but not one. Love, Protection
Uses:	Powdered roots added to Pot Pourri. Flowers used in cosmetics.

PULSE (Lens esculenta) Lentils

Planet:	Venus
Medicinal:	Loose Bowels, Ulcers, Abscesses.
Culinary:	Staple food, soups, stews, pottages, many other dishes.
History:	Name also embraces Peas, Beans and other Leguminous plants. Used as ballast for ancient ships.

PURSLANE (Portulaca oleracea) Purslain, Summer Purslane, Pigweed, Garden Purslane

Planet:	Moon
Element:	Water
Gender:	Female
Medicinal:	Fatigue
Powers:	Sleep, Love, Luck, Protection, Happiness
Culinary:	Salad and Pot Herb.
History:	Protection against Witchcraft.
Magical:	Protection against Evil Spirits and to attract love and luck

QUINCE (Cydonia speciousa)

Planet:	Saturn
Element:	Earth
Gender:	Female
Deity:	Venus
Powers:	Protection, Love, Happiness

RADISH, Garden (Raphanus sativus) Wild Radish (Raphanus raphanistrum)

Planet:	Mars
Element:	Fire
Gender:	Male
Care Doll:	Protection
Powers:	Protection, Lust
Medicinal:	Coughs, Bronchitis, Asthma, Rheumatism, Gout, Respiratory Complaints, Digestive Disorders, Provokes Urine and Kidney Stones
Culinary:	Raw, Pottages, Sauces, Stews, Porrays, Salads History: Used by the Anglo Saxons. Harvested from the wild.
Magical:	Protection, Lust

RAGWORT (Senecio jacobaea) St James Wort, Ragweed,

Stinking Nanny, Staggerwort, Cankerwort. Oxford Ragwort (Senecia squalidus)

Planet:	Venus
Element:	Water
Gender:	Female
Powers:	Protection
Medicinal:	Astringent, Wounds, Ulcers, Sores, Burns, Inflammations, Cancerous Ulcers, Aching Joints, Swellings, Rheumatic Pains, Sciatica, gout.
History:	Starts flowering 25th July, St James the Greater. Leaves give of an unpleasant odour. Harmful to cattle, even dry. Oxford Ragwort escaped from the City's Botanical Garden in the Nineteenth Century.

RASPBERRY (Rubus idaeus) European Raspberry, Red

Raspberry

Planet:	Venus
Element:	Water
Gender:	Female
Powers:	Protection, Love

REED, Common (Phragmites communis or Phragmites australis)

Planet:	Sun
Element:	Fire
Gender:	Male
Totem Animal:	Fox, Salmon
Deities:	Faunus, Pan, The Pharoah, Ra, Sun Gods, Taliesin
Medicinal:	Fevers, Coughs, Phlegm, Lung Complaints, Urinary Problems, Nausea, Arthritis.
Culinary:	Roots, shoots and leaves eaten in time of famine. Stems sweet edible sap.
History:	Helps to cure erosion of river banks they also choke waterways. Harvested and used for thatching.

Uses: Matting, Pipes and Fuel.

ROSE (Rosa) Apothecary's Rose or Red Rose of Lancaster (Rosa gallica officinalis) White Rose (Rosa alba semi-plena) Damask Rose (Rosa damascena)

Planet: Moon (White Rose), Jupiter (Red Rose),
                 Venus (Damask Rose)
Element: Water
Gender: Female
Gemstone: Emerald, Turquoise
Tarot: Seven of Cups
Deities: Adonis, Aphrodite, Bacchus, Blodeuwedd, Christ, Cupid,
                 Demeter, Eros, Flora, Freya, Hathor, Hulda, Hymen, Isis,
                 Nike, Venus, Vishnu
Care Doll: Love, Protection, Good Luck, Healing
Powers: Love, Psychic Powers, Healing, Divination, Luck,
                 Protection
Medicinal: Diarrhoea, Bronchial Infections, Coughs, Colds, Chest
                 Complaints, Nervous Tension, Lethargy, Eye
                 Inflammation, Refresh the Spirits, Strengthen the Heart,
                 Rose Oil for chapped skin. Staunch bleeding.
Culinary: Salads, crystallized, syrup, jams, preserves, vinegars.
                 Rose water to flavour confectionery, jellies, sauces,
                 sweet and savoury dishes.
History: Oldest cultivated rose is the red (Rosa gallica), ancestor
                 of all Medieval roses. Introduced into Britain by the
                 Romans. Emblem of England. Symbol of Love and
                 Secrecy (things spoken under a rose carved on the
                 ceiling of a dining room are "sub rosa" "Under the
                 Rose" and in strict confidence). Damask Rose one of
                 the most fragrant. Introduced from Persia by returning
                 Crusaders.
Magical: Love, Protection, Good Luck, Healing, Dreams, Sleep,
                 Money, Psychic Powers, Divination
Uses: Damask Oil used for flavouring and perfumes. Rose

petals were used in soaps, cosmetics and pot pourri.

Essential Oil: Love, Romance, Happiness, Contentment

ROSEMARY (Rosmarinus officinalis) Incensier, Dew of the Sea,

Rose of the Sea, Sea Mint, Sea Dew, Ros Maris, Rosemarie, Guardrobe,
Mary's Mantle, Polar Plant, Compass Plant, Rosmarin, Roero,
Rosemarino POISONOUS IN LARGE DOSES

Planet:	Sun
Element:	Fire
Gender:	Male
Sign:	Aries
Rune:	Jera
Deities:	Fairies, The Virgin Mary
Care Doll:	Love, Protection, Healing
Powers:	Protection, Love, Lust, Mental Powers, Exorcism, Purification, Healing, Sleep, Youth
Medicinal:	Pain, nervous tension, headaches, flatulence, promote liver function, improve blood circulation, increase flow of bile, Rheumatism, Ulcers, Eczema, Sores, Wounds, Hair Tonic, Antiseptic, Tea for digestive complaints, Stuffy Head, Gentle Bitter Tonic, Stimulates Circulation, Antiseptic, Antibacterial, Antifungal, Diuretic, Relieves Stress, Lifts the Spirits, Tones Skin, Digestive, Antispasmodic, Disinfectant, Mild Depression, Stress Related Headaches, Sore Throats, Hair Loss, Hair Growth after chemotherapy stress and worry, Poor Digestion, Gall Bladder, Liverishness, Hair Conditioner, Dandruff, Glossy Hair, Low Blood Pressure, Muscle Fatigue, Poor Circulation, Aches, Pains, Strains, Mental Exhaustion, Mental Clarity, Tones the Skin, Acne, Eczema, Lice, Fluid Retention, Painful Menstruation, Vaginal Discharge, Digestive Spasms, Relieves Wind, Digestion, Catarrh, Coughs, Colds Headaches.
Culinary:	Aromatic herb, soup, stew, fish, meats, eggs, vegetables. Flowers and leaves in salads, sprigs used in

stuffing. Jams, Jellies, Biscuits, Cordials, Vinegars and Wines

History: Worn by Ancient Greeks to improve memory especially by students studying for examinations. Introduced to Britain by the Romans. Symbol of Remembrance and Friendship.
Carried by wedding couples as a sign of love and fidelity.

Magical: Placed under pillow to ward off evil spirits and bad dreams. Love, Protection, Healing, Sleep, Banishment, Lust, Mental Powers, Exorcism, Purification, Youth.

Uses: Strewing herb. In wardrobes discourages insects and moths. Wood used to make lutes and similar musical instruments. Burnt instead of incense. Essential oil in perfumes, cosmetics, disinfectants and herbal shampoos.

Essential Oil: Healing, Love, Protection, Purification

RUE, Garden (Ruta graveolens)

Herb of Grace, Herbygrass, Herb of Repentance, Ruta, Basboush, Garden Rue, Rewe POISONOUS IN LARGE DOSES.
SHOULD NOT BE TAKEN DURING PREGNANCY.

Planet: Sun in Leo, Mars
Element: Fire
Gender: Male
Deities: Diana, Aradia, Hermes, Horus, Mars, Menthu, Mercury, Odysseus
Care Doll: Protection, Healing
Powers: Healing, Health, Mental Powers, Exorcism, Love
Medicinal: Headaches, Strained Eyes, Colic, Indigestion, Flatulence, Heart Palpitations, Menstrual Problems, Intestinal Worms, Sprains, Bruises, Rheumatic Pains, Gout, Chilblains, Skin Diseases, Poison Antidote, Improve Vision.
Culinary: Strong Aromatic Herb for food and alcoholic drinks, grappa. Salads.

170

History:	Introduced into Britain by the Romans. Leonardo da Vinci and Michelangelo took the herb to enhance visions. Symbol of sorrow and repentance. Herb of Grace. Brushes of rue used to sprinkle holy water in Exorcisms and before Mass. Only herb blessed by Mohammad. Rue the day comes from the custom of throwing a bunch of rue in the face of an enemy while cursing them.
Magical:	Worn for luck and protection against Witchcraft, the evil eye and plague. Protection, Healing, Health, Mental Powers, Exorcism, Love.
Uses:	Hung in houses to repel insects. Perfumes and Cosmetics.

RUSH Common (Juncus conglomeratus) Soft Rush (Juncus effusus), Common Bulrush (Scirpus lacustris)

Planet:	Saturn
Medicinal:	Coughs, Sleep, Drowsiness, Dead Sleep History: Derived from the German for to bind or plait.
Magical:	Made into crosses and hung over doors to protect against evil.
Uses:	Matting, Baskets, Wickerwork. Strewn on the stone floor of churches, castles and houses. Pith made into wicks for candles and lamps. Dipped into animal fat as domestic lighting.

RYE (Secale)

Planet:	Venus
Element:	Earth
Gender:	Female
Powers:	Love, Fidelity

SAFFRON (Crocus sativus) Saffron Crocus, Meadow Saffron
(Colchicum autumnale), False Saffron (Carthamus tinctorius) Crocus
(Crocus vemus) POISONOUS Autumn Crocus, Karco, Korkos, Spanish
Saffron

Planet:	Sun in Leo, Meadow Saffron (Saturn) Crocus (Venus)
Element:	Water, Fire
Gender:	Male
Sign:	Leo
Deities:	Amun Ra, Ashtoreth, Eos, Indra, Jupiter, Zeus
Care Doll:	Happiness, Love, Visions
Dye:	Yellow
Powers:	Love, Healing, Happiness, Wind Raising, Lust, Strength, Psychic Powers
Medicinal:	Fevers, Increase Perspiration, Relieve Cramps, Calm Nerves, Life Depression, Aid Digestion, Remedy Menstrual Disorders, Cure Yellow Jaundice, Balancing, Warming, Digestive, Aphrodisiac, Stimulant, Rejuvenating, Antispasmodic, Expectorant, Emmenagogue, Aids Digestion, Improves Appetite, Gastro-Intestinal Complaints, Colic, Chronic Diarrhoea, Menstrual Pain, Menopause, Impotency, Infertility, Calms Hysteria, Depression, Insomnia, Coughs, Asthma, Neufalgia, Lumbago, Rheumatism, Anemia, Enlarged Liver, Balancing, Warming, Digestive, Aphrodisiac, Stimulant, Rejuvenating, Antispasmodic, Expectorant, Emmenagogue, Aids digestion, Improves Appetite, Gastro-Intestinal Complaints, Colic, Chronic Diarrhea, Menstrual Pain, Menopause, Impotency, Infertility, Calms Hysteria, Depression, Insomnia, Coughs, Asthma, Neuralgia, Lumbago, Rheumatism, Anemia, Enlarged Liver.
Culinary:	Stigmas used to colour and flavour wide variety of dishes, cakes, bread, confectionery, liqueurs.
History:	It took over 4000 flowers to produce one ounce of

spice. Those who adulterated the product were buried alive. Introduced from the Holy Land either by the Knights of St John, or by a pilgrim who stole a bulb from the Arabs and hid it in the head of his staff. Grown in Essex around Walden now called Saffron Walden.

Uses: Cosmetics and Perfumes.

SAGE Common (Salvia officinalis)   Purple Sage (Salvia officinalis)

Garden Sage, Red Sage, Sawge LARGE DOSES CAN BE DANGEROUS

Planet: Jupiter
Element: Air
Gender: Male
Care Doll: Protection, Healing, Money
Powers: Immortality, Longevity, Wisdom, Protection, Wishes
Medicinal: Antiseptic, astringent properties, coughs, colds, headaches, epilepsy, lethargy, palsy, menstruation problems, liver complaints, hair conditioner, soothe nerves, stimulate the digestive system, cleanse the blood, sore throats, Laryngitis, tonsillitis, mouth ulcers, infected gums, whiten yellowing teeth, Calminative, Antispasmodic, Nervine, Strengthening, Women's Tonic, Depression, Nervous Exhaustion, Post-viral Fatigue, Debility, Anxiety, Confusion (elderly), Exhaustion, Weakened States, Indigestion, Wind, Loss of Appetite, Stomach Mucus, Sweating, Night Sweats, Weak Lungs, Coughs, Allergies, Hot Flushes, Menstrual Cramps, Premenstrual Painful Breasts, Dry up Breast Milk, Sore Throat, Laryngitis, Mouth Ulcers, Inflamed Gums, Antiseptic for Wounds
Culinary: Salads, stuffing, pottages, soups, pickles, cheeses, desserts, jellies, vinegars, wines, liqueurs, ales.
History: Sacred of Ancient Greeks and Romans. Gathered with a special knife as it reacts with iron salts. Salvia derives from the Latin for "to be saved". Introduced into Britain by the Romans.

Magical:	When sage flourishes in a garden the owner's business would prosper. When it withers the business will fail. Protection, Healing, Money, Banishment, Success, Longevity, Wisdom, Wishes
Uses:	Soaps, Perfumes, Cosmetics, Pot Pourri.

ST JOHN'S WORT Common (Hypericum perforatum)

Perforate St John's Wort POISON Amber, Fuga daemonum, Goat Weed, Herba St John's Wort, Klamath Weed, Sol Terrestis, Tipton Weed

Planet:	Sun in Leo
Element:	Fire
Gender:	Male
Dye:	Yellow with alum. Violet-red with alcohol.
Medicinal:	Nervous Exhaustion, Epilepsy, Depression, Insomnia, Bronchial Catarrh, Stomach Complaints, Madness, Wounds (particularly deep sword wounds), Sores, Burns, Bruises, Inflammations, Sprains, Hemorrhoids, Nerve Pains, Neuralgia, sciatica.
Culinary:	Salads
History:	Native of Britain. Powers derived from John the Baptist. Spots on its leaves supposed to appear on 29 August, the day he was beheaded. Yellow flowers produce red juice. Glandular dots were supposed to have been caused by the devil trying to destroy the plant with a needle.
Magical:	Those treading on the plant after sunset would be carried away by a fairy horse on a wild journey that would last the entire night.

SANICLE (Sanicula europoea) Wood Sanicle

Planet:	Mars
Medicinal:	Wound herb, Ulcerations of the Kidney, Ruptures, Burstings, Diarrhoea, Dysentery, Coughs, Catarrh, Chest Complaints, Urinary Disorders, Liver Disorders, Sore Throats, Skin Diseases.

History:	Held to be a panacea. The name is said to come from the Latin for sound or healthy. It may be a derivation of St Nicholas (Santa Claus) the patron saint of Apothecaries.

SAVORY Garden or Summer (Satureja hortensis) Winter or

Mountain Savoury (Satureja montana) SHOULD NOT BE TAKEN DURING PREGNANCY

Planet:	Mercury
Element:	Air
Gender:	Male
Powers:	Mental Powers
Medicinal:	Stomach and Bowel Complaints, Intestinal Disorders,
Flatulence.	Tired Eyes, Insect Stings, Stimulate the Appetite, Indigestion, Sore Throats
Culinary:	Hot Peppery Herb. Added to salads, sauces, stews, soups, stuffing, liqueurs, bean sauces.
History:	Introduced into Britain by the Romans. Satureja is thought to be derived from the Latin for satyr due to its aphrodisiacal reputation.
Used:	Perfumes and strewing herb.

SAXIFAGE (Pimpinella saxifraga) Burnet Saxifrage. Greater

Burnage Saxifrage (Pimpinella major)

Planet:	Moon
Medicinal:	Stimulate Digestion, Ease Respiratory Infections, Treat Kidney and Urinary Complaints, Cure Flatulence, Protect against the Plague, Slow Healing Wounds, Gargle for Sore Throats, Toothache, Paralysis of the Tongue.
Culinary:	Salads, Cakes, Sauces, Soups, Fish and Vegetable Dishes, flavour Alcoholic drinks.
History:	Native of Britain.

SCULLCAP (Scutellatia lateriflora)

Greater Scullcap, Helmet Flower, Hoodwort, Madweed, Quaker Bonnet

Planet:	Saturn
Element:	Water
Gender:	Female
Powers:	Love, Fidelity, Peace

SELFHEAL (Prunella vulgaris) Carpenter's Herb, Hook Heal,

Sicklewort

Planet:	Venus
Medicinal:	Sore Throats, Wound Herb, Headaches. Culinary: Salads or cooked as a vegetable
History:	Name derived from the German for quinsy.

SENNA (Cassia marilandica) Locust Plant, Wild Senna

Planet:	Mercury
Element:	Air
Gender:	Male
Powers:	Love

SHALLOT (Allium)

Planet:	Mars
Element:	Fire
Gender:	Male
Powers:	Purification

SKULLCAP (Scutellaria lateriffIora/Scutellaria galericulata)

Virginia Skullcap, Mad-dog, Madweed, Hoodwort, Helmet Flower, Blue Pimpernell WHEN TAKEN IN LARGE DOSES CAN CAUSE GIDDINESS, STUPOR AND TWITCHING. DO NOT TAKE WITH PRESCRIBED TRANQUILIZERS

Planet:	Saturn
Element:	Water
Gender:	Female

| Powers: | Love, Fidelity, Peace |
| Medicinal: | Antispasmodic, Anxiety, Tension Headaches, Premenstrual Syndrome, Examination Nerves, Post-Examination Depression, Insomnia, Disturbed Sleep, Tranquilizer withdrawal, Relaxing without a sedative. |

SLIPPERY ELM (Ulmus fulva)

Planet:	Saturn
Element:	Air
Gender:	Female
Powers:	Halts Gossip

SLOE (Prunus spinosa) Blackthorn, Mother of the Wood, Wishing Thorn

Planet:	Mars
Element:	Fire
Gender:	Male
Powers:	Exorcism, Protection

SOLOMON'S SEAL (Polygonatum officianle) Dropberry, Lady's Seal, St Mary's Seal, Sealroot, Sealwort, Solomons Seal

Planet:	Saturn
Element:	Water
Gender:	Female
Care Doll:	Protection
Powers:	Protection, Exorcism
Magical:	Banishment, Success, Exorcism

SORREL Common or Garden (Rumex acetosa)

Green Sauce, Sour Leaves, Cockoo's Meat, Cuckoo Sorrow, Sour Sud, Green Sauce, Ver Juice, Sour Sabs, Sour Grabs, Cowke-meat

LARGE DOSES CAN BE POISONOUS

| Planet: | Venus |
| Element: | Earth |

Gender:	Female
Deities:	Aphrodite, Venus
Care Doll:	Love, Healing, Health
Medicinal:	Cleanse blood, ease constipation, reduce fever, treat jaundice, urinary disorders, kidney disorders, liver disorders, infected wounds, boils, ulcers, various skin complaints, treat leprous sores, strengthen loose teeth
Culinary:	Vinegar and Pot Vegetable, salads, sauces, porrays, soups, stews and other dishes, verjuice.
Magical:	Love Healing Health

SOW-THISTLE Smooth (Sonchus oleraceus) Hare's Lettuce

Planet:	Venus
Medicinal:	Fevers, Urinary Disorders, Stomach Complaints, Stones, Deafness, Inflammation, Swelling, Haemorrhoids, Short windedness and wheezing
Culinary:	Salads, soups, vegetable
History:	Native of Britain, Eaten by sows to increase milk production. Favourite food of hares and rabbits.
Magical:	Power to repel witches and increase strength and stamina. Pliny mentioned it was eaten by Theseus who slew the Minotaur.
Uses:	Milky juice was used as a cosmetic.

SPIKENARD (Nardostachys grandiflora or Nardostachys jatamansi) Nard

Planet:	Venus
Element:	Water
Gender:	Female
Powers:	Fidelity, Health
Medicinal:	Nervous headaches, Indigestion, Insomnia, Depression, Skin rashes, Inflammations, Provokes Urine, Stomach Pains
History:	Mentioned in the Bible. Used to anoint the feet of Jesus at the Last Supper.

Uses: Perfume

STAR ANISE (Illicum verum) Badiana

Planet: Jupiter
Element: Air
Gender: Male
Powers: Psychic Powers, Luck

STRAW

Powers: Luck, Image Magic

STRAWBERRY, Wild (Fragaria vesca) Wood Strawberry.

Alpine Strawberry, Woodman's Delight

Planet: Venus
Element: Earth
Gender: Female
Deities: Fairies, Freya, The Mother Goddess, Virgin Mary
Care Doll: Love, Luck
Medicinal: Wounds, stomach and urinary disorders, dysentery, diarrhoea, liver complaints, digestive upsets. Tonic after Illness, anaemia, bad nerves. Soothe sunburn, whiten discoloured teeth
Culinary: Raw, sauces, desserts, jams, syrups, flavour liquours, cordials, cooked meat.
History: Native of Britain. Comes from the Old English for "strew" and refers to its roots creeping.
Magical: Symbol of perfection and righteousness, dedicated to the Virgin Mary.
Uses: Cosmetics, pot pourri

SUNFLOWER (Helianthus annus) Marigold of Peru

Planet: Sun
Element: Fire
Gender: Male
Sign: Leo

Gemstone:	Tiger's Eye
Totem Animal:	Dragon
Tarot:	The Sun
Deities:	Apollo, Demeter, Helios, Venus
Care Doll:	Protection, Good Luck
Powers:	Fertility, Wishes, Health, Wisdom
Magical:	Protection, Good Luck, Fertility, Happiness, Success

SWEET CICELY (Myrrhis odorata) Sweet Chervil, The Roman

Plant, British Myrrh, Cow Chervil, Smooth Cicely, Sweet Fern, British
Myrrh, Shepherd's Needle, Sweets, Fernleaved Chervil, Wild Myrrh,
Sweet Cus, Sweet Hemlock, Beaked Parsley

Planet:	Jupiter
Element:	Air
Festival:	Midsummer
Deities:	St Cecilia, The Virgin Mary, The Summer Goddess
Medicinal:	Flatulence, Digestive Complaints, Epilepsy, Rheumatism, Coughs, Pleurisy, Protection against the Plague, Bruises, Swellings, Green Wounds, Sores, Ulcers, Gout,
Culinary:	Fruit and vegetable salads, pot herb. Added to acid fruits to reduce amount of sugar needed. Seeds to flavour liqueurs. Roots cooked or grated raw into salads.
History:	Introduced into Britain by the Romans. "Myrrhis odorata" means "the fragrant perfume of myrrh".
Uses:	Seeds used for scent and to polish furniture.

SWEETGRASS (Hierochloe odorata)

Powers:	Calling Spirits

SWEETPEA (Lathrus odoratus)

Planet:	Venus
Element:	Water
Gender:	Female
Powers:	Friendship, Chastity, Courage, Strength

TANSY (Tanacetum vulgare or Crysanthemum vulgare)

Garden Tansy (Tanacetum hortis)   Buttons, Butter Buttons, English Cost, Ginger Plant, Batchelor's Buttons, Joynsons Remedy Cheese, Travellers Rest, Stinking Willie SHOULD NOT BE TAKEN DURING PREGNANCY. OVERDOSE CAN BE POISONOUS

Planet:	Venus
Element:	Earth
Gender:	Female
Festival:	Ostara
Deity:	Ganymede
Care Doll:	Protection, Healing
Dye:	Yellow-Orange
Powers:	Health, Longevity
Medicinal:	Expel worms, Aid Digestion, Relieve Flatulence, Treat Gout, Dissolve Concealed Blood and Promote Menstruation, Swellings, Sprains, Bruises and Varicose Veins, General Tonic, Stimulate Appetite, Treat Jaundice, Reduce Blood Pressure, Strengthen the Heart,
Culinary:	Stewed with Rhubarb, sauces, salads, cakes, creams, omelettes, possets, custards. Pancakes to mark the end of the Lenten fast. Substitute for Nutmeg or Cinnamon. Leaves around meat acted as a preservative and fly repellant.
History:	Native of Britain. Flowers long lasting when dried. Ancients used the plant for embalming or preserving corpses. In Greek Mythology Ganymede cup bearer of Zeus was made immortal by drinking the juice of Tansy.
Magical:	Easter Rituals, Protection, Healing, Health, Longevityf.
Uses:	Strewing herb and Insect Repellant. Added to Pot Pourri.

TARE, Hairy (Vicia hirsuta)

Planet: Moon
Medicinal: Smallpox and Measles
History: Common in Britain. Pea Family. Improving the Fertility
               of poor soils. Reduced the crop yield of cornfields and
               made harvesting more difficult.

TARRAGON (Artemisia dracunculus (French

Tarragon)/Artemisia dracunculiases (Russian Tarragon) Little Dragon,
Dragon, Serpentaria, Estragon

Planet: Mars
Element: Fire
Gender: Female
Totem Animal: Dragon
Deity: Lillith

THISTLE Carline Thistle (Carlina vulgaris) Holy Thistle (Carbenia

benedicta) Scotch/Cotton/Woolly Thistle (Onopordon acanthium), Milk
Thistle (Silybum marianum) Dwarf Thistle (Carduus acaulis)

Planet: Mars
Element: Fire
Gender: Male
Gemstone: Black Diamond
Sign: Aries
Deity: Bacchus, Pan, Priapus, Thor, Vesta, Minerva
Care Doll: Protection
Powers: Strength, Protection, Healing, Exorcism, Hex-Breaking
Magical: Protection, Banishment, Strength, Healing, Exorcism,
               Hex

THISTLE, MILK (Carduus marianus) Marian Thistle

Planet:	Mars
Element:	Fire
Gender:	Male
Powers:	Snake Enraging

THYME Common (Thymus vulgaris)

Garden Thyme, Wild Thyme, Mother of Thyme (Thymus praecox or Thymus serpyllum), Mother Thyme, Shepherd's Thyme SHOULD NOT BE TAKEN DURING PREGNANCY

Planet:	Venus
Element:	Water
Gender:	Female
Sign:	Aries
Deities:	Ares, Fairies, Mars
Care Doll:	Love, Healing
Powers:	Health, Healing, Sleep, Psychic Powers, Love, Purification, Courage, Medicinal: Antiseptic, disinfectant, indigestion, flatulence, gastric upsets, bronchial troubles, coughs, colds, laryngitis, colic, rheumatism, menstrual disorders, hangovers, flu, mouth infections, gum infections and throat infections. Melancholy, hypochondria, aberrations of the mind, epilepsy, Antibacterial, Antifungal, Expectorant, Digestive Tonic, Antirheumatic, Soothing, Rubifacient, Diuretic, Cough, Asthma, Indigestion, Wind, Intestinal Infections, Cystitis, Intestinal Worms in Children, Nightmares, Colds, Flu, Catarrh, Athlete's Foot, Thrush, Depression, Headaches, Stress, cleaning wounds, Burns, Bruises, Clearing Lice, Abscesses, Gum infections, Anti Rheumatic, Antitoxic, Arthritis, Gout, Cellulite, Muscle Pain, Joint Pain, Poor Circulation, Coughing,
Culinary:	Pot herb, stimulates the appetite, helps digestion of

fatty meats such as mutton or pork, salads, stews, soups, stuffing, vegetables, pickles, sauces, cheeses, omelettes, various other dishes, flavour liqueurs.

History: Embalming the dead. Introduced into Britain by the Romans. Presented to knights with favours embroidered with a sprig of thyme. Carried by judges to ward off gaol fever.

Magical: Associated with death. Flowers were said to be the resting place for the souls who had died. Favourite flower of the fairies. Has the power to make fairies visible to humans. Love, Healing, Sheep, Confidence, Courage, Health, Psychic Powers, Purification

Uses: Pillow (giddiness and nightmares). Strewn on floors. Burned to fumigate houses and repel insects. In wardrobes to keep moths away from linen. Used in soaps, cosmetics, perfumes and pot pourri.

TOADFLAX, Common (Linaria vulgaris) Flaxweed, Lion's Mouth, Devil's Head   SHOULD NOT BE TAKEN DURING PREGNANCY

Planet: Mars
Element: Fire
Gender: Male
Powers: Protection, Hex Breaking
Medicinal: Constipation, Dropsy, Kidney Complaints, Liver Diseases, Scrofula, Enteritis, Hepatitis, Gall Bladder Problems, Cuts, Haemorrhoids, Sores, Malignant Ulcers, Skin Rahes, Conjunctivitis.
History: Native to Britain.
Uses: Laundry starch, fly poison.

TOMATO (Lycopersicon esculentum)

Planet: Venus
Element: Water
Gender: Female
Care Doll: Prosperity, Protection, Love

Powers: Prosperity, Protection, Love

TREFOIL, Heart (Trifolium cordatis)

Planet: Sun
Medicinal: Strengthener of the Heart, Fainting, Remedy against
                 Poison and Pestilence

TULIP (Tulipa)

Planet: Venus
Element: Earth
Gender: Female
Care Doll: Love, Prosperity, Protection
Power: Love, Prosperity, Protection

TURNIP (Brassica rapa)

Planet: Moon
Element: Earth
Gender: Female
Care Doll: Protection, Ending Relationship

VALERIAN (Valeriana officinalis) St George's Herb, Setwell,

Setwall, Setewale, Cat's Valerian, All Heal, Phu, Phew, Phu Plant, Fu,
Great Wild Valerian, Amantilla, Garden Heliotrope, Vandal, Vandal Root,
Bloody Butcher, English Valerian, Capon's Tail, Herb of Witches,
Graveyard Dust, Bouncing Bees, Pretty Betsy TAKEN OVER AN
EXTENDED PERIOD OF TIME CAN CAUSE HEADACHES AND STUPOR

Planet: Mercury
Element: Water
Gender: Female
Sign: Virgo
Humour: Cold
Deity: St Bernard
Care Doll: Protection, Love, Sleep, Purification
Powers: Love, Sleep, Purification, Protection
Medicinal: Sedative, Nerve Restorative, Calms the heart,

Antispasmodic, Carminative, Anxiety, Confusion, Migraines, Insomnia, Depression, Withdrawal from Tranquilizers, High Blood Pressure, Stress Palpitations, Colic, Nervous Indigestion

VERVAIN (Verbena officinalis) Verbena (not Lemon Verbena), Holy Herb, Herb of Grace, Enchanter's Plant, Herb of the Cross, Juno's Tears, Van Van, Fer Faen, Llystaur Hudol, Enchanting Herb, Lustral Water, Holy Vertain, European Vervain, Simpler's Joy, Herbine, Pigeon Grass, Pigeon's Meat, Pogeonwood, Herb of Enchantment, Devil's Hate, Wizard's Plant, Brittanica.

Planet:	Venus
Element:	Water
Gender:	Female
Totem Bird:	Hawk
Gemstone:	Opal, Agates
Deities:	Aphrodite, Aradia, Cerridwen, Diana, galahad, Horus, Isis, Jupiter, Mars, Ra, Thor, Venus, Zeus
Care Doll:	Protection, Healing
Powers:	Love, Protection, Purification, Peace, Money, Youth, Chastity, Sleep, Healing
Medicinal:	Tonic, Reduced Fever, Nerve restorative, Antispasmodic, Carminative, Diuretic, Lactagogue, Emmanagogue, Exhaustion, Post-Viral Fatigue, Post-Operative Tiredness, Overwork, Nervous Depression, Postnatal Depression, Insomnia, Headaches, Fevers, Flu, Indigestion, Digestive Discomfort, Liverishness, Irritable Bowel Syndrome, Menstrual Cramps, Inflamed Eyes

VETCH Common (Vicia sativa) Tufted Vetch (Vicia cracca)

Planet:	Moon
Powers:	Fidelity
Medicinal:	Hard to digest,
History:	Only really common in South Eastern England. Introduced into Britain by the Romans. Grown for

Sileage and Fodder. Seeds feed domestic pigeons.
Adds colour to hedges.

VIOLET Sweet (Viola odorata) Dog Violet (Viola riviniana) Sweet

Violet, Apple-leaf, Bairnwort, Banwort, Blaver, Bessy Banwood, Vilip,
Blue Violet, Cookoo's Shoe, Sweetling, Garland-flower, English Violet

Planet:	Venus
Element:	Water
Gender:	Female
Totem Animal:	Cow
Deities:	Aphrodite, Io, Orpheus, Venus
Care Doll:	Protection
Dye:	Purple
Powers:	Protection, Luck, Love, Lust, Wishes, Peace, Healing
Medicinal:	Mild Laxative, Respiratory Disorders, Hot Swellings, Coughs, Colds, Mouth and Throat Infections, Catarrh, Headaches, Insomnia, Quinsy, Pleurisy, Epilepsy, many other ailments.
Culinary:	Petals in salads, crystallized for cake and pudding decorations, sweet syrup for flavouring custards and omelettes. Flavour wine.
History:	Cultivated for over 2000 years. Hangovers and Headaches, Emblem of Athens.
Magical:	Flower of Aphrodite Goddess of Love. Love Potions. Symbol of purity and humility. Associated with Virgin Mary. Violets blooming in Autumn foretell the arrival of some kind of epidemic.
Uses:	Perfume

WALNUT, English (Juglans regia) Tree of Evil, English Walnut,

Common Walnut, Jupiter's Nuts

Planet:	Sun
Element:	Fire
Gender:	Male
Deities:	Adonis, Apollo, Jupiter

Care Doll:	Fertility

Care Doll: Fertility

Powers: Health, Mental Powers, Infertility, Wishes Dye: Brown once used to colour hair.

Medicinal: Stomach complaints, kidney and urinary stones, flatulence, intestinal worms, hair loss, bite of mad dog or man. Tonic, Stimulate the Appetite, Rheumatism, Gout, Swellings, Scrofula, Skin Complaints, Eczema, Herpes, Mange, Hardness of Hearing, Astringent, Cleansing, Anti-inflammatory, Discourages Milk Flow, Aphrodisiac, Mildly Laxative, Antiparasitic, Digestive, Protective, Fatigue, Strengthens Body, Gums anti inflammatory (bark), Circulation, Heart, Rheumatism, Muscles, Joints, Swellings, Skin Problems, Heartburn, Diarrhea, Gas, Intestinal Worms, Irritable Bowel Syndrome, Mild Laxative, De Flea Pets

Culinary: Raw, pickled, preserved in syrup, added to cakes, stuffing, salads and sauces. Fruit pies, nut comfit, nut jam, sweet and sour meat dishes, cordials, liqueurs, wine. Cooking oil.

History: Introduced into Britain by the Romans. Royal nut of Jove "Jupiter's Nuts". Comes from the German for foreign.

Magical: Wards off lightning. If put under a Witch's chair it will rob her of mobility. Fertility, Health, Mental Powers, Infertility, Wishes

Uses: Leaves repel flies and moths. Wood for furniture, cabinets and interior panelling. Oil used in lamps, wood polish and artist's paints.

WATER-WEED Curled Pondweed (Potaogeton crispus)

Broad-leaved Pondweed (Potamogeton natans)

Planet: Moon

Medicinal: Itch, Ulcers, Inflammation of the Legs.

History: Found in the mud at the bottom of ponds, lakes, canals, ditches.

WHEAT, Common (Triticum vulgare)

Planet:	Venus
Medicinal:	Inflammations, Swellings, Eczema, Ringworm, Painful Joints, Wounds, Ulcers, Boils, Sores, Gout,
Culinary:	Flour, Cooking, Bread, Cakes, Pastries, Wheatgerm.
History:	Cultivated in Britain since Prehistoric Times. Grew in the Holy Land 9000 years ago. Discovered in Egyptian Tombs.
Magical:	Corn Dolly plaited from straw of the last sheaf of wheat, stored over Winter and ploughed into the ground the following spring. Contained the Harvest Spirit.
Uses:	Reed used in thatching.

WILLOW White (Salix Alba) Crack Willow (Salix fragilis) Common Osier (Salix viminalis) Pussy Willow (Salix caprea) Sallow Willow (Saliz caprea)

Planet:	Moon
Element:	Water
Gender:	Female
Gemstone:	Peridot, Moonstone, Blood Red Carbuncle, Crystal
Totem Bird:	Swan, Wryneck
Colour:	Yellow
Rune:	Lagu
Deities:	Artemis, Belili, Belin, Belinos, Brigantia, Brighid, Callisto, Ceres, Circe, Europe, Hecate, Hera, Hermes, Isis, Kundalini, Lakshmi, Mercury, Moon Goddess, Osiris, Persephone, Poseidon, Psyche, Zeus
Care Doll:	Love, Protection, Healing
Dye:	Purple
Powers:	Love, Love Divination, Protection, Healing
Medicinal:	Alleviate Pain, Relieve Headaches, Reduce Fevers, Rheumatism, Arthritis, Internal Bleeding, Inflammations, Gout, Heartburn, Colds, Nervous

Insomnia, Digestive Problems, Stomach Complaints, Burns, Sores, Cuts, Skin Rashes

History:	Native to Britain since the Ice Age. Salix is derived from the Celtic for near water. Sprigs worn as a sign of mourning. "To wear the Willow".
Magical:	Sorrow and lost love. To make wands. Love, Protection, Healing
Uses:	Baskets, Fish Traps, Fences, Coracles, Tanning, Fodder, to Attract Bees, Artist's Charcoal. Down of seeds used as mattress stuffing.

WILLOWHERB Rosebay (Epilobium augustifolium) Fireweed.

Broad Leaved Willowherb (Epilobium montanum) Great Hairy Willowherb (Epilobium hirsutum)

Medicinal:	Hemorrages, Migraine, Dropsy, Stomach Disorders, Urinary Disorders, Asthma, Whooping Cough, Skin Inflammations and Infections.
Culinary:	Shoots boiled and used like asparagus. Leaves used as Tea Substitute.
History:	Colonized land cleared by fire, hence "Fireweed"
Use:	Smoke when burnt drives away flies and gnats and venomous beasts.

WOAD (Isatis tinctoria) POISONOUS

Planet:	Saturn
Element:	Water
Gender:	Female
Festival:	Lughnasa
Deities:	Robin Hood, Warrior Gods
Dye:	Blue
Medicinal:	Astringent, Stem Flow of Blood, Heal Wounds, Ulcers, Inflammations.
History:	Celts painted themselves with Woad before battle. Depletes land.
Uses:	Wool and cloth dye.

WOODRUFF (Asperula oderata/Galium oderatum) Sweet

Woodruff, Woodrove, Wuderove, Cordialis, Herb Walter, Master of the
Woods, Star grass, Hey Plant, Sweetgrass, Sweet Hair-hoof, Woodrowe,
Mugwet, Moth-herb, Woodruffe, Musk-of-the-woods, Sweet Woodruff,
Woodward LARGE AMOUNTS MAY CAUSE VOMITING AND DIZZINESS

Planet:	Mars
Element:	Fire
Gender:	Male
Festival:	Beltane
Tool:	The Wheel
Care Doll:	Healing, Victory, Protection, Money Powers:
	Healing, Victory, Protection, Money

WORMWOOD Common (Artemisia absinthium) Absinthe,

Green Ginger Roman Wormwood (Artemista pontica) Sea Wormwood
(Artemisia maritima) OVERDOSE IS DANGEROUS. SHOULD NOT BE
TAKEN IF PREGNANT OR BREAST FEEDING

Planet:	Mars
Element:	Air
Gender:	Male
Gemstone:	Ruby
Humour:	Red
Care Doll:	Protection
Deities:	Aesculapis, Artemis, Castor, Diana, Horus, Isis, Iris, Menthu, Pollux
Powers:	Psychic Powers, Protection, Love, Calling Spirits
Medicinal:	Childbirth, Appetite, Ailing Digestion, Jaundice, Constipation, Kidney Disorders, Reducing Fevers, Expelling Intestinal Worms, Remedying Liver and Gall Bladder Complaints, Flatulence, Improving Blood Circulation, Sprains, Bruises, Inflammation, Rheumatism, Lumbago,
Culinary:	Flavour Alcoholic Drinks e.g. Vermouth and Absinthe
History:	Native of Britain. Comes from the Greek God Artemis.

Absinthium derived from the Greek for without sweetness. Protection, Banishment, Divination, Psychic Powers, Love, Calling Spirits

Magical: Sprang up from the tracks of the serpent leaving the Garden of Eden. Bunches hung up to ward off evil.

Uses: Pillows for insomnia. Bunches hung up to repel moths, fleas and insects and to prevent infection. Strewing Herb. Hair Dye. Added to ink to repel mice. Incense

YELLOW EVENING PRIMROSE (Oenothera

biennis) War Poison, Sundrop, Tree Primrose, Evening Primrose

Powers: Hunting

YEW (Taxus baccata) English Yew POISONOUS

Planet: Saturn

Medicinal: Purgative, Heart and Liver Diseases, Gout, Rheumatis, Arthritis, Urinary Infections.

History: Native of Britain. Yew Spear found near Clacton on Sea 150,000 years old. Greek for Arrow.

Magical: Sacred Tree. Potent protection against evil. Symbol of Immortality. To bring cuttings into the house will lead to the death in the family. Damaging the tree will bring bad luck.

Uses: Making longbows and axe handles. Crushed seeds used for Arrow Poison. Smoke from burning leaves will repel gnats and mosquitoes and will kill rats and mice.

PLANT REMEDIES

Note: All information about plants and their uses is purely for information and amusement purposes only. We do not suggest that you use these remedies unless you find a reputable source of information about how to use them and in what quantity etc.

ABSCESS:	Marshmallow, Wild Indigo
ACNE:	Myrtle, Lemon Balm, Burdock, Nettle, Blackberry, Sage, Primrose, Thyme, Feverfew, Dock, Elecampane, Calendula
ADRENALS:	Borage
ALOPECIA:	Nettle, Rosemary
APPETITE:	Tarragon, Alfalfa, Bergamot, Angelica
ANXIETY:	Lemon Balm, Rosemary, Mint, Betony, Chamomile, Hop, Damiana, St John's Wort, Scullcap, Valerian, Vervain
ARTHRITIS:	Tarragon, Agrimony, Balm of Gilead, Chervil, Bistort, Mustard, Nettle, Fumitory, Hop, Garlic, Hemp, Dandelion
ASTHMA:	Mullein, Betony, Coltsfoot, Sage, Ox-Eye Daisy, Thyme, Marjoram, Mint, Lemon Verbena, Elecampane, St John's Wort, Garlic, Hollyhock, Honeysuckle
BITES:	Lemon Balm, Coltsfoot, Sage, Feverfew, Marjoram, Parsley, Garlic, Calendula
BLADDER:	Meadowsweet, Madder
BLOOD	
TONIC:	Agrimony, Purslane, Rosemary
BLOOD PRESSURE	
HIGH:	Rue, Yarrow, Hawthorn
LOW:	Hawthorn, Broom
BOILS:	Lemon Balm, Chicory, Clary Sage, Marshmallow, Hop, Flax, Garlic
BRONCHIAL:	Mullein, Violet, Balm of Gilead, Sunflower, Ox-Eye Daisy, Mustard, Thyme, Marjoram, Mint, Nasturtium,

	Elecampane, Flax, Clover, St John's Wort, Garlic, Caraway, Dog Rose, Fenugreek
BURNS:	Aspen, Vervain, Marshmallow, Mallow, Willow, Houseleek, Calendula, Cleavers.
BRUISES:	Houseleek, Elecampane, Hyssop, Hollyhock, Daisy, Myrtle, Tansy, Violet, Borage, Balm of Gilead, Soapwort, Comfrey, Vervain, Mallow, Feverfew, Mint, Parsley, Lady's Mantle, Hop
CANDIDA:	Garlic
CATARRH:	Mullein, Tarragon, Avens, Lemon Balm (1), Bergamot, Betony, Poppy, Mint, Holly, Hyssop, St John's Wort, Hemp, Agrimony, Honeysuckle, Horehound, Flax
CELLULITE:	Ivy
CHILBLAINS:	Mustard, Horseradish, Garlic, Honeysuckle, Calendula
CHAPPED SKIN:	Alder, Yarrow
HIGH CHOLESTEROL:	Apple, Garlic
CIRCULATION:	Hawthorn, Ginger
COLDS:	Myrtle, Lavender, Bayberry, Sunflower, Coltsfoot, Angelica, Sage, Thyme, Marjoram, Mint, Nasturtium, Yarrow, Garlic, Hemp, Agrimony, Catnip, Dog Rose, Eyebright.
COLD SORES:	Bergamot, Elecampane
COLIC:	Lavender, Basil, Parsley, Lovage, Hop, Fennel, Valerian, Caraway, Catnip, Dill
COLITIS:	Periwinkle, Marshmallow
CONJUNCTIVITIS:	Calendula, Eyebright
CONSTIPATION:	Violet, Apple, Nasturtium, Hollyhock, Feverfew
COUGH:	Myrtle, Balm of Gilead, Sunflower, Bistort, Sage, Purslane, Primrose, Ox-Exe Daisy, Mustard, Marshmallow, Mallow, Poppy, Thyme, Mint, Hyssop, Sweet Cicely, Garlic, Hemp, Agrimony, Honeysuckle, Horehound, Dog Rose, Fenugreek.
CRAMP:	Saffron, Valerian

CUTS:	Chickweed, Betony, Comfrey, Vervain, Mallow.
CYSTITIS:	Angelica, Juniper, Yarrow, Burdock, Blackberry.
DANDRUFF:	Oak, Fenugreek
DEPRESSION:	Lavender, Lemon Balm, Mugwort, Sage, Rosemary, Thyme, Nasturtium, Lemon Verbena, Damiana, St John's Wort
DIARHHOEA:	Meadowsweet, Buckwheat, Sage, Cinquefoil, Apple, Blackberry, Marshmallow, Periwinkle, Strawberry, Lady's Mantle, Nettle, Hollyhock, Caraway, Dog Rose
DIABETES:	Nettle, Herb Robert
DIGESTIVE TONIC:	Chervil, Basil, Angelica, Rosemary, Thyme, Mint, Hop, Elecampane, Vervain, Hyssop, Ground Ivy, Caraway, Eyebright
DERMATITIS:	Aloe Vera
DYSENTRY:	Sunflower, Bistort, Blackberry
EARACHE:	Tansy, Basil
ECZEMA:	Violet, Burdock, Chickweed, Chicory, Bistort, Nettle, Sage, Periwinkle, Fumitory, Dock, Yarrow, Horehound, Daisy
EPILEPSY:	Mugwort
EYE PROBLEMS:	Violet, Agrimony, Chervil, Angelica, Marshmallow, Rue, Daisy, Eyebright
FEVER:	Meadowsweet, Borage, Cinquefoil, Apple, Sage, Saffron, Catnip, Sorrel, Strawberry, Oak, Holly
FLATULENCE:	Tarragon, Lavender, Bergamot, Angelica, Thyme, Mint, Parsley, Lovage, Lemon Verbena, Lady's Mantle, Fennel, Caraway, Dill
FUNGAL INFECTIONS:	Tarragon, Nasturtium, Calendula
GALL BLADDER:	Nettle
GASTRITIS:	Meadowsweet

GASTRO
ENTERITIS: Hollyhock
GINGIVITIS: Dog Rose
GOUT: Tarragon, Violet, Meadowsweet, Betony, Nettle
HAEMORRHOIDS: Lesser Celandine, Parsley, Calendula
HALITOSIS: Tarragon, Lavender, Dill Fennel
HANGOVER: Thyme, Fennel
HAYFEVER: Mullein, Marjoram, Eyebright
HEADACHE: Violet, Lavender, Lemon Balm, Bergamot, Betony, Basil,
               Primrose, Marshmallow, Periwinkle, Rue, Willow, Ivy,
               Ground Ivy, Catnip
HEARTBURN: Meadowsweet, Marshmallow
HICCUPS: Tarragon, Dill
INDIGESTION: Lemon Balm, Mugwort, Centaury, Apple, Sage, Mint,
               Nasturtium, Lovage, Lemon Verbena, Horehound
INFECTIONS: Garlic, Nasturtium, Parsley
INFLAMMATIONS: Mullein, Violet, Woad, Agrimony, Borage, Chicory,
               Cinquifoil, Coltsfoot, Apple, Angelica, Marshmallow,
               Madonna Lily
INFLUENZA: Meadowsweet, Lavender, Cinquefoil, Coltsfoot,
               Angelica, Nasturtium, Garlic, Dog Rose, Thyme,
               Marjoram
IMMUNE
SYSTEM: Hemp, Agrimony
INSOMNIA: Mint, Hop, Vervain, Woodruff, St John's Wort, Dill,
               Valerian, Hollyhock, Chamomile, Cleavers, Tarragon,
               Agrimony, Lavender, Bergamot, Saffron, Primrose,
               Marshmallow, Rosemary, Marjoram
ITCHING: Chickweed, Angelica, Calendula
JAUNDICE: Alfalfa, Chicory, Bistort, Fumitory
KIDNEY
PROBLEMS: Meadowsweet, Sunflower, Betony
KIDNEY
STONES: Chicory, Madder, Lady's Mantle

LARYNGITIS:	Agrimony, Balm of Gilead, Blackberry
LIVER TONIC:	Centuary, Peony, Nettle
LUMBAGO:	Daisy
MENOPAUSE:	Mugwort
MENSTRUAL PROBLEMS:	Tarragon, Mugwort, Bergamot, Nettle, Sage, Periwinkle, Thyme, Marjoram, Mistletoe, Parsley, Lady's Mantle, Hop, Valerian, Calendula, Caraway, Daisy
MIGRAINE:	Basil, Sage, Rosemary, Feverfew
MILK STIMULATION:	Borage, Buckwheat, Basil, Nettle, Hop, Caraway, Fenugreek
MOUTH ULCERS:	Bistort, Nettle, Vervain, Sage, Periwinkle, Sorrel, Strawberry, Mint, Herb Robert, Daisy, Fenugreek
NAUSEA:	Betony, Vervain, Lemon Verbena
NERVOUS COMPLAINTS:	Violet, Lavender, Mugwort, Basil, Peony, Ox-Eye Daisy, Strawberry, Thyme, Marjoram, Mint, Hop, Valerian, Chamomile
NOSEBLEED:	Nettle
PAINKILLER:	Meadowsweet, Willow, Scullcap, Valerian
PRE-MENSTRUAL TENSION:	Scullcap, Valerian
PSORIASIS:	Myrtle, Burdock, Chickweed, Bistort, Marshmallow, Periwinkle, Dock, Horehound
PNEUMONIA:	Mullein
PLEURISY:	Mullein, Borage, Holly
RHEUMATISM:	Tansy, Tarragon, Agrimony, Mugwort, Chervil, Chickweed, Betony, Bistort, Columbine, Nettle, Apple, Sage, Angelica, Mustard, Rosemary, Willow, Holly, Hop, Dock, Horseradish, Garlic, Hemp, Agrimony, Dandelion
SCABIES:	Angelica
SCIATICA:	Horseradish, Yarrow
SHINGLES:	Bergamot

SINUS PROBLEMS:	Myrtle, Coltsfoot, Marshmallow
SORES:	Lemon Balm, Betony, Coltsfoot
SORE THROATS:	Violet, Agrimony, Bergamot, Betony, Bistort, Nettle, Apple, Vervain, Blackberry, Sage, Purslane, Periwinkle, Willow, Strawberry, Thyme, Mint, Oak, Elecampane, Vervain, Herb Robert, Chamomile
SPRAINS:	Tansy, Comfrey, Vervain, Parsley
STINGS:	Betony, Basil, Sage, Mallow, Parsley
STRESS:	Lavender, Borage, Lemon Balm, Vervain, Scullcap, Mint, Hop, Woodruff, Damiana, Valerian
SUNBURN:	Marshmallow, Fumitory, Ivy, Calendula
SWELLINGS:	Tansy, Violet, Clary Sage, Comfrey
THRUSH ORAL:	Lavender, Basil, Marjoram
TONIC:	Thyme, Mint, Nasturtium, Elecampane, Vervain, Sweet Cicely
TONSILITIS:	Vervain, Cleavers
TOOTHACHE:	Tansy, Tarragon, Angelica, Thyme, Mint, Parsley, Yarrow
TRAVEL SICKNESS:	Angelica
PEPTIC ULCERS:	Meadowsweet, Alfalfa
SKIN ULCERS:	Woad, Meadowsweet, Burdock, Betony, Coltsfoot, Madonna Lily, Willow, Flax, Calendula
UPSET STOMACH:	Mugwort, Basil
URINARY INFECTION:	Violet, Flax, Ground Ivy
VARICOSE VEINS:	Buckwheat, Burdock, Betony, Coltsfoot, Lesser Celandine, Calendula
VOMITING:	Mustard, Marshmallow, Peppermint
WARTS:	Mullein, Greater Celandine

WATER
RETENTION: Tarragon, Meadowsweet, Bindweed, Alfalfa, Purslane,
              Parsley, Fumitory, Gorse, Holly, Vervain, Dandelion
WHOOPING
COUGH: Mullein, Violet, Sunflower, Ox-Eye Daisy, Marjoram,
              Elecampane, Garlic
WORMS: Betony, Horehound
WOUNDS: Burdock, Chickweed, Betony, Coltsfoot, Comfrey

ESSENTIAL OILS

Almond: (Carrier Oil)
                Wealth, Wisdom
Anise: Balance, Energy
Bergamot: Friendship, Happiness, Depression
Catnip: Cats, Luck, Love
Camphor: Disenchantment
Cedar: Balance, Grounding
Chamomile: Health, Healing, Calmness, Balance
Cinnamon: Relaxing, Stimulating, Aphrodisiac, Concentration
Citronella: Control, Insect Repellant
Clary Sage: Purification, Stress, Healing, Strength, Dream Magic
Cloves: Abundance, Gossip
Copal: Purification, Clarity
Cypress: Anger, Grief, Change
Fennel: Courage, Energy
Frankincense: Abundance, Concentration, Spirit, Gods, Goddesses
Gardenia: Fear
Geranium: Harmony, Friendship, Calmness, Positive Energy,
                Addictions
Grapefruit: Energy
Heliotrope: Abundance
Hyssop: Grief
Jasmine: Balance, Confidence, Dreams, Sensuality, Relaxation,

	Protection
Lavender:	Balance, Clarity, Forgiveness, Healing
Lemon:	Stimulating, Cleansing
Mastic:	Abundance
Mint:	Disenchantment
Myrrh:	Abundance, Concentration
Neroli:	Courage, Creativity, Overcoming Depression
Olive:	(Carrier Oil)
	Abundance, Wisdom, Fertility, Purity, Victory, Peace
Orange Blossom: Abundance, Happiness
Patchouli:	Creativity, Grounding, Sensuality
Pepper:	Abundance, Heat, Warding Spells
Peppermint:	Dreams, Calming, Cooling
Pine:	Disenchantment, Cleansing
Rose:	Love, Romance, Happiness, Contentment
Rosemary:	Healing, Love, Protection, Purification
Sandalwood:	Psychic Abilities, Success
Vanilla:	Love, Sensuality, Peace, Dreams, Luck, Success
White Sage:	Purification, Cleansing, Negative Energy, Blessing, Healing, Calming
Vertivert:	Grounding, Earthiness, Calming
Ylang Ylang:	Confidence, Sensuality, Passion, Romance

6 ANIMALS

MINERALS and MEDICINAL PLANTS RICH IN THEM: THEIR ACTION

CALCIUM: Chamomile, Chicory, Cleavers, Coltsfoot, Dandelion, Meadowsweet, Mistletoe, Mustard, Plantain, Sorrel, Toadflax, Watercress, Willow

Builds and maintains bones, teeth and nails, gives vitality, promotes healing of wounds, reduces acidity, prevents faulty food assimilation, safeguards health of the embryo.

CHLORINE: All Herbs Contain Chlorine as Sodium Chloride

Maintains suppleness of joints and tendons, removes toxic elements, prevents the formation of fatty tissue, promotes health of teeth and hair.

COPPER: Burdock, Chickweed, Chicory, Cleavers, Dandelion, Fennel, Garlic, Horseradish, Houseleek, Sorrel.

Aids digestive organs, tones the nerves, clears septic conditions of the tissues, strengthens and brightens hair.

FLUORINE: Beet leaves, Garlic

Anti-infective, maintaining whole body and tissue health, keeps bones disease free, teeth, nails, ears and eyes.

IODINE: Asparagus, Cleavers, Garlic, Seaweed,

Gland builder and conditioner, reduces excess fatty tissue, safeguards
the brain from toxins, removes toxic elements, promotes strong hair.

IRON: Artichoke, Asparagus, Bilberry, Blackberry, Burdock,
                 Chicory, Comfrey, Cornflower, Dandelion, Dock,
                 Gentian, Groundsel, Ground Ivy, Hawthorn, Hops,
                 Nettle, Parsley, Periwinkle, Raspberry, Rose, Scabious,
                 Scullcap, Strawberry, Toadflax, Vervain, Wormwood

Important to the blood, promotes oxygen absorption, builds red
corpuscles, good pigment, maintains disease resistance, feeds nerve
tissues, aids hair growth.

MAGNESIUM: Alder, Artichoke, Birth, Broo, Carrot Leaves, Cowslip,
                 Dandelion, Hop, Marshmallow, Meadowsweet,
                 Mistletoe, Mullein, Oak, Poppy, Primrose, Orchid,
                 Scabious, Rose, Toadflax, Walnut leaves.

Promotes cleansing and restoration, reduces excess acidity, calms the
nerves, promotes skin health and fine texture.

PHOSPHORUS: Asparagus, Calamus, Chickweed, Cornflower, Dill,
                 Fenugreek, Linseed, Marigold, Meadowsweet,
                 Sunflower, Sorrel, Watercress

Builds and maintains the brain, teeth and hair and all bony structure.
Promotes keen eyesight and good nerve cocoordination.

POTASSIUM: Birch, Borage, Calamus, Carrot Leaves, Chamomile,
                 Coltsfoot, Comfrey, Couch Grass, Cowslip, Dandelion,
                 Elder, Eyebright, Fennel, Honeysuckle, Lady's Mantle,
                 Meadowsweet, Mistletoe, Mullein, Nettle, Oak, Peony,
                 Peppermint, Plantain, Primrose, Rhubarb, Scullcap,
                 Toadflax, Walnut Leaves, Wormwood General healing of

the tissues, tones the bowels, gall bladder and liver. Encourages healing of diseased tissues, relieves pain.

SILICON: Asparagus, Cleavers, Dandelion, Flax, Holly, Strawberry, Thistle, Stalks of grasses and Cereals including wheat and oat straw

Promotes and maintains strength of hair, hardens teeth and nails, strengthens the eyes. Maintains suppleness of limbs, ligaments and skin.

SODIUM: Alder, Cleavers, Clover, Comfrey, Dill, Fennel, Garlic, Marshmallow, Meadowsweet, Mistletoe, Nettle, Violet, Woodruff

Alkalizer of the body, strengthens the digestive juices, aids iron assimilation, reduces premature hardening of the tissues, prevents catarrh and disease of the mucous membranes. Maintains health of the urinary system and kidneys

SULPHUR: Broom, Cabbage, Calamus, Cowslip, Coltsfoot, Daisy, Eyebright, Fennel, Garlic, Marigold, Meadowsweet, Mullein, Nettle, Plantain, Poppy, Primrose, Scabious, Seaweed, Toadflax, Watercress

Acts as a purifier and tonic for the entire system, especially the blood. Maintains health of skin and hair, strengthens glandular system and promotes flow of bile. Keeps the liver healthy.

WOOD ASH: Ash of wood, charcoal.

Cleanser of the body. Highly absorbent and will take in impurities. Laxative to pass impurities out of the system. Worms and worm ova are removed to some extent by charcoal. Wild animals eat it and when they smell smoke they will come to eat the resulting charcoal. Burn clean and dry tree branches slowly in deep pits. Scoop it up and mix with bran and milk. One dessertspoon of charcoal twice daily.

HERBAL GOAT MANAGEMENT

This is something I've long wanted to try. It wasn't something to undertake lightly but I've long been frustrated by the amount of chemicals that have to be poured down a goat's throat. Wave tried worming less and watching their "poo" to make sure there aren't any signs of worm infestation.

Goats need exercise for good health. That bore out at the last place where the weather was harsher and they spent more time captive in the shed. Now that they can roam, even if it is a few hours before rain drives them stampeding back, they are much healthier.

Goats thrive on dry, coarse mountain grasses and herbs like thyme, marjoram, save and lavender. Damp pasture can cause lung weakness. So if you are thinking of keeping goats, pick a smallholding which is dry.

Goats enjoy twigs, branches and bark of woodland trees for a balanced diet and they suffer ill health if they cannot get their regular fill of these things. They are not grazing animals, they are more like deer and browse.

Goats also need plenty of sunlight but shelter from the sun if it gets too hot. They enjoy a huge elderly oak tree here and will be found laying around in their family groups in its shade on particularly hot days.

Rock salt is important in a goat's diet and woodland grazing is perfect for them. Crops to grow for goats are oats, vetches, barley, alfalfa, sunflower, linseed, corn including the inner cobs. They like flaked barley and rolled oats, wheat bran and dried beet pulp.

WORMS (The Goat Killer)

Many species of worms can attack goats and they are the most common cause of ailments and the cause of the greatest losses. If they don't kill directly the debilitate the animal which makes him or her prone to other diseases.

Pasture maintenance is the best way to guard against worms. There is no point in worming and then putting the animal back on infected pasture. Grazing a large area can help but if you are tied to a small amount of land there are ways to "cure" the land by natural methods such as liming heavily, growing a thick crop of mustard and ploughing it in, heavily planting with garlic or spreading with soot.

SYMPTOMS: Discharging eyes, husky cough and scour.

TREATMENT: Garlic is a great start, aided by molasses. Garlic is also a good preventative.

The garlic referred to is the wild variety and it was pleasant to see that it has begun to grow prolifically on our land last year. They can eat the whole plant.

 If they are not naturally grazing it they will need it to be fed finely chopped and mixed with bran and molasses or can be made into medicine balls for those who are "difficult". One large or two small plants finely chopped and mixed with flour and black treacle into balls the size of a walnut would make a good way of giving it to your goats. Flaked garlic root can be used throughout the year and tablets of compressed garlic can be given. Tapeworm and Liver Fluke can be treated the same way. There are other methods if there is an "issue" which involves terpentine but I haven't used this method so I cannot comment on it.

LIVER FLUKE: This parasite infests damp pastures as it needs ill drained places to complete its life cycle. Garlic is a preventative. Centaury herb is an ancient peasant remedy. One ounce of the herb being given daily in small balls with fat and flour. Lumps of rock salt should be available in the pastures.

SYMPTOMS: A jaundiced look to the eyes, rapid wasting and loss of hair. The back becomes roached and the abdomen drops.

TREATMENT: As per worms. Give as much chopped raw dandelion and centaury and flaked gentian root.

SCOUR (Diarrhoea): This is a common ailment especially during prolonged very cold and wet weather.

TREATMENT: I have read that a laxative drench should be given. One to two full ounces of Epsom Salts dissolved in half a pint brew of Dill seed water or Senna Pods. One small handful of Dill Seed boiled for five minutes in one pint of water, brewed for two hours. The goat should be fasted for 24 hours following the drench and given a garlic brew or tablets for internal disinfecting in the evening.

Slippery Elm (Red Elm) is recommended by one book I've read as it acts as an internal poultice. Keep the goat penned in a warm and dry place. Only feed flaked barley with boiled beets and parsnips.

LICE: Garlic given to the goat can repel the parasites.

PLANTS POISONOUS TO GOATS

Buttercup, Greater Celandine, Foxglove, Ragwort, Larkspur, Deadly Nightshade, Henbane, Wild Arum, Good King Henry, Honeysuckle, Morning Glory, Bryony (White), Bindweed, Bracken and most ferns, Winter Heliotrope, Monkshood, Belladonna, Greater Fennel, Castor Oil Leaves and fruits. Yew, Laburnum, Rhododendrum, Berries of Laurel, Elder and Alder.

SYMPTOMS: General Symptoms are violent vomiting and diarrhoea, abnormal thirst, discomfort accompanied by incessant bleating, striking the ground with feet, cold extremities, body swelling, violent nervous spasms.

TREATMENT: I have read to give the animal a teaspoon size piece of washing soda which produces instant vomiting. Make sure it is pure washing soda not caustic soda! Give the animal a drench three times daily of: two tablespoons of honey mixed in half pint of skimmed raw milk.

RECOMMENDED BOOKS:

The Complete Herbal Handbook for Farm and Stable by Juliette de Bairacli Levy

Diseases of the Goat by John Matthews

Goat Husbandry by David Mackenzie

Goats: Homoeopathic Remedies by George Macleod

.

7 MAGIC, CORRRESPONDENCES AND DEITIES

ADONIS: Greek Vegetation God: Fir, Myrrh, Anemone, Rose, Frankincense, Dog Rose, Acacia, Bay, Laurel, Vine, Snowdrop, Narcissus, Lily, Walnut.

AEACUS: Greek Son of Zeus: Aloe

AESCULAPIUS: Greek God of Medicine: Bay, Laurel, Mustard, Cinnamon, Orchid, Wormwood, Peony, Lily of the Valley.

AENGUS Irish God of Love: Hazel

AGNI: Hindu Fire God: Red Poppy, Nettle, Hibiscus

AINE: Irish Moon Goddess: Meadowsweet

ALCESTIS: Greek Floral Goddess: Daisy

AMUN RA: Egyptian Sun God: Amaranth, Olive, Aloe, Saffron, Reed

ANNA PERENNA: Roman Goddess of the Year: Barley

ANUBIS: Egyptian Jackal Headed God: Opium Poppy

APHRODITE: Greek Goddess of Love: Cypress, Myrtle, Marjoram, Dog Rose, Parsley, Rose, Apple, Clover, Cinnamon, Iris, Columbine, Vervain, Daisy, Geranium, Coriander, Marshmallow, Sorrel, Violet

APOLLO: Geek and Roman God of the Sun, Poetry and Medicine: Apple, Bay Laurel, Sunflower, Heliotrope, Peony, Fenugreek, Aspen, Daisy, Frankinsense, Anise, Cypress, Fennel, Mistletoe, Vine, Acacia, Rush, Bistort, Fennel, Walnut, Lily of the Valley.

ARACHNE: Greek Spider Goddess: Flax

ARADIA: Italian Witch Goddess: Rue, Vervain

ARES: Greek God of War: Pepper, Dragon's Blood

ARIANRHOD: Welsh Goddess of the Moon, Initiation and Rebirth): Ivy, Oak, Flax.

ARTEMIS: Greek Goddess of the Moon: Myrtle, Ox-Eye Daisy, Hazel, Mugwort, Willow, Wormwood, Almond, Amaranth, Rush, Cypress, Wormwood, Lesser Celandine, Dairy, Mandrake, Oak, Damiana, Almond, Jasmine, Ginseng, Camphor, Aloe, Lemon Balm, Beech, Fir, Birthwort.

ARTHUR: Celtic Sun God: Apple, Alder

ASTARTE: Canaanite Fertility Goddess: Acacia, Myrtle, Pine

ATROPOS: Greek, One of the Fates: Belladonna

ATHENE: Greek Warrior Goddess of Wisdom: Apple, Olive, Geranium, Amaranth, Ash, Cypress, Yew, Hellebore, Belladonna, Dragon's Blood, Asafoetida, Mulberry.

ATTIS: Anatolian Vegetation God: Pine, Almond, Snowdrop,

Lily, Narcissus, Fir, Heather.

BACCHUS: Roman God of Wine: Ivy, Hemp, Fir, Vine, Orchis Root, Thistle, Rose

BALDUR: Scandanavian Sun God: Mistletoe, St John's Wort, Oak

BAST: Egyptian Cat Goddess: Catnip, Valerian.

BEL: Sumerian Sun God: Frankincense, Bistort.

BELIDIS: Greek Dryad: Daisy

BELILI: Sumerian Underworld, Moon Goddess: Willow

BELINOS: Celtic Sun God: Willow, Daisy, Celandine

BELLONA: Roman Battle Goddess: Belladonna

BHAVANI: Tantric Mother Goddess: Cypress, Opium Poppy, Myrrh

BLODEUWEDD: Welsh Spring Goddess: Broom, Bean, Horse Chestnut, Oak, Meadowsweet, Nettle, Primrose, Hawthorn, Burdock, Blackthorn, Corn Cockle.

BRAN: Raven, Welsh Oracular God: Alder

BRANWEN: Welsh Goddess, Sister of Bran: Alder

BRIGHID: Irish Triple Goddess: Rowan, Blackberry, Birch, Willow, Bistort, Oak, Snowdrop, Hop, Flax

BRIGANTIA: British Goddess: Rowan, Birch, Willow, Blackberry, Oak, Snowdrop, Bistort

CALLISTO: Greek Moon Goddess: Willow

CARDEA: Roman Goddess of the Hinges: Hawthorn, Bean

CASTOR: Greek and Roman, One of the Heavenly Twins: Orchid, Wormwood

CENTAURS: Greek race of beings, half man, half horse: Fir

CERBERUS: Greek Guardian of the Underworld: Aconite

CERES: Roman Corn Goddess: Bay, Laurel, Corn, Poppy, Willow, Chaste Tree, Snowdrop, Lily, Narcissus.

CERIDWEN: Welsh Goddess of the Moon, Grain, Initiation, Underworld: Bay, Laurel, Corn, Ivy, Oak, Vervain, Chervil, Honeysuckle, Catnip, Mistletoe, Apple, Blackthorn

CERNUNNOS   Celtic Horned God: Betony, Pine, Oak, Chamomile, Yarrow, Lavender, Ash, Bistort, Nettle

CHANDRA: Hindu Moon God: Almond, Mugwort, Hazel, Camphor, Aloe

CHIRON: Greek, The Wise Minotaur: Centuary, Fir

CIRCE: Greek Witch Goddess: Willow, Belladonna, Garlic, Mandrake, Lavender, Mullein

CONNLA: Irish: Hazel

CONSUS: Roman God of the Harvest: Sage, Dogwood

CREIDDYLAD: Welsh Maiden Goddess: Hawthorn, Oak

CUCHULAIN: Irish Hero: Rowan

CUPID: Roman God of Love: Rose, Cypress, Bay, Dog Rose

CYBELE: Phrygian Goddess of Caverns: Oak, Pine, Garlic, Myrrh, Heather, Fir

CYPARAISSUS: Greek, Friend of Apollo: Cypress

DAGDA: Irish principle of God: Oak

DAPHNE: Greek Nymph: Bay, Laurel

DEMETER: Greek Corn Goddess: Corn, Rose, Frankincense, Myrrh,
               Dog Rose, Pennyroyal, Sunflower, Bean, Red Poppy,
               Cypress, Wheat, Opium Poppy

DIANA: Roman Goddess of the Moon/Hunt: Acacia, Apple,
               Hazel, Mugwort, Rue, Wormwood, Jasmine, Mandrake,
               Vervain, Cypress, Damiana, Almond, Lemon Balm,
               Lesser Celandine, Beech, Birthwort

DIANUS: Roman Oak God: Oak

DIONYSUS: Thracian/Greek God of Vegetation/Wine/Fertility:
               Apple, Ivy, Pine, Fir, Belladonna, Fennel, Vine

DONAR: Teutonic Thunder God: Oak

DRUANTIA: Gaulish Goddess: Fir

EOS: Greek Goddess of the Dawn: Saffron

EOSTRE: Teutonic Earth Goddess: Pasque Flower

ERATO: Greek Muse: Oak

EROS: Greek God of Love: Rose, Bay, Dog Rose

ERZULIE: Haitian Voodoo Goddess of Love: Basil

EUPHROSYNE: Greek, One of the Graces: Eyebright

EUROPA: Greek, Mother of the Minotaur: Willow

EVE: Canaanite Mother Goddess: Apple

FATES: Greek Goddesses of Destiny: Cyrpess

FAUNUS: Roman Nature God: Bay, Reed

FLORA: Roman Goddess of Vegetation: Hawthorn, Cereals,

Fruit Trees, Vine, Rose, Dock, Cornflower

FREYA: Teutonic Moon/Love Goddess: Primrose, Cowslip, Catnip, Cypress, Mistletoe, Opium Poppy, Rose, Daisy, Strawberry, Myrtle, Clover, Myrrh, Red Sandalwood

FURIES: Greek Goddesses of Divine Retribution: Juniper, Cypress, Oak

GAIA: Greek Earth Goddess: Cereals, Fruits

GANESHA: Hindu God of Good Fortune: Banyan, Mandrake, Damiana, Jasmine

GANYMEDE: Greek, Cup Bearer of Zeus: Olive, Tansy

GODA/GODIVA: British Beltane Goddess: Apple

GRANNOS: Celtic God of Springs: Apple

GUINIVERE: Early Celtic Triple Goddess of Sovereignty: Alder

GWYDION: Welsh God, brother of Arianrhod: Ash

HADES: Greek, God of the Underworld: Oak, Nux Vomica, Nettle, Red Poppy, Hibiscus, Frankincense, Cypress, Fern

HANUMAN: Hindu Monkey God: Vertain, Palm, Storax, Mastic, White Sandalwood, Mace.

HATHOR: Egyptian Sky Goddess: Mandrake, Sandalwood, Myrtle, Rose, Myrrh, Clover, Dog Rose

HECATE: Greek/Thracian Moon/Witch/Underworld Goddess: Garlic, Mandrake, Willow, Aconite, Almond, Lavender, Myrrh, Cypress, Opium Poppy, Mugwort, Hazel, Belladonna, Hemlock, Mint, Dandelion, Lesser Celandine, Hellebore, Yew

HELIOS:	Greek Sun God: Sunflower, Laurel, Heliotrope, Frankincense, Cinnamon, Bistort,
HERA/ HERAKLES:	Greek, Queen of Heaven: Apple, Willow, Iris, Cypress, Opium Poppy, Myrrh
HERCULES:	Greek Deified Hero: Apple, Cypress, Oak, Aspen, Olive
HERMES:	Greek, Messenger of the Gods: Lotus, Storax, Willow, Vervain, Palm, Mastic, White Sandalwood, Mace, Anise, Apple, Lily of the Valley, Rue
HERNE:	British Horned God: Oak, Yarrow, Betony, Pine, Ash
HOLDA:	Teutonic Moon/Witch Goddess: Elder
HORUS:	Egyptian Falcon Headed God: Horehound, Oak, Nux Vomica, Nettle, Wormwood, Rue, Pepper, Dragon's Blood
HULDA:	Teutonic Goddess of Marriage and Fertility: Flax, Rose, Dog Rose, Elder
HYMEN:	Roman Maiden Goddess: Hawthorn, Rose, Ivy.
HYPNOS:	Greek God of Sleep: Poppy, Opium Poppy
IDUNA:	Teutonic Keeper of the Apples of Youth: Apple
INANNA:	Sumerian Queen of Heaven: Grains, Date Palm, Vine, Flax
INDRA:	Hindu God of Battles/Rain: Olive, Aloe, Saffron, Oak
IRIS:	Greek Goddess of the Rainbow: Wormwood, Iris
ISHTAR:	Semitic Queen of Heaven: Acacia, Grains, Date Palm, Vine

ISIS: Egyptian Queen of Heaven: Heather, Myrrh, Rose, Vervain, Wormwood, Iris, Lotus, Narcissus, Onion, Lily, Ivy, Geranium, Horehound, Olive, Willow, Snowdrop, Amaranth, Cypress, Opium Poppy, Dittany of Crete, Dragon's Blood

JANICOT: Basque God: Oak

JANUS: Roman Good of Doorways: Oak, Amaranth

JUNO: Roman Queen of Heaven: Myrrh, Olive, Iris

JUPITER: Roman chief God: Oak, Vervain, Ox-Eye Daisy, Marjoram, Carnation, Lily, Cypress, Vervain, Saffron, Hibiscus, Nettle, Gorse, Sage, Mullein, Almond, Olive, Aspen, Red Poppy, Houseleek, Walnut

KHEPHERA: Egyptian Scarab God of the Dawn/Sun: Lotus, Cactus, Opium Poppy, Opoponax

KRISHNA: Hindu, Incarnation of Vishnu: Basil

KUNDALINI: Hindu, Feminine Serpent Force: Willow, Lily, Ivy

LADY HORSE
HEAD: Chinese patroness silkworms: Mulberry

LAKSHMI: Hindu Goddess of Good Fortune: Willow, Lily, Ivy, Dittany of Crete, Basil

LATTIS: British Goddess of the Pool/Beer

LIBER PATER: Roman Fertility God: Vine

LILLITH: Hebrew, Adam's First Wife: Tarragon

LIR/LLYR   Welsh, Father of Bran: Ash, Oak

LLEU LLAW
GYFFES: Welsh, Son of Arianrhod: Borage, Hazel, Holly

LOKI: Scandanavian Trickster God: Storax

LUGH: Irish God of the Tuatha de Dannan: Borage, Hazel, Holly

LETO: Greek, Mother of Apollo and Artemis: Palm, Peony, Hop

MABON: Welsh, Son of the Great Mother: Apple

MAIA: Roman, Mother of Mercury: Lily of the Valley

MANANNAN: Manx Sea God: Hazel

MARIAN: Traditional British Witch Name for the Lady: Myrrh,
Myrtle

MARS: Roman God of War: Rue, Ash, Vervain, Holly, Thyme

MEDEA: Greek Goddess, In later legends a mortal sorceress:
               Aconite, Lavender

MENTHU: Egyptian War God: Geranium, Wormwood, Rue,
               Dragon's Blood, Pepper

MERCURY: Roman Messenger God: Willow, Storax, Vervain, Palm,
               Lotus, Anise, Lily of the Valley, Rue.

MINERVA: Roman Goddess of Wisdom: Mulberry, Geranium,
               Dragon's Blood

MINOS: Greek, Originally God of Cretan Bull Cult: Aloe,
               Galbanum

MINTHA: Greek, Nymph: Mint

MITHRAS: Persian God of Light/Purity, Later God of Sun/Victory:
               Cypress

MODRON: Welsh, Great Mother: Apple

MORRIGAN: Pre-Caltic Moon Goddess, Later Irish War Goddess:
              Belladonna

MUT: Egyptian Mother Goddess: Aspen

NUN: Egyptian God of the Primordial Waters: Aspen

NEPHTHYS: Egyptian, Sister of Isis: Cypress, Opium Poppy, Oak,
              Rush, Myrrh, Dittany of Crete

NEPTUNE: Roman God of the Sea: Lotus, Myrrh, Opium Poppy, Fir

NIKE: Greek Goddess of Victory: Rose

NUT: Egyptian Sky Goddess: Amaranth, Olive

ODIN: Scandinavian Chief God: Ash, Mistletoe, Oak,
              Amaranth, Sorax, Elm

ODYSSEUS: Greek hero: Garlic, Mullein, Rue

OGMA: Irish God of Wisdom/Writing: Hazel

OLWEN: Welsh Beltane Goddess: Hawthorn, Apple, Trefoil

ORPHEUS: Greek God of Music: Alder, Vine, Violet, Elm

OSIRIS: Egyptian Vegetation God: Acacia, Ivy, Marjoram, Dittany
              of Crete, Lotus, Vine, Horehound, Nettle, Willow, Lily,
              Mallow, Storax, Fir, Iris, Heather, Acacia, Pine

PAN: Greek Nature God: Pine, Blessed Thistle, Juniper, Reed,
              Honeysuckle, Oak, Hemp, Orchis Root, Yarrow

PAEON: Greek: Peony

PERSEPHONE: Greek/Phoenician Goddess of the Underworld: Cypress,
              Pomegranate, Willow, Dittany of Crete, Parsley, Ivy, Red

Poppy, Forget me Not

PHILYRA: Greek, Mother of Chiron: Linden

PLUTO: Roman God of the Underworld: Cypress, Mint,
                Peppermint, Red Poppy, Fig, Poplar, Oak, Hyssop,
                Nettle, Frankincense, Fern

POLLUX   Greek/Roman, one of the Heavenly Twins: Wormwood

POSEIDON: Greek Sea God: Ash, Olive, Pine, Fir, Willow

PRIAPUS: Greek Fertility God: Fig, Hemp, Orchis Root, Thistle,
                Asafoetida

PROMETHEUS: Greek, Son of the Titans: Fennel

PROSERPINA: Roman Goddess of the Underworld: Red Poppy,
                Cypress, Pomegranate, Willow, Dittany of Crete,
                Parsley, Ivy, Forget me Not

PSYCHE: Greek, Wife of Eros: Willow, Lily, Ivy, Dittany of Crete

PYTHIA: Greek Serpent Goddess: Bistort

QUAN YIN: Chinese Goddess of Good Fortune: Jasmine

RA: Egyptian Sun God: Acacia, Mandrake, Chamomile,
                Frankincense, Myrrh, Bay, Vine, Cinnamon, Reed

RHADAMANTHUS: Greek, Son of Zeus, tutor of Herakles: Aloe

RHEA: Cretan Mother Goddess, Mother of Zeus: Oak, Myrrh,

Cyress,   Opium Poppy, Pine

RHIANNON: Welsh Fertility/Otherworld Goddess

ROBIN: Traditional Witch name for the Lord: Herb Robert,
                Woad

SATURN: Roman, Originally a God of Plenty and Harvest: Cypress, Lavender, Mandrake, Myrrh, Holly, Opium Poppy, Ash, Hellebore, Yew, Asafoetida, Indigo, Ivy

SCATHACH: Irish Warrior Goddess: Yew

SEKMET: Egyptian Lion Goddess: Catnip, Valerian

SELENE: Greek Moon Goddess: Mugwort, Red Rose, Frankincense, Marshmallow

SHIVA: Hindu, Lord of the Dance: Dragon's Blood, Amaranth, Geranium, Mallow, Storax

SIEN-TSAN: Chinese Goddess of Silkworm Culture: Mulberry

SINGARMATI: Hindu Goddess of Silkworm Culture: Mulberry

SOMNOS: Roman God of Sleep: Red Poppy, Opium Poppy

SYLVANUS: Roman Nature God: Pine

TALIESIN: Welsh, Originally a Barley God, later perhaps the title of Chief Bards: Reed, Barley, Hazel

TANNUS: Gaulish/British Thunder God: Holly, Oak

TARAN/TARANIS: Gaulish Lightening God: Holly, Oak

THESEUS: Greek Hero: Dandelion

THOR: Scandanavian Good of the Sky/Thunder: Ash, Holly, Hazel, Oak, Ox-Eye Daisy, Rowan, Vervain, Birch, Marjoram, Daisy, Gorse, Nettle, Thistle, Hawthorn.

THOTH: Egyptian God of Wisdom/Writing: Storax, Almond

TYPHON: Greek Storm God: Cactus, Opoponax

URANUS: Greek Sky God: Ash, Amaranth

VALKYRIES: Scandanavian, Originally Priestesses of Freya, Later they carried the souls of slain warriors to Odin: Aspen

VENUS: Roman Goddess of Love, originally Goddess of Spring/Vegetation: Anemone, Parsley, Rose, Angelica, Elder, Marjoram, Dog Rose, Myrtle, Pine, Vervain, Violet, Quince, Sandalwood, Apple, Heather, Elder, Clover, Mallow, Marshmallow, Sunflower, Frankincense, Cinnamon, Lily, Columbine, Apricot, Mistletoe, Daisy, Geranium, Coriander, Isis, Meadowsweet, Sorrel, Heather.

VESTA: Roman Goddess of Fire: Hemp, Orchis Root, Thistle

VISHNU: Hundu Sun God: Apple, Rose, Basil, Jasmine, Banyan, Mandrake, Damiana, Ginseng, Sandalwood, Oak, Nettle, Rush, Palm, Mace, Storax, Acacia, Bay, Frankincense

VULCAN: Roman Smith God: Aloe, Red Poppy, Nettle, Frankincense

WODEN: Anglo-Saxon Chief God: Ash

WOTAN: Germanic Chief God:

YAMA: Hindu, the first man: Red Poppy, Aloe, Nettle, Frankincense

YMIR: Scandinavian, Father of the Giants, Originator of the World Tree: Ash

ZEUS: Greek, Chief God: Oak, Almond, Ox-Eye Daisy, Olive, Peppermint, Mandrake, Damiana, Aspen, Hyssop, Oak, Poplar, Fig, Jasmine, Saffron, Alexanders, Apple, Ash, Sage, Willow.

8 ELEMENTAL CORRESPONDENCES

EARTH

NORTH

Green/Brown

Money, Prosperity, Fertility, Healing, Employment

Stability, Money, Home, Strength, Grounding, Protection, Nature,

Material Matters, Career, Death and Rebirth

Physical Realm, Bodies, Making things solid and real, Place of Power,
Evening, Winter, Age, Wisdom, Salt, Rocks, Trees

Alfalfa, Bistort, Fir, Soapwort, Briony, Fumitory, Primrose, Vervain,
Clover, Barley, Buckwheat, Honeysuckle, Rhubarb, Vetivert, Sorrel,

Blackthorn, Hollyhock, Sage, Tansy, Strawberry

AIR

EAST

Yellow

Mental Powers, Visions, Psychic Power, Wisdom

Intellect, Intuition, Thought, Mental Power, Communication, Travel, Divination, Teaching, Freedom, Beginnings, Creativity, Phychic Powers, Thoughts, Morning, Spring, Youth, First Steps

Agrimony, Bergamot, Chicory, Dandelion, Lavender, Sweet Cicely, Marjoram, Mint, Caraway, Comfrey, Fenugreek, Lemon Verbena, Elecampane, Fern, Bean, Clary Sage, Mulberry, Sage, Dock, Clover, Parsley, Chervil, Dill, Horehound, Hop.

FIRE

SOUTH

Red

Lust, Courage, Strength, Exorcism, Protection, Health

Passion, Creativity, Action, Will, Sex, Anger, Desire, Energy, Work, Purification, Destruction, Strength, Enthusiasm, Action, Midday, Afternoon, Summer, Adulthood, Parenthood, Candles, Light, Sun, Red Flowers, Red Hot Poker.

Centaury, Coriander, Garlic, Horseradish, Mustard, Oak, Sunflower, Rue, Lily of the Valley, Avens, Betony, Dill, Gorse, Hyssop, Madder,

Peony, Tarragon, Clover, Aspen, Ash, Cinquefoil, Fennel, Holly, Juniper, Nettle, Rue, Woodruff, Rosemary, Nasturtium, Flax, Angelica, Basil,

Celandine, Lovage, Saffron, St John's Wort

WATER

WEST

Blue

Sleep, Meditation, Purification, Prophetic Dreams, Healing, Love, Friendships, Fidelity

Emotions, Love, Dreams, Compassion, Psychic Work, Healing, Cleansing, Subsconscious, Ealy Evening, Autumn, Maturity, Hopes and Fears, Purification, Death and Rebirth, Shells and Sea Items, Water, Willow and Reeds, Blue Flowers.

Ash, Burdock, Chervil, Dog Rose, Hellebore, Herb Robert, Lady's Mantle, Orris (Iris), Rose, Rowan, Poppy, Clover, Forget Me Not, Aconite, Burdock, Cleavers, Coltsfoot, Foxglove, Indigo, Marsh Mallow, Myrtle, Ox-Eye Daisy, Snowdrop, Ivy, Thyme, Cornflower, Apple, Chamomile, Columbine, Damiana, Feverfew, Hemp, Jasmine, Mallow, Mugwort, Valerian, Periwinkle, Violet, Woad, Blackberry, Catnip, Camphor, Daisy, Geranium, Henbane, Lily, Meadowsweet, Mullein, Purslane, Yarrow, Willow, Scullcap.

SPIRIT

Violet, Electric Blue, White, Black.

Goddess and God, Inner essence, Centre of the Circle, Lavender,

Rosemary, Jasmine, Honeysuckle, Night Scented Stock, Night Jasmine

.

9 RITUALS AND FESTIVALS

HANDFASTING

Broom, Lavender, Meadowsweet, Strawberry, Marjoram, Myrtle, Saffron, Rosemary, Apple, Sorrel, Mallow, Dill, Coriander, Rue, Violet.

MOON RITUALS

WANING MOON: Garlic

DARK MOON: Garlic, Parsley, Willow, Forget Me Not

WAXING MOON: White Rose, Mugwort, Lily, Ox-Eye Daisy, Cinquefoil, Poppy

FULL MOON: Cinquefoil, Red Rose, Marshmallow, Mugwort, Poppy, Dandelion

FESTIVAL HERBS

SAMHAIN 31st October

Beginning and Ending of the Year. All Souls. All Hallows Eve, Halloween Goddess Returns as Crone or Wise One

Aconite, Henbane, Mullein, Valerian, Parsley, Thistle, Apple, Dimiana, Fumitory, Hellebore, Blackthorn, Catnip, Dittany of Crete, Honeysuckle,

Pumpkin, Hop, Chervil, Ivy, Juniper,

YULE 21st December, Winter Solstice. Rebirth of the Sun. Christmas

Ivy, Violet, Fern, Apple, Calendula, Juniper, Hop, Bayberry, Blackthorn, Holly

IMBOLC

2nd February. First Buds, Return of the Goddess as the Maiden. Oimelc, Festival of Bride, Festival of Bridgit, Candlemas

Chickweed, Willow, Alfalfa, Snowdrop, Periwinkle, Tansy, Hop, Lily of the Valley, Willow, Woad

OSTARA The Spring Equinox, 21st March, Day and Night are Equal Balance, throwing out the old and taking on the New, Oestre, Eostar

Apple, Celandine, Daisy, Lemon Verbena, Tansy, Forget me Not, Calendula, Mugwort, Bluebell, Caraway, Gorse, Nettle, Blackthorn, Bistort, Cleavers, Coltsfoot, Ground Ivy, Violet

BELTANE 1st May. Marriage of the Goddess and God, Goddess becomes the Mother. God returns to reign beside her. Beltan, Bealtaine, Walpurgisnacht, May Day

Apple, Cinquefoil, Dog Rose, Honeysuckle, Primrose, Daisy, Rose, Dandelion, Mallow, Sweet Cicely, Celandine, Dill, Hawthorn, Willow, Oak, Woodruff, Lily of the Valley, Sorrel, Clover

LITHA Summer Solstice, 21st June. Height of the Sun King's power. Days begin to Shorten.

LAMMAS 1st August, First Harvest. Feast of the Sacrificial God. Lughnasadh. Loaf Mass

MADRON Autumn Equinox, 21st September. Day and Night Equal. Time of Balance. Height of the Harvest. Modron. Harvest Festival

COAHAIN

Angelica, Celandine, Calendula, Dog Rose, Fennel, Lavender, St John's Wort, Elecampane, Strawberry, Chamomile, Feverfew, Marjoram, Sweet Cicely, Mint, Daisy, Honeysuckle, Yarrow, Apple, Violet, Fern, Dill, Oak

LUGHNASA

Apple, Bean, Fenugreek, Honeysuckle, Mugwort, Sunflower, Borage, Woad, Marshmallow, Chicory, Fennel, Poppy, Oak, Basil, Daisy, Gorse, Ivy, Nasturtium

HERFEST

Basil, Corn, Apple, Bean, Chicory, Cornflower, Rose, Buckwheat, Dog Rose, Parsley, Hawthorn, Acorn, Blackberry, Calendula, Daisy, Poppy, Ivy.

10 SOLAR SYSTEM AND ASTROLOGY

PLANETARY MAGICAL ASSOCIATIONS

JUPITER

Truth, Knowledge, Religion, Education, Language, Foreign Countries, Faith, Philosophy, Publications, Reading, Banking, Judgement, Justice,

Optimism, Compassion, Law and Legal Action, Politics, Leadership, Honour, Public Acclaim, Wealth, Responsibility, Conceit, SelfIndulgence, Excessive Optimism.

THE SUN

Health, Success, Career Goals, Ambition, Money and Wealth, Law, Buying and Selling, Strength, Leadership, Men's Mysteries, Children.

SATURN

Tenacity, Law, Dentistry, Construction, Real Estate, Thriftiness, Reliability, Self-Discipline, Patience, History and Time, Order, Slow Change, Inhibition, Intolerance, Dogmatism, Depression, Obstacles, Isolation.

MERCURY

Communication, Travel, Intellect and Learning, Mental Perception, Teaching, Writing, Creativity, Memory, Cleverness, Reasoning, Arguments, Sarcasm and Cynicism, Trickery and Thievery.

URANUS

Eccentric Ideas, Inventiveness, Electricity, Bizarre Occurrences, Reform, Unexpected Change.

VENUS

Feminine Qualities and Pursuits, Harmony, Partnerships, Art, Beauty and Fashion, Peace, Pleasures, Tact and Adaptability, Friendships and Affection, Love and Romance, Sexuality and Lust, Luxury, Impracticality, Indecisiveness, Possessiveness, Excessive Romanticism.

NEPTUNE

Dreams, Visions, Ideal, Fantasy, Art, Healing, Illusion, Psychic Knowledge, Alchemy.

MARS

Aggressive Masculine Energy, Weapons and Tools, Impulsiveness, Loyalty, Sports, Initiative, Action, Freedom, Pioneers, Decisiveness, Selfishness, Brutality, Lust, Conflict, Struggle, Disharmony, Anger, War.

MOON

Female Mysteries, Psychic Knowledge, Psychology, Dreams, Imagination,

Reincarnation, Women, Birth and Children, Domestic Concerns, Emotions, Spirituality, Nursing, Initiation, Healing, Instinct, Memory, Virginity, Purity, Protection, Intuition, Beauty.

NEW MOON (DARK MOON), WAXING MOON, FULL MOON, WANING MOON

January:	Wolf Moon
February:	Snow Moon
March:	Worm Moon
April:	Pink Moon
May:	Flower Moon
June:	Strawberry Moon
July:	Mead Moon
August:	Red Moon
September:	Harvest Moon
October:	Blood Moon
November:	Frost Moon
December:	Cold Moon

ASTROLOGY

ARIES Ram 21 March – 20 April. Courage, Fire, Mars

Energy, Encouragement, Unstoppable, Bold, Caring, Devoted, Proud, Impulsive, Stubborn, Reckless, Leadership, Jealous.

Diamond, Rock Crystal, Sapphire

TAURUS Bull 21 April – 21 May. Strength, Earth, Venus

Beauty, Love, Patience, Organisation, Support, Romance, Careful, Dedication, Stubborn, Lazy, Vain, Overcautious, Stability, Over Indulgent.

April: Rose Quartz, Orange Carnelian, Sapphire

May: Emerald, Chrysoprase

GEMINI Twins 22 May – 21 June. Adaptable, Air, Mercury
Communication, Fascination, Originality, Adventure, Versatile, Wisdom, Charm, Resourceful, Restless, Distraction, Judgement, Depression.

May: Citrine, Agate, Tigereye

June: Pearl, Moonstone, Agate

CANCER Crab 22 June – 22 July Caring, Water, The Moon

Emotions, Helpful, Support, Patience, Compassion, Romance, Creativity, Nurturing, Gossip, Isolation, Overly Sensitive, Intuition, Psychic Awareness, Lack of Communication, Competitive.

June: Emerald, Crysoprase, Green Adventurine

July: Ruby, Carnelian, Onyx, Turquoise

LEO Lion 23 July – 22 August Generosity, Fire, The Sun

Courage, Generosity, Protection, Loyalty, Kindness, Bare Truth, Entertainment, Arrogant, Jealous, Power, Optimism, Aggressive, Wasteful.

July: Citrine, Rock Crystal, Onyx

August: Peridot, Aventurine, Sardonyx

VIRGO Virgin 23 August – 23 September Organised, Earth, Mercury

Communication, Dedication,   Hardworking,   Practical, Humour, Resourceful, Self Destruction, Uptight, Critical, Self Pity

August: Yellow Agate, Citrine, Carnelian

September: Sapphire, Lapis Lazuli, Crysolite (peridot)

LIBRA Scales 24 September – 23 October Fairness, Air, Venus

Charm, Loveable, Fairness, Sincerity, Sharing, Romantic, Vain, Spoiled, Delusions of Grandeur, Balance, Harmony, Manipulation, Indecision, Drama Queen.

September: Smoky Quartz, Orange Citrine, Chrysolite

October: Opal, Tourmaline, Beryl

SCORPIO Scorpion 24 October – 22 November Willpower, Water, Pluto

Power, Rebirth, Magnetism, Passion, Loyalty, Protection, Bravery, Trendy, Obsession, Possession, Organisation, Transformation, Jealousy, Secrets, Revenge, Manipulation

October: Red Carnelian, Sard, Aquamarine

November: Topaz, Tigereye

SAGITTARIUS Archer 23 November – 21 December Enthusiastic, Fire, Jupiter

Honesty, Inspiration, Optimism, Fair, Enthusiasm, Encouraging, Dedication, Independence, Education, Arguments, Recklessness, No tact, Over confidence, Flaky

November: Chalcedony, Blue Quartz, Topaz

December: Turquoise, Zircon, Ruby

CAPRICORN Goat 22 December – 20 January Determination, Earth, Saturn

Discipline, Maturity, Loyalty, Family, Hard Work, Devotion, Honesty, No Fear, Pessimism, No Forgiveness, Cold, Materialistic, Fairly Hopeless, Snob

December: Onyx, Cat's Eye, Ruby

January: Garnet, Rose Quarts

AQUARIUS Water Carrier 21 January – 19 February Ingenuity, Air, Uranus

Communication, Fair, Logical, Welcoming, Open Mind, Detachment, Self Destruction, Irrational, Desperation, Guarded, Out of Touch with reality

January: Garnet, Turquoise, Hawkeye

February: Amethyst, Onyx

PISCES Fish 20 February – 20 March Empathy, Water, Neptune Romance, Wisdom, Comfort, Help, Imagination, Self Pity, Self Destruction, Gullible, Clingy, On another planet.

February: Amethyst

March: Aquamarine, Red Jasper, Bloodstone

11 GEMSTONES

AMBER: Wisdom, Witchcraft, Ancestral
                  Knowledge, Healing, Love, Soothing Nightmares
AMETHYST: Spirituality, Addictions, Clear Head
BLACK
TOURMALINE: Protection
BLOODSTONE: General
CARNELIAN: Career, Ambition
CITRINE: Abundance, Money, Luck
CLEAR QUARTZ: General, Health, Luck, Psychic Development
FLOURITE: Mental Clarity
JET: Purification, Protection, Healing Grief, Spiritual
                  Advancement, Witchcraft
LAPIS LAZULI: Healing, Psychic Knowledge
MALACHITE: Willpower, Resolve
OBSIDIAN: Grounding, Protection
ONYX: Self-Control, Decision Making, Luck
ROSE QUARTZ: Love, Romance, Friendship
SMOKY QUARTZ: Protection, Grounding
TIGER'S EYE: (Agate) Prosperity
TOPAZ: Balancing, Healing
ONYX: Black, Protection, Psychic Protection, Root Chakra,
                  Mental, Physical Imbalance

An old fashioned Nineteenth Century rhyme "Lucky Birth Stones"

By her in January born
No gem save Garnets shall be worn
They ensure her constancy
True friendship and fidelity

The February born shall find
Sincerity and peace of mind
Freedom fro passion and from care
If they the Amethyst will wear

Who in this world of ours, her eyes
In March first opens, shall be wise
In days of peril, firm and brave
And wear a Bloodstone to her grave

She who from April dates her years
Diamonds shall wear, lest bitter tears
For vain repentance flow, this stone
Emblem for innocence is known

Who first beholds the light of day
In spring's sweet flowery month of May
And wears an Emerald all her life
Shall be a loved and happy wife.

Who comes with summer to this earth
And owes to June her hour of birth
Will ring of Agate on her hand
Can health, wealth and long life command

The glowing Ruby shall adorn

Those who in warm July are born
Then will they be exempt and free
From love's doubt and anxiety

Wear Sardonyx or for thee
No conjugal fidelity
The August born without this stone
'Tis sat, must live unloved and lone.

A maiden born when autumn leaves
Are rustling in September's breeze
A Sapphire on her brow should bind
'Twill cure diseases of the mind.

October's child is born for woe
And life's vicissitudes must know
But lay an Opal on her breast
And hope will lull those foes to rest

Who first comes to this world below
With drear November's fog and snow
Should prize the Topaz's amber hue
Emblem of friends, and lovers true

If cold December gives you birth
The month of snow, and ice and mirth
Place on your hand a Turquoise blue
Success will bless whate're you do

SAINTS AND STONES

10th Century

Peter	Jasper	Peter
Paul	Sapphire	Andrew
Andrew	Calcedony	James
John	Emerald	John
James	Sardonyx	Philip
Philip	Sardius	
Bartholomew	Chrysolite	Mathias
Thomas	Beryl	Thomas
Matthew	Topaz	James the Less
Thaddeus	Chrysoprase	Thaddeus
Simon Zelotes	Jacinth	Simon
Matthias	Amethyst	Matthew
	Carnelian	Bartholomew

ANGELS AND GEMSTONES

Malchediel	Ruby
Asmodel	Topaz
Ambriel	Carbuncle (Garnet)
Muriel	Emerald
Herchel	Sapphire
Humatiel	Diamond
Zuriel	Jacinth
Barbiel	Agate
Adnachiel	Amethyst

Humiel	Beryl
Gabriel	Onyx
Barchiel	Jasper

MINERAL HARDNESS SCALE

10	Diamond
9	Corundum (Sapphire, Ruby)
8	Topaz
7	Quartz
6	Microcline feldspar (or orthoclase)
5	Apatite
4	Fluorite
3	Calcite
2	Gypsum
1	Talc

GEMSTONES - The Minerals

Adamite	(Hydrous Zinc Arsenate)
Agate	(Silicon Dioxide)
Alexandrite	(Beryllium Aluminum Oxide)
Amazonite	(Potassium Aluminium Silicate)
Amber	(Organic Material)
Amethyst	(Silicon Dioxide)
Apatite	(Calcium Strontium, Lead, Sodium and/or Potassium Fluorine-Chlorine-Hydroxyl Phosphate)
Apophyllite	(Hydrous Potassium Calcium Fluorsilicate)
Aquamarine	(Beryllium Aluminum Silicate)
Aragonite	(Calcium Carbonate)
Atacamite	(Hydrous Copper Chloride)

Aventurine	(Silicon Dioxide)
Azurite	(Copper Hydroxyl Carbonate)
Barite	(Barium Sulfate)
Benitoite	(Barium Titanium Silicate)
Beryl	(Beryllium Aluminum Silicate)
Bloodstone or Heliotrope	(Silicon Dioxide)
Brazilianite	(Sodium Aluminum Hydroxyl Phosphate)
Calcite	(Calcium Carbonate)
Carnelian	(Silicon Dioxide)
Celestite	(Strontium Sulfate)
Cerussite	(Lead Carbonite)
Chabazite	(Hydrous Calcium Aluminum Silicate)
Chalcanthite	(Hydrous Copper Sulfate)
Chalcedony	(Silicon Dioxide)
Charloite	(Complex Potassium/Sodium, Calcium/Barium/Strontium Hydrous Silicate)
Chiasolite	(Aluminum Silicate)
Chrysoberyl	(Beryllium Aluminum Oxide)
Chrysocolla	(Hydrous Copper Hydroxyl Silicate)
Chrysoprase	(Silicon Dioxide)
Cinnabar	(Mercury Sulfide)
Citrine	(Silicon Dioxide)
Coal	(Organic Material)
Copper	(Element)
Coprolite	(Silicon Dioxide)
Coral	(Organic Material)
Crocoite	(Lead Chromate)
Cubic Zircona	(Stabilized Cubic Zirconium Oxide)
Danburite	(Calcium Borosilicate)
Datolite	(Calcium Hydroxyl Borosilicate)
Diamond	(Elemental Carbon)
Diopside	(Calcium Magnesium Silicate)
Dioptase	(Hydrous Copper Silicate)

Dolomite	(Calcium Magnesium Carbonate)
Emerald	(Beryllium Aluminum Silicate)
Enhydros	(Silicon Dioxide)
Enstatite	(Magnesium Silicate)
Epidote	(Calcium Aluminum Iron Hydroxyl Silicate)
Fire Agate	(Silicon Dioxide)
Fire Opal	(Hydrous Silicon Dioxide)
Fluorite	(Calcium Fluoride)
Galena	(Lead Sulfide)
Garnet	(Calcium, Aluminum, Magnesium, Manganese, Chromium and/or Iron
Silicate Geode	(Silicon Dioxide)
Gold	(Element)
Goldstone	(Glass)
Halite	(Sodium Chloride)
Hematite	(Iron Oxide)
Hemimorphite	(Hydrous Zinc Hydroxyl Silicate)
Herkimer Diamond	(Silicon Dioxide)
Heulandite	(Hydrous Sodium Calcium Aluminum Silicate)
Hexagonite	(Calcium Magnesium Iron Silicate)
Hiddenite	(Lithium Aluminum Silicate)
Ice	(Hydrogen Oxide)
Iceland Spar	(Calcium Carbonate)
Iron	(Element)
Ivory	(Organic Material)
Jade	
Nephrite	(Calcium Magnesium Iron Silicate)
Jadeite	(Sodium Aluminum Silicate)
Jasper	(Silicon Dioxide)
Jet	(Organic Material)
Kaemmererite	(Magnesium Iron Aluminum Hydroxyl Silicate)
Kunzite	(Lithium Aluminum Silicate)
Kutnohorite	(Calcium Manganese Carbonate)
Labradorite	(Sodium Calcium Aluminum Silicate)
Lapis Lazuli or Lazurite	(Sodium Calcium Aluminum Sulfate Silicate)

Lead	(Element)
Lepidolite	(Potassium Lithium Aluminum Hydroxyl Fluorsilicate)
Lodestone or Magnetite	(Iron Oxide)
Malachite	(Copper Hydroxyl Carbonate)
Marble	(Calcium Carbonate)
Mercury	(Element)
Meteorite	(Elements: Nickel-Iron)
Mica	(Complex Potassium Sodium Magnesium Iron Aluminum Hydroxyl Silicates)
Moldavite	(Glass)
Moonstone	(Adularia Orthoclase: Potassium Aluminum Silicate Albite Plagioclase: Sodium Aluminum Silicate)
Obsidian	(Glass)
Onyx	(Silicon Dioxide)
Opal	(Hydrous Silicon Dioxide)
Orpiment	(Arsenic Trisulfide)
Paste	(Glass)
Pearl	(Organic Material)
Peridot	(Magnesium Iron Silicate)
Petrified Wood	(Silicon Dioxide)
Prehnite	(Calcium Aluminum Hydroxyl Silicate)
Pumice	(Glass)
Pyrite	(Iron Sulfide)
Quartz	(Silicon Dioxide)
Rhodochrosite	(Manganese Carbonate)
Rhodonite	(Manganese Silicate)
Rose Quartz	(Silicon Dioxide)
Ruby	(Corundum: Aluminum Oxide)
Rutile	(Titanium Oxide)
Sapphire	(Corundum: Aluminum Oxide)
Sard	(Silicon Dioxide)
Sardonyx	(Silicon Dioxide)

Scapolite	(Complex Sodium-Calcium Aluminosilicate)
Selenite	(Gypsum: Hydrous Calcium Sulfate)
Shattuckite	(Copper Hydroxyl Silicate)
Siderite	(Iron Carbonate)
Silver	(Element)
Smithsonite	(Zinc Carbonate)
Smoky Quartz	(Silicon Dioxide)
Sodalite	(Sodium Aluminum Chlorine Silicate)
Sphalerite	(Zinc Sulfide)
Spinel	(Magnesium Aluminum Oxide)
Staurolite	(Iron Aluminum Hydroxyl Silicate)
Stibnite	(Antimony Sulfide)
Stichtite	(Hydrous Magnesium Chromium Carbonate)
Stilbite	(Hydrous Sodium Calcium Aluminum Silicate)
Sugilite	(Potassium Sodium Iron Lithium Silicate)
Sulfur	(Element)
Tanzanite	(Calcium Aluminum Hydroxyl Silicate)
Tektite	(Glass)
Thulite	(Calcium Aluminum Hydroxyl Silicate)
Tigereye	(Silicon Dioxide with inclusions)
Tin	(Element)
Topaz	(Aluminum Hydroxyl-Fluorine Silicate)
Tourmaline	(Complex Borosilicate)
Turquoise	(Hydrous Copper Aluminum Phosphate)
Ulexite	(Hydrous Sodium Calcium Borate)
Vanadinite	(Lead Chlorovanadate)
Variscite	(Hydrous Aluminum Phosphate)
Wavellite	(Hydrous Aluminum Phosphate)
Willemite	(Zinc Silicate)
Witherite	(Barium Carbonate)
Wulfenite	(Lead Molybdate)
Zincite	(Zinc Oxide)
Zircon	(Zirconium Silicate)

POT POURRI HERBS & PLANTS

Rose, Lavender, Bay, Anise Seed, Cloves, Nutmeg, Cinnamon, Allspice, Mace, Coriander, Orris Root, Sandalwood, Oakmoss, Orange Leaves, Sweet Woodruff, Moss, Thyme, Cornflowers, Peppermint, Violets, Anise, Lemon Verbena, Rose Geranium, Vertiver.

POT POURRI OILS

Jasmine, Rose   Geranium, Patchouli, Rosemary, Eucalyptus, Peppermint, Lavender, Cinnamon, Rose, Sandalwood, Bergamot and Lemon.

13 DYE PLANTS

Vervain, Angelica, Sage, Strawberry, Thyme, Marjoram, Mint, Parsley, Lady's Mantle, Woodruff, Calendula, Chamomile

ALDER:	Bark:	Red
	Flowers:	Green
	Twigs:	Brown
ALKANET:	Roots:	Red
AGRIMONY:	Flowering Tops:	Butter Yellow (Mordant: Alum)
APPLE:	Bark:	Tan (Mordant: Alum)
BAYBERRY:	Berries:	Blue
	Root Bark:	Red
BEDSTRAW:	Roots:	Light Red (Mordant: Alum)
	Roots:	Purplish Red (Mordant: Chrome)
	Flowering Tops:	Yellow (Mordant: Alum/Chrome)
BILBERRY:	Berries:	Pink-Purple

| BIRCH: | Bark: | Brown (Mordant: Alum) |
| | Roots: | Reddish-Brown (Mordant: Alum) |

BLACKBERRY: Young Shoots: Light Grey (Mordant: Alum)

| BLACKTHORN: | Bark: | Reddish-Brown |
| | Bark: | Black (Mordant: Copper) |

BRACKEN:	Roots:	Yellow (Mordant: Chrome)
	Young Shoots:	Yellowish-Green (Mordant: Alum/Chrome)
	Young Shoots:	Grey (Mordant: Copper)

| BROOM: | Bark: | Yellow |

| CALENDULA: | Petals: | Yellow |

| CHICORY: | Leaves: | Blue |

| CLEAVERS: | Roots: | Red (Mordant: Alum) |

| COLTSFOOT: | Whole Plant: | Yellow-Green (Mordant: Alum) |
| | Whole Plant: | Green (Mordant: Copper) |

COMFREY: Fresh Green Shoots: Yellow (Mordant: Alum)

| CORNFLOWER: | Flowers: | Blue |

| CRAB APPLE: | Bark: | Pink (Mordant: Alum) |

| DANDELION: | Whole Plant: | Reddish-Purple |

| DOCK: | Roots: | Dark Yellow (Mordant: Alum) |

| ELECAMPANE: | Roots: | Blue |

ELDER:	Bark:	Black (Mordant: Alum)
	Roots:	Black (Mordant: Alum)
	Leaves:	Green (Mordant: Alum)
	Leaves:	Olive Green (Mordant: Copper)
	Berries:	Purple/Blue
	Berries:	Lilac (Mordant: Alum or Salt)
	Juice:	Violet (Mordant: Alum)
FENUGREEK	Seeds:	Yellow
FOXGLOVE:	Whole Plant:	Black
FUMITORY:	Whole Plant:	Yellow or Green
GOLDEN ROD:	Flowers:	Yellow or Tan (Mordant: Alum)
	Flowers:	Gold (Mordant: Chrome)
HEATHER:	Young Tips:	Yellow (Mordant: Yellow)
	Branches:	Green (Mordant: Alum or Iron)
HOLLYHOCK:	Flowers:	Blue
HORSERADISH:	Leaves:	Yellow
INDIGO:	Roots:	Blue
IRIS:	Roots:	Black
JUNIPER:	Berries:	Brown or Khaki
LADY'S MANTLE:	Leaves:	Green
LARCH:	Needles:	Brown

LARKSPUR:	Flowers:	Green (Mordant: Alum)
LILY OF THE VALLEY:	Leaves:	Green (Mordant: Lime Water)
	Young Shoots:	Greenish-Yellow (Mordant: Chrome)
	Autumn Leaves:	Gold (Mordant: Chrome)
MADDER:	Leaves or Roots:	Pink or Red or Brown
	Roots:	Crimson Red (Cold Water)
	Roots:	Rich Brown (Hot Water)
MARJORAM:	Young Tops:	Purple or Reddish Brown
MEADOWSWEET:	Flowering Tops:	Greenish-Yellow (Mordant: Alum)
	Roots:	Black
MULLEIN:	Whole Plant:	Purple
NETTLE:	Roots:	Yellow
	Leaves:	Green
	Whole Plant:	Grey-Green (Wool)
	Whole Plant:	Cream (Silk)
	Whole Plant:	Greeny-Grey
	Whole Plant:	Soft Grey (Mordant: Copper)
OAK:	Bark:	Black (Mordant: Iron)
	Bark:	Brown
	Bark:	Yellow (Mordant: Tin or Zinc)
ONION:	Skins:	Orange (Mordant: Alum)

	Skins:	Yellowy-Brown (Mordant: Copper)
PARSLEY:	Leaves or Stems:	Cream
RUE:	Roots:	Red
SAFFRON:	Stamens:	Golden Yellow
SORREL:	Aerial Parts:	Greyish-Brown (Mordant: Alum)
STJOHNS WORT:	Roots:	Pink
	Young Tops:	Yellow (Mordant: Alum)
SUNFLOWER:	Flowers:	Yellow
TANSY:	Flowers:	Golden Yellow
	Leaves:	Green-Yellow
	Roots:	Green
TEA:	Leaves:	Rose-Tan
WOAD:	Whole Plant:	Blue
	Whole Plant:	Pink (Mordant: Alum)

14 CHAKRAS AND COLOUR

CHAKRAS

CROWN: "I AM", Purple, Wisdom, Spirit, Enlightenment, Transcendence, Source Energy.

    Herbs: Lavender, Lotus Flowers

    Gemstones: Amethyst, Diamond, Clear Quartz, Selenite

    Sound: "Om"

THIRD EYE: "I KNOW", Indigo, Perception, Intuition

    Herbs: Clover, Lemon Balm, Eucalyptus, Lemongrass, Peppermint, Coltsfoot, White Sage

    Gemstones: Aquamarine, Lapis Lazuli, Sodalite, Turquoise, Aventurine, Amazonite, Blue Calcedony

    Sound: "Ham"

HEART   "I LOVE", Green, Heart, Compassion, Love

    Herbs: Hawthorn, Marjoram, Rose, Basil, Thyme, Sage, Cilantro, Jasmine, Parsley, Cayenne

    Gemstones: Green Tourmaline, Jade, Rose Quartz,

Aventurine, Strawberry Quartz, Green Calcite.

Sound: "Yam"

SOLAR PLEXUS: "I DO", Yellow, Power, Will, Socialization, Ego,
Impulse

Herbs: Lavender, Bergamot, Rosemary, Mint,
Ginger, Fennel, Marshmallow, Celery, Lily,
Lemon Balm, Anise

Gemstones: Orange Calcite, Citrine, Sunstone,
Red Agate, Topaz

Sound: "Ram"

SACRAL: "I FEEL", Orange, Emotions, Creativity,
Sexuality, Self-worth

Herbs: Sandalwood, Calendula, Licorice,
Cinnamon, Paprika, Gardenia, Sesame,
Coriander, Hibiscus, Vanilla

Gemstones: Carnelian, Sunstone, Snowflake
Obsidian, Citrine, Coral, Moonstone,

Sound: "Vam"

ROOT: "I AM", Red, Earth Connection, Survival Instinct,

Grounding

Herbs: Dandelion, Cloves, Burdock, Valerian
Root, Elderflower

Gemstones: Red Agate, Bloodstone, Black
Tourmaline, Hematite, Garnet, Red Aventurine,
Onyx, Smoky Quartz, Tigers Eye.

Sound: "Lam"

COLOUR THERAPY

Colour fills our lives. It is everywhere and we associate different colours with different things as those are the colours we see in those places etc. Colour can also be used to make you feel in a different way. There are many books on this and much has been written about it.

When I went to a Colour Therapy Workshop at the College of Psychic Studies I learnt a fair bit about colour and my near black wardrobe began to take on many other colours. I went out and bought some silk scarves so that it was easy to add those colours and those moods to my day.

Ancient cultures worshipped the Sun where all colour came from. The use of colour in the Ancient World can be traced in the teachings of Thoth who was known as Hermes by the Greeks. They used different coloured ointments and salves as remedies. They practiced in treatment rooms painted in specific colours to promote healing. Through the years there are many who have written about and used the properties of colour.

Then these things could be seen as "Pagan". Now in our enlightened age there is no need for the Church or anyone else to be worried about the "Pagan" aspects of such beliefs. We have science to prove that certain colours and herbs can be beneficial. It doesn't take any Pagan Practice to make them work so there is no need to fear them anymore. So a vast array of beneficial materials can now be used.

Colour Therapy is not new. In 1878 Edwin Babbitt published The Principles of Light and Colour and achieved world renown with his comprehensive theory, prescribing specific colours for specific conditions.

In the Modern world practices such as Aura Soma show how the body craves certain colours when there is a need. The mind interpreting this by being drawn to certain colours when they are needed.

There are now many theories and colour is used in many ways now that it can be better understood and quantified in a scientific way e.g. Yellow and Red Light raises blood pressure, blue light lowers it. Blue light is also used to treat neonatal jaundice and has also been effective in pain relief to assist with rheumatoid arthritis.

Colour Therapy aims to balance and enhance your body's energy centers (Chakras) by using the seven colours of the light spectrum. This can help to stimulate our body's own healing process. It is also possible to introduce colours into your life to bring about specific feelings and promote different emotions. This is where the constructive use of colour can be a valuable tool, especially in the workplace, where facing something that you need a little support with. It is also useful when you need to relax and find peace when there is very little time or space to do so.

Each of the seven colours resonates with one of the main seven chakras.

Each of the spectrum colours is simply light of varying wavelengths, thus each colour has its own particular energy and vibration.

The energy relating to each of these spectrum colours resonates with the energy of one of the seven main chakras of the body.

Included here also are colour correspondences.

RAINBOW

>Spirit in Nature, Happiness, Opens Mystical Realm

>Spirit, Fairies, Angels, Creativity

VIOLET/PURPLE – Crown Chakra

>Brain, Higher Spirit.

>CANDLE: Wisdom and Spirituality

Jupiter, Thursday, Water, Air

Spirituality, Higher Mind, Psychic Pursuits, Dreams, Spiritual Communication, Career Ambition, Protection against ghosts and astral nasties, Expansion of Business and Wealth, Protection of the Innocent.

INDIGO - Third Eye, Forehead,

Intuition CANDLE: Intuition, Psychic Abilities

Moon, Mercury, Monday, Wednesday, Water and Air.

TURQUOISE - Throat, Communication:

GEMSTONE: Turquoise, Aquamarine, Lapis Lazuli, Angelite, Blue Lace Agate

CANDLE: Communication, Spirituality, Peace, Harmony, Dreams, Sea and Sky.

Protection, Harmony, Healing (Women and Children), Sympathy,

Compassion, Devotion, Understanding, Vitality, Calms nervous people, Calms manic people, Calms overexcited people, Antiseptic, Burns, Bleeding, Fevers, Increase Metabolism, Mental Pursuits, Commanding, Safety of Hearth and Home, Healing.

GREEN – Heart Chakra

Healing, Growth, Nervous System, Heart, Circulatory System, Liver,

Lowering Blood Pressure, Releasing Frustration and Anger, Meditation, Healing, Stimulates Growth, Healing Broken Bones

GEMSTONE: Malachite, Aventurine, Green Calcite, Peridot, Green Tourmaline, Moss Agate, Serpentine

CANDLE: Nature, Environmental Issues, Erath, Health, Wealth, Love and Luck

YELLOW - Solar Plexus

Digestive System, Intellect/Ego: Yellow Topaz, Citrine

ORANGE - Abdomen

Reproductive Organs, Sexuality, Reproduction:

Carnelian, Fire Opal, Orange Calcite, Sunstone, Orange Topaz, Amber

CANDLE: Energy, Encouragement, Recovery

RED - Root

Waste System, Lower Limbs, Security, Life Force:

Ruby, Garnet, Fire Agate, Red Jasper, Bloodstone.
CANDLE: Passion, Sex, Love, Courage, Fire.

PINK

Romance, Friendship, Emotional Wellbeing, Friendship, Partnership, Harmony, Healing, Affection, Compassion, Kindness, Good Health, Unconditional Love, Opening Your Heart, Healing Heart Problems, Releasing Emotional Challenges, Tranquility, Insomnia, Manifestation of Dreams

Venus, Friday, Air

BROWN

Miracles, Fertility, Hidden Wealth, Hidden Information,
Secrets, Confusing an Enemy, Earthiness, Animal
Wisdom, Universal Wisdom, Bringing an object into
manifestation (Mind to Physical), Garden blessing and
plant spirits, Materialising a desire, Magical Boost,
Patchouli adds to vibration, Nature Healing, Revive
energy and creativity, Connection to Earth Animals and
Earth, Saturn, Saturday, Earth

BLACK

CANDLE: Purification, Protection, Hidden Things,
Mourning and the Dead

Protection, Strength, Retreat, Gateway to new
Experiences

OCHRE: Earth and Animals

GREY

CANDLE: Neutrality, Balance

Secrets, Illusion, Glamour, Neutrality, Fog, Enemy to see
your way, Information about mental emotional and
physical state, Alternative point of view

Neptune, Wednesday, Saturday, Water

15 DAYS OF THE WEEK

MONDAY

Planet: Moon

Colours: Silver, White, Blue

Deities: Diana, Artemis, Selene, Luna

Correspondences: Illusion, Sleep, Peace, Beauty, Prophecy,
                    Dreams, Emotions, Travel, Fertility, Insight,
                    Wisdom

TUESDAY

Planet: Mars

Colours: Red, Black, Orange

Deities: Mars, Ares, Tiwaz

Correspondences: Battles, Courage, Victory, Success, Strength,
                    Conviction, Rebellion, Defence, Wards,
                    Protection, Military

WEDNESDAY

Planet:	Mercury
Colours:	Purple, Orange
Deities:	Mercury, Hermes, Woden
Correspondences:	Arts, Chance, Change Luck, Communication, Fortune, Gambling, Transport, Creativity, Deals, Writing

THURSDAY

Planet:	Jupiter
Colours:	Blue, Purple, Green
Deities:	Thor, Jupiter, Juno
Correspondences:	Abundance, Protection, Prosperity, Strength, Wealth, Healing, Management

FRIDAY

Planet:	Venus
Colours:	Pink, Aqua, Green
Deities:	Venus, Aphrodite, Freya
Correspondences:	Love, Birth, Fertility, Romance, Gentleness, Pregnancy, Friendship, Passion, Happiness

SATURDAY

Planet: Saturn

Colours: Black, Purple

Deities: Saturn, Hecate

Correspondences: Banishing, Protection, Wisdom, Spirituality, Cleansing, Astral Magic, Weeding the Garden, Gathering Crops, Remembering the Dead

SUNDAY

Planet: Sun

Colours: Gold, Yellow

Deities: Brigit, Helios, Apollo

Correspondences: Success, Fame, Wealth, Prosperity, Promotion, New Job

REIKI THERAPY

Reiki is a healing technique based on the principle that the therapist can channel energy into the patient by means of touch to activate the natural healing processes of the patient's body and restore physical and emotional well-being.

Reiki encourages the individual to heal the spirit by consciously deciding to improve themselves which is necessary for the healing process.

I can only write from the experience of the Reiki Therapy Sessions I provide but when a client has their first Reiki Therapy they will be asked to complete a "Client Questionnaire" which starts their file and gives an indication of what they would like to address. Notes from the session are kept on the Client Record Sheet which is put into the file at the end of the session.

Client Records are held in the strictest confidence and are kept locked away. The client always has a right to see their own records. In the event of a client changing practitioner the records can be handed back to the client. If they do not wish to have the records returned they can be destroyed after seven years.

No records are kept electronically. All records are either handwritten or where they are typed they are printed out and the original file deleted. The records are then put on the client's personal file for future reference.

I did find when I had a practice in London that some clients asked for no records to be taken or kept. This was where they were busy executives who didn't want their stress mentioned or known about by their employers. I was happy to do this but it did mean that I had to cease my membership of the Reiki Federation. I totally understood their position and was happy to continue under those circumstances.

When you are looking for a Reiki Therapist it is best to check their credentials first and whether they have trained officially. Asking for their Master Lineage in the Usui System of Natural Healing is not unreasonable.

You should expect an initial therapy to be one and a half hours to allow for registration. About forty minutes of this will be the Reiki Therapy.

The Principles of the Usui System of Natural Healing

Just for today I will live the attitude of gratitude
Just for today I will not worry
Just for today I will not anger
Just for today I will do my work honestly
Just for today I will show love and respect for every living thing

To have lasting results a client must accept responsibility and take an active part in the healing process. In this process the client is invited to take care of their thoughts.

They are invited to stand back and create space for themselves. To stand back from their mind and thoughts. To observe without judgment and watch to see how they are thinking, their attitude, their perception, their beliefs and to direct their thoughts in a positive way.

The recommendations of my Reiki Teacher involved standing back and letting those who needed help come to me. The hand was offered, it was up to the client to take that hand.

History of Reiki

Dr Mikao Usui or Usui Sensei as he was referred to by his students in Japan was the founder of the Usui System of Reiki. He was born in 1865 in the Village of Yago in the Yamagata district of Gifu prefecture, Japan. It is believed that he entered a Tendai Buddhist School on or near Mount Kurama at the age of four. He also studied Kiko, the Japanese version of Quigong.

The young boy found that these healing methods required the practitioner to build up and then deplete his own life energy when giving treatments. This made him wonder if it would be possible to do healing work without depleting his own energy. He went on to study in Japan, China and Europe and ended up receiving Reiki during a meditation practice on Mount Kurama.

Usui Sensei had a great interest in learning and worked hard at his studies. He traveled to Europe and China to further that education. He learnt about medicine, psychology and religion as well as fortune telling.

It is thought that he came from a wealthy family as in Japan only the wealthy could afford to send their children to school. He became the Secretary to Pei Gotoushin, Head of the Department of Health and Welfare who later became the Mayor of Tokyo.

The connections Usui Sensei made at this job helped him to become a successful businessman. Usui Sensei was also a member of the Rei Jyutu Ka, a metaphysical group dedicated to the development of psychic abilities.

In 1914 Usui Sensei's personal and business life were not doing well. As a sensitive spiritualist Usui Sensei had spent much time meditating at power spots on Mount Kurama where he had received his early Buddhist training. He decided to travel again to this Holy Mountain where he enrolled in Isyu Guo, a 21 day training course sponsored by the Tendai Buddhist Temple which is located there. Nothing is known about his training but it is likely that it involved fasting, meditation, chanting and prayers.

It is known that there is a small waterfall on Mount Kurama where even today people go to meditate. This meditation involves standing under the waterfall and allowing the waters to flow over the top of the person's head. This practice is said to activate the Crown Chakra.

Japanese Reiki Masters believe that Usui Sensei may have used this meditation as part of his practice as it was during the Isyu Guo training that the Reiki Energy entered his Crown Chakra. This greatly enhanced his healing abilities and he realized he was receiving a wonderful new gift which is the ability to give healing to others without depleting his own energy.

In 1925 Dr Chujiro Hayashi, a retired Naval Officer, received his Reiki Master Initiation from Dr Usui.

Up to this point the Usui System of Healing consisted of the energy itself, the symbols, the attunement process and the Reiki Ideals. This was what Dr Usui had received during his mystical enlightenment. Dr Hayashi went on to develop the Usui System of Healing and opened a Reiki Clinic in Tokyo. He kept detailed records of the treatments given and used this information to create the Standard Hand Positions, the system of Three Degrees and the Initiation Procedures.

Hawayo Takata

Hawayo Takata was born on 24th December 1900 on the island of Kauai, Hawaii. Her parents were Japanese Immigrants and her father worked in the sugar cane fields. She worked hard as she was growing up and eventually married the Bookkeeper of the plantation where she worked. His name was Saichi Takata and they had two daughter together.

In October 1930 Saichi died at the age of 34 leaving Mrs Takata to raise their children.

In order to provide for the family she worked very hard with little rest. After five years she developed severe abdominal pain, a lung condition and had a nervous breakdown.

Soon after this one of her sisters died and it was her responsibility to travel to Japan to visit her parents who had moved there to deliver the news. She also felt she could receive help for her health while in Japan.

She therefore took a steamship, accompanied by her sister in law, and after informing her parents she entered a hospital. It was then found that she had a tumour, gallstones and appendicitis and after resting for several weeks she was ready for the needed operation.

While she was on the operating table, just before surgery, Hawayo heard a voice which said that "The operation is not necessary". She had never heard a voice speak to her like this before and wondered what it meant. As the voice repeated the message three times she took notice. She knew she was awake and had not imagined it. It was so unusual yet so compelling that she decided to ask the doctor about it. So she got off of the operating table, wrapped herself in a sheet and went to ask him.

The doctor knew of Dr Hayashi's Reiki Clinic and told Hawayo about it and she decided she wanted to try it.

At the Reiki Clinic she began receiving treatments. The Practitioners could sense what was wrong and their diagnoses closely matched that of the doctors in the hospital. This impressed her and gave her confidence to continue.

Two Reiki Practitioners treated her each day. The heat from their hands was strong and she thought they were using some sort of equipment. She thought it was hidden up the large kimono sleeves and grabbed at them trying to find out what was hidden there. She found nothing. The startled Practitioner asked her what she was doing, she explained and he laughed. He then explained Reiki and how it worked.

Mrs Takata received daily treatments and got gradually better. In four months she was completely healed. She was impressed with the results and wanted to learn Reiki. However, it was explained that Reiki was Japanese and that it was intended to stay in Japan. It could not be taught to an outsider.

Mrs Takata talked to the surgeon at the hospital and convinced him to ask Dr Hayashi to allow her to learn Reiki. Since Dr Hayashi actually wanted to teach Reiki to another woman besides his wife and since she was so persistent he decided she should be the one.

In the Spring of 1936 Mrs Takata received her First Degree Reiki training. She worked with Dr Hayashi for one year and then received her Second Degree Reiki.

She returned to Hawaii in 1937 and was soon followed by Dr Hayashi and his daughter who came to help establish Reiki in Hawaii. In the Winter of 1938 Hawayo Takata was initiated as a Reiki Master. She was the thirteenth and last Reiki Master Dr Hayashi initiated.

Between 1970 and her death on 11th December 1980 Mrs Takata initiated 22 Reiki Masters. This is the list of them and Reiki Masters today can trace their lineage back to one of these.

George Araki, Barbara McCullough, Beth Grey, Ursula Baylow, Paul Mitchell, Iris Ishikura, Fran Brown, Barbara Weber Ray, Ethel Lombardi, Wanya Twan, Virginia Samdahl, Phyllis Lei Furumoto, Dorothy Baba, Mary McFaden, John Gray, Rick Bockner, Bethel Phaigh, Harry Kuboi, Patricia Ewing, Shinobu Saito, Kay Yamashita (Takata's Sister) and Barbara Brown.

The original 22 teachers have taught others and in the decade since Mrs Takata died Reiki rapidly spread in the West and is now practiced throughout the world.

(This information is taken from Reiki the Healing Touch by William Rand kindly provided by Xenia Tran of Tranformation).

The Ethical Principles of Reiki

During a meditation several years after developing Reiki, Dr Usui decided to add the Reiki Ideals to the practice of Reiki. The Ideals came in part from the Meiji Emperor of Japan whom Dr Usui admired.

The Ideals were developed to add spiritual balance to Usui Reiki. Their purpose is to help people realise that the conscious decision to improve yourself is a necessary part of Reiki. The client must accept responsibility for their own healing and take an active part in it.

Printed in Great Britain
by Amazon

19271130R00159